States a

Political Evolution and Institutional Change
Bo Rothstein and Sven Steinmo, editors

Exploring the dynamic relationships among political institutions, attitudes, behaviors, and outcomes, this series is problem-driven and pluralistic in methodology. It examines the evolution of governance, public policy, and political economy in different national and historical contexts.

It will explore social dilemmas, such as collective action problems, and enhance understanding of how political outcomes result from the interaction among political ideas—including values, beliefs, or social norms—institutions, and interests. It will promote cutting-edge work in historical institutionalism, rational choice and game theory, and the processes of institutional change and/or evolutionary models of political history.

Also in the series

Restructuring the Welfare State: Political Institutions and Policy Change
Edited by Bo Rothstein and Sven Steimo

The Problem of Forming Social Capital: Why Trust?
By Francisco Herreros

The Personal and the Political: How Personal Welfare State Experiences Affect Political Trust and Ideology
By Staffan Kumlin

Building a Trustworthy State in Post-Socialist Transition
Edited by János Kornai and Susan Rose-Ackerman

Creating Social Trust in Post-Socialist Transition
Edited by János Kornai, Bo Rothstein, and Susan Rose-Ackerman

States and Development: Historical Antecedents of Stagnation and Advance
Edited by Matthew Lange and Dietrich Rueschemeyer

States and Development

Historical Antecedents of Stagnation and Advance

Edited by
Matthew Lange and Dietrich Rueschemeyer

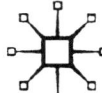

STATES AND DEVELOPMENT
© Matthew Lange and Dietrich Rueschemeyer, 2005.

All rights reserved. No part of this book may be used or reproduced in any manner whatsoever without written permission except in the case of brief quotations embodied in critical articles or reviews.

First published in 2005 by
PALGRAVE MACMILLAN™
175 Fifth Avenue, New York, N.Y. 10010 and
Houndmills, Basingstoke, Hampshire, England RG21 6XS
Companies and representatives throughout the world.

PALGRAVE MACMILLAN is the global academic imprint of the Palgrave Macmillan division of St. Martin's Press, LLC and of Palgrave Macmillan Ltd. Macmillan® is a registered trademark in the United States, United Kingdom and other countries. Palgrave is a registered trademark in the European Union and other countries.

ISBN 1–4039–6492–0
ISBN 1–4039–6493–9

Library of Congress Cataloging-in-Publication Data

    States and development : historical antecedents of stagnation and advance / edited by Matthew Lange and Dietrich Rueschemeyer.
      p. cm.—(Political evolution and institutional change)
    Includes bibliographical references and index.
    Revisions of papers presented at a one-day conference held in Oct. 2003 at the Watson Institute of International Studies, Brown University.
      ISBN 1–4039–6492–0
      ISBN 1–4039–6493–9 (pbk.)
      1. State, The—Congresses. 2. Nationalism—Congresses. 3. Economic development—Congresses. 4. Political development—Congresses. 5. Comparative government—Congresses. I. Lange, Matthew. II. Rueschemeyer, Dietrich. III. Series.

JA77.S73 2005
320.1—dc22
                                                2004065496

A catalogue record for this book is available from the British Library.

Design by Newgen Imaging Systems (P) Ltd., Chennai, India.

First edition: August 2005

10 9 8 7 6 5 4 3 2 1

Printed in the United States of America.

CONTENTS

List of Tables and Figures vii
Notes on Contributors ix
Preface xii

PART I   States and Development: An Introduction   1

One   States and Development   3
Matthew Lange and Dietrich Rueschemeyer

Two   Harnessing the State: Rebalancing
Strategies for Monitoring and Motivation   26
Peter Evans

Three   The Rule of Law and Development: A
Weberian Framework of States and
State-Society Relations   48
Matthew Lange

PART II   Long-Lasting Effects of States on Development   67

Four   State Effectiveness, Economic Growth,
and the Age of States   69
Areendam Chanda and Louis Putterman

Five   Colonial States and Economic Development
in Spanish America   92
James Mahoney and Matthias vom Hau

Six	British Colonial State Legacies and Development Trajectories: A Statistical Analysis of Direct and Indirect Rule *Matthew Lange*	117
PART III	**Building States—Inherently a Long-Term Process?**	**141**
Seven	Building States—Inherently a Long-Term Process? An Argument from Theory *Dietrich Rueschemeyer*	143
Eight	Building States—Inherently a Long-Term Process? An Argument from Comparative History *Thomas Ertman*	165
Nine	How Fast Can You Build A State? State Building in Revolutions *Jaime Becker and Jack A. Goldstone*	183
Ten	State Building in Korea: Continuity and Crisis *Bruce Cumings*	211
PART IV	**Conclusion**	**237**
Eleven	States and Development: What Insights Did We Gain? *Matthew Lange and Dietrich Rueschemeyer*	239
Index		259

LIST OF TABLES AND FIGURES

Tables

3.1	Four coordination structure ideal types	50
4.1	Regional averages of *statehistn05* and *statehist1500* (weighted by 1960 population)	76
4.2	Income levels and growth: correlations with *statehistn05* and *statehist1500*	76
4.3	Political, institutional, demographic and geographical variables: correlations with *statehistn05* and *statehist1500*	78
4.4	Regressions with per capita GDP growth rate (1960–1995) as dependent variable	80
4.5	Regressions with per capita GDP growth rate (1960–1995) as dependent variable, developing country sample only	83
4.6	Regressions using log of per capita GDP (1995) as dependent variable	85
4.7	Regressions using institutional quality (1982–1995) as dependent variable	87
A	Additional correlations	89
6.1	Former British colonies used in analysis: dates and duration of colonialism	123
6.2	Bivariate correlation between the extent of indirect rule and various postcolonial development indicators	127
6.3	Multivariate analysis of state governance among former British colonies, 1997–1998	129
6.4	Multivariate analysis of democracy among former British colonies	130

6.5	(a) Multivariate analysis of per capita GDP in 1960 (log) (b) Multivariate analysis of average annual per capita GDP growth, 1961–2000	132
6.6	(a) Multivariate analysis of life expectancy, 1960 (b) Multivariate analysis of change in life expectancy, 1960–1990	134
7.1	Summary of factors slowing state development	154
9.1	Time-spans from state collapse to revolutionary consolidation	185
9.2	Major social revolutions' time-span to consolidation	190

Figures

2.1	The tripod model of state control	30
2.2	Total percent change in unexplained growth in per capita GDP (1970–1990) by "Weberianness" scale score	33
2.3	Virtuous circle of intangible compensation	35
2.4	Quality of government institutions (ICRG) by relative income conversion efficiency (RICE)	40
3.1	Three types of structural synergy	60

NOTES ON CONTRIBUTORS

Jaime Becker is a graduate student at the University of California at Davis. Her research is on social movements and revolutions. Current research is focused on transnational flows of anarchist ideology, activists, and organizing frameworks in the Mexican Revolution.

Areendam Chanda is currently Assistant Professor of Economics at Louisiana State University. His research focuses on a variety of issues related to economic growth and development.

Bruce Cumings is the Norman and Edna Freehling Professor of History at the University of Chicago. His publications include *Parallax Visions: American–East Asian Relations at the End of the Century* (Durham, NC, London: Duke University Press, 1999); *Korea's Place in the Sun: A Modern History* (New York, London: Norton, 1997); *The Origins of the Korean War* (2 vols., Princeton, NJ: Princeton University Press, 1981, 1990). He is currently completing a book entitled *Industrial Behemoth: The Northeast Asian Political Economy in the 20th Century*.

Thomas Ertman is Associate Professor of Sociology at New York University. He is the author of *Birth of the Leviathan: Building States and Regimes in Medieval and Early Modern Europe* (Cambridge, UK, New York: Cambridge University Press, 1997), winner of the Barrington Moore Jr. Prize. He is completing a successor volume on liberalization and democratization in Europe from the French Revolution until World War II tentatively entitled "Taming the Leviathan."

Peter Evans is Professor of Sociology at the University of California, Berkeley and holds the Eliaser Chair of International Studies. His publications include *Livable Cities? Urban Struggles for Livelihood and*

Sustainability (editor, Berkeley, CA: University of California Press, 2001); *Embedded Autonomy: States and Industrial Transformation* (Princeton, NJ: Princeton University Press, 1995), winner of the book prizes in Political Sociology and in Political Economy of the World System of the American Sociological Association; *Bringing the State Back In* (co-editor with D. Rueschemeyer and T. Skocpol, Cambridge, UK, New York: Cambridge University Press, 1985); and *Dependent Development: The Alliance of Multinational, State, and Local Capital in Brazil* (Princeton, NJ: Princeton University Press, 1979). He currently works on a set of interrelated projects on the political economy of development in the context of globalization.

Jack A. Goldstone is the Virginia E. and John T. Hazel Jr. Professor of Public Policy at George Mason University. His publications include *States, Parties, and Social Movements* (editor, New York: Cambridge University Press, 2003); *Encyclopedia of Political Revolutions* (editor, Washington, DC: CQ Press, 1998); and *Revolution and Rebellion in the Early Modern World* (Berkeley, CA: University of California Press, 1991), winner of the Distinguished Publication Award of the American Sociological Association. He currently works on causes of revolutionary and ethnic wars.

Matthew Lange is Assistant Professor of Sociology at McGill University. His dissertation "The British Colonial Lineages of Despotism and Development" (Department of Sociology, Brown University) analyzed the long-term consequences of direct and indirect rule in British colonies. It combines quantitative cross-national analysis with case studies of Botswana, Guyana, Mauritius, and Sierra Leone.

James Mahoney is Associate Professor of Sociology at Brown University. His monograph on *The Legacies of Liberalism: Path Dependence and Political Regimes in Central America* (Baltimore, MD: Johns Hopkins University Press, 2001) won the Barrington Moore Jr. Prize. He coedited with Dietrich Rueschemeyer *Comparative Historical Analysis in the Social Sciences* (Cambridge, UK, New York: Cambridge University Press, 2003), which won the Giovanni Sartori Book Award of the Qualitative Methods Section of the American Political Science Association. His current research deals with long-term development and the legacy of colonialism in Spanish America.

Louis Putterman is Professor of Economics at Brown University. A past president of the Association for Comparative Economic Studies, he has published numerous papers on a wide variety of issues including preferences and values, economic organization and the firm, cooperation and worker participation, experimental economics, economic development and growth, and economic issues in China and Africa. His books include *Dollars and Change: Economics in Context* (New Haven, CT: Yale University Press, 2001); *Economics, Values, and Organization* (coeditor with A Ben-Ner, Cambridge, UK, New York: Cambridge University Press, 1998); *Continuity and Change in China's Rural Development* (New York: Oxford University Press, 1993); *State and Market in Development* (coeditor with D. Rueschemeyer, Boulder, CO: Rienner, 1992); *Division of Labor and Welfare: An Introduction to Economic Systems* (Oxford, New York: Oxford University Press, 1990); and *Peasants, Collectives, and Choice: Economic Theory and Tanzania's Villages* (Greenwich, CT: JAI Press, 1986).

Dietrich Rueschemeyer is Professor of Sociology and Charles C. Tillinghast Jr. Professor of International Studies Emeritus at Brown University. He currently holds a research professorship at Brown's Watson Institute for International Studies. His publications include *Comparative Historical Analysis in the Social Sciences* (coeditor with James Mahoney, Cambridge, UK, New York: Cambridge University Press, 2003, winner of the Giovanni Sartori Book Award of the Qualitative Methods Section of the American Political Science Association); *Capitalist Development and Democracy* (coauthor with E.H. Stephens and J.D. Stephens, Chicago: University of Chicago Press, 1992, winner of the book prize in Political Sociology of the American Sociological Association); *Power and the Division of Labour* (Stanford, CA: Stanford University Press, 1986), and *Bringing the State Back In* (coeditor with P. B. Evans and Th. Skocpol, Cambridge, UK, New York: Cambridge University Press, 1985). He currently works on a book tentatively titled *Usable Theory: Analytic Tools for Social Research*.

Matthias vom Hau is completing his dissertation at Brown University. The project analyzes the sociopolitical mechanisms involved in transformations of nationalism in three Latin American countries—Argentina, Mexico, and Peru—from a comparative perspective.

PREFACE

This volume grew out of a study group on states and development that the editors organized at Brown University's Watson Institute of International Studies between 2001 and 2004. The project, dubbed "Effective and Defective States," sponsored presentations and discussions of a wide scope, including historic state making in Europe, the Middle East, Africa, and Japan as well as the trajectory of state functioning in Russia in the nineteenth and twentieth centuries. Reflections on historical developments were juxtaposed to research reports on current instances of developmental success and disaster, to quantitative studies that compared many countries, and to theoretical modeling.

A common theme repeatedly emphasized by the research group was the dimension of time, both the historical aspects of state building and the long-term effects states have on development. This was not by chance, as the concern with time informed the conception of the "Effective and Defective States" project from the start and was central to several independently conceived research projects at Brown, including Louis Putterman's quantitative studies of the relation between age of states and the pace of development, Jim Mahoney's research on the influence of Spanish colonialism on subsequent development in Latin America, and Matt Lange's dissertation research on the impact of British colonialism on later political and socioeconomic development. Quite befitting to its focus, the study group also built on a longer tradition. Since the 1970s, Peter Evans, Morris D. Morris, Louis Putterman, Dietrich Rueschemeyer, and others had initiated strong interdisciplinary research activities at Brown University on development. The role of states in development was a major focus of this work (cf. Evans, Rueschemeyer, and Stephens 1985; Rueschemeyer and Evans 1985; Putterman and Rueschemeyer 1992).

Against this background, we held a one-day conference in October 2003 at the Watson Institute that explored rigorously three issues: (1) the ways in which states affect developmental processes, (2) the long-term effects of states on development, and (3) the historical nature of state building. This volume maintains the same three-part organization, and the chapters that follow are revised versions of the papers presented at the conference.

At the conference, an intense dialogue developed among the participants, and these exchanges were of great value to the final set of contributions presented here. Several participants who did not present papers—such as Fernando Henrique Cardoso, who with perfect timing entered during a discussion of dependency and globalization—also joined in the conversations and provided considerable insight. We give special thanks to Patrick Heller, Eun Mee Kim, Zeev Rosenhek, and Marilyn Rueschemeyer for their contributions.

We are grateful to Brown's Watson Institute for International Studies for generously funding the conference as well as the project as a whole. We thank Ellen Carney for her work on the logistics of the conference, making it a most pleasurable occasion. Dietrich Rueschemeyer would like to give special thanks the Social Science Research Center Berlin (WZB) for its support while he worked on this project. Finally, we are grateful to Bo Rothstein, Sven Steinmo, and David Pervin for including our book in Palgrave Macmillan's series on "Political Evolution and Institutional Change" and to Heather Van Dusen and Maran Elancheran for guiding us through the publication process.

Providence, September 2004
Matthew Lange and Dietrich Rueschemeyer

References

Evans, Peter, Dietrich Rueschemeyer, and Evelyne H. Stephens (eds). 1985. *States Vs. Markets in the World System*, Beverly Hills, CA: Sage Publications.

Putterman, Louis, and Dietrich Rueschemeyer (eds). 1992. *State and Market in Development: Synergy or Rivalry?* Boulder, CO: Lynne Rienner.

Rueschemeyer, Dietrich and Peter Evans. 1985. "The State and Economic Transformation: Toward an Analysis of the Conditions Underlying Effective Intervention." In *Bringing the State Back In*, edited by P. Evans, D. Rueschemeyer, and T. Skocpol. New York and Cambridge: Cambridge University Press, 44–77.

PART I

States and Development: An Introduction

CHAPTER ONE

States and Development

MATTHEW LANGE AND
DIETRICH RUESCHEMEYER

The Contribution of States to Social and Economic Development

Why are states important for economic growth and for the social transformations that go with it? Adam Smith (1776) and the Scottish enlightenment gave a first answer: the state can guarantee the institutions enabling individuals and firms to engage in economic activities that bring economic growth. The institutional infrastructure around contract, property, tort law, and incorporation allows the exchange of goods and services as well as the accumulation, lending, and investing of capital to proceed with a reasonable degree of ease, security, and predictability. This idea is also at the core of Max Weber's (1968) analysis of the role of law in the rise of capitalism, and it is similarly central to the theoretical framework of the economic historian and Nobel Laureate Douglass North (e.g., 1981).

A second answer is of equal weight. Although the rational pursuit of economic gain in markets for goods, capital, land, and labor is critical to economic growth, it stands at odds with powerful interests, and it disrupts established social relations. Consequently, states are of great importance for socioeconomic development in two seemingly contradictory ways: they can break down resistance to the market, but they can also moderate the impact of the market through regulation and social policy and thus make a market economy sustainable. Resistance to the market comes from powerful interests—above all large landlords, aristocratic or not—that benefit from a stagnant status quo and gain from the dependence of peasants and serfs. In addition, various bodies of custom stand against the extension of market exchange. Grounded in community and kinship standards of mutuality and protecting individuals against some of the major risks of life, these norms and institutions tend to be undermined by radical extensions of market exchange.

The fact that states played an important role in breaking down resistance to the capitalist penetration of traditional economies was recognized clearly by Weber. But the dual role of states in overcoming this resistance and in moderating the impact of market exchange on social life became a central theme only in Karl Polanyi's study of the *Great Transition* (1957). On the one hand, he insisted that the "laissez faire economy was the product of deliberate state action": "The road to the free market was opened and kept open by an enormous increase in continuous, centrally organized and controlled interventionism" (pp. 140, 141). At the same time, he viewed the self-adjusting market as "a stark utopia" that "could not exist for any length of time without annihilating the human and natural substance of society; it would have destroyed man and transformed his surroundings into a wilderness" (p. 3). Social responses seeking to protect the security of people as well as the environment against the unregulated market first arose spontaneously, but then they acquired a standard place among the expectations to be met by states.

Finally, social scientists studying the latecomers to capitalist development have noted that states in continental Europe and elsewhere acted in yet another—and more directly economic—way to stimulate economic growth. In Germany and Russia, and later in countries such as Japan and South Korea, states have intervened in the mobilization of capital when individual firms were not able to meet the capital needs of advanced technology, and they have developed a variety of other proactive policies seeking advance economic growth that departed from a pure market model of economic development (see, e.g., Amsden 1989, 2001; Evans 1979, 1995; Gerschenkron 1962; Hirschman 1958; Johnson 1982; Wade 1990). These interventions have been the subject of extended and often heated debate, an issue to which we will return.

States and the "Collective Action Problem"

What accounts for such a central role of states in social and economic development? Joseph Strayer, in the preface to his lectures *On the Medieval Origins of the Modern State* (1970, p. vi), points to the fundamental answer: "Cooperation in the effort to achieve common goals has been responsible for most human achievements, and the state offers one way of securing this cooperation. It is certainly not the only way of securing cooperation, but at present it is the dominant way." Cooperation—especially cooperation on a large scale—must not be taken for granted. The fact that a large number of people have common interests does not mean that they will band together to achieve their goals. Even if it is clear that joining together can create such "public goods" as a clean environment, an irrigation system, or a legal order easing economic transactions, one cannot assume that collective action will emerge. This has come to be called the "collective action problem."

Why should this be a pervasive problem? Once an outcome that serves common interests is achieved, people can often benefit from it whether they have contributed or not. Examples are the results of agricultural research, a clean center of town, and the higher wages prevailing in a unionized industry. A large number of actors faced with such a prospect will *refrain* from contributing to the cause for the simple reason that they can benefit without contributing if enough others play a part in the action, while their contribution would be futile if too few joined in. Collective action of large numbers of actors, Mancur Olson argued in his pathbreaking *The Logic of Collective Action* (1965), requires that the cost-benefit calculus of potential participants shows it to be beneficial to join in the action despite the uncertainty of success. This might be the case because they have individual incentives that favor participation aside from the prospect of the "collective good" in question; early unions, for example, offered a life insurance to cover the funeral expenses of their members. An important alternative to such incentives is that those who fail to participate can be threatened with sanctions.

The role of punitive sanctions in the creation of public goods is, of course, the main reason why states are so central to securing social cooperation. Even though they can devise effective incentive schemes as well, the threat of punishment corresponds to the distinctive strength of states, their capacity for coercion. Being threatened with coercion makes people cooperate when they otherwise might not—laboring on common projects, serving in armies, obeying laws and regulations, and paying taxes. The successful extraction of taxes in turn gives states the chance to offer incentives as well as to underwrite the creation of public goods directly.

Noncoercive ways of attaining cooperation in the pursuit of common goals are also of great importance. The extended discussion and research following Olson's book (see, e.g., Hardin 1982; Taylor 1987) has further elucidated these other, noncoercive bases of cooperation, which may be activated by states as well. Mancur Olson had already pointed to a few of these conditions. A group may be "privileged" to have one or more members who by themselves benefit sufficiently from the collective good to cover its costs even if no one else contributes. Equally important, small groups may be able to monitor the behavior of their members to prevent them from "free riding." Olson also stressed that collective action in small groups is promoted by the fact that each individual's contribution has a visible impact on the outcome. Under certain conditions these small group effects may result in quite extensive outcomes: if a network of similar small groups exists, this may enable collective action even in large social aggregates. Furthermore, preexisting norms may induce people to cooperate even when the chances of monitoring their behavior are limited. Partly because of such norms and partly because of positive experiences in the past, people may give cooperation a try even when they cannot be sure about the cooperation of others; subsequent positive experience can then result in extended cooperation.

There is one further consideration that is relevant to the role of states in solving collective action problems. Multitask institutions have a special role in overcoming the collective action problem in the pursuit of public goods. Often it is far from clear which collective good is suited to satisfying an emergent set of interests. We will see that this is frequently the case in economic policy. It is obviously difficult to mobilize cooperation for an as yet unclear cause. However, existing institutions that have the capacity either to provide a variety of collective goods by themselves or to induce people to participate in their creation can explore different solutions for new problems and then proceed to mobilize resources once a promising course of action is identified. States are, of course, prime examples of such multipurpose institutions that can directly provide solutions or activate collective action once a goal has been determined. They and their non-state counterparts (such as religious bodies) might be considered prefabricated problem solvers, as it were.

States, then, are major facilitators of collective action. However, the simple fact that states play a critical role in creating social cooperation does not mean that they will seek to advance economic growth. Nor can we assume that the policies they pursue will actually be adequate to the goal. States may not only create collective goods; they can also generate public failures (see, e.g., Scott 1998). Before we turn to these questions, however, we must inquire into the characteristics of the state that are most conducive to effective state action.

What Kind of State Does It Take?

The state's capacity to overcome collective action problems depends on its internal quality as well as on its relations to society. A first condition is that the state's own personnel *act as a corporate group*. The left hand must not undo what the right hand does, a requirement that is anything but trivial in a large and variegated organization. This coordination depends largely on the state's internal organization and the norms and outlooks of state actors. Internal organization and the orientations of officials also determine to a large extent a second important internal issue—whether the state becomes *an effective instrument* of administration and rule. Externally, states depend for successful action on a multitude of *ties to societal actors for information and resource flows*. They must be able to engage and guide societal actors as well as to oppose and negotiate with them. At the same time, states need *a certain autonomy* from actors whose interests may be at odds with chosen policy goals and who may be bent on using parts of the state apparatus for their own purposes.

Max Weber (1968) recognized that the organization of the state along bureaucratic lines is a vital condition for coordinated and effective state action. Although bureaucracy has become a popular byword for red tape and unresponsive administration, what Weber identified in his theoretical model or "ideal type" was the form of organization that is characteristic of the modern state and the contemporary corporation. Most basically, corporately coherent and effective state action requires (1) the rational organization of social relations, which is necessary for the transfer of information and resources that makes possible effective and coordinated action, and (2) control over state actors, which is necessary for actually getting state agents to act as required for the goals pursued. The six basic components of bureaucratic organization outlined by Weber—formal rules prescribing the duties attached to positions within the bureaucracy, hierarchical organization, record keeping, meritocracy, full-time employment, and salary-based compensation—promote these two requirements in a number of ways.

Formal rules defining duties and coordinating agents make possible an organizational structure that facilitates effective state action. In the extreme formulation of the model of bureaucracy, organizational rules create a gapless institutional framework dictating how agents act under all possible circumstances and thereby making state agents impersonal cogs within a preprogrammed organizational machine. Filing and record keeping are central to bureaucracy's rational character—they create organizational memory and allow actors to monitor the functioning of the organization and the performance of agents through the constant collection of data. Similarly, hierarchical organization establishes a chain of command and thereby endows officials with the authority to preside over certain organizational functions or to oversee the agents performing them, or both. In this way, hierarchical organization provides a formal means of decision-making as well as a check on the seeking of individual gain. Full-time employment and salary-based compensation provide additional limits to insubordination by making state agents dependent on their positions for their livelihood. At the same time, they support the autonomy of the organization from the surrounding society, and autonomy helps to prevent individuals with common class, religious, or political loyalties from usurping the state apparatus to serve these loyalties. Such autonomy, in turn, helps to ensure that agents act with organizational interests in mind. Meritocracy, while obviously enhancing effectiveness, also promotes a special kind of group coherence that strengthens organizational autonomy.

Obviously, the complete subordination of state agents to a gapless system of bureaucratic rules is an ideal type—we will never see the impersonal cogs that Weber envisioned and feared. State agents will always have considerable room to maneuver given such difficulties as imperfect monitoring, imprecise regulatory rules, and the night-watchman problem. This opens the door to uncoordinated action and, equally important, the abuse of office for private gain. The problem can be contained if officials are committed to advancing the goals of the state organization and if these commitments are embedded in an organizational culture and supported by a certain *esprit de corps* (Rueschemeyer and Evans 1985). In his comparative-historical analysis of state building in Europe, Philip Gorski (1993) argues that common religious-based identities and values shared by state officials in Holland and Prussia promoted a "disciplinary revolution" and thereby effective corporate action: state officials followed norms of individual subordination to organizational rules and regulated their own actions as well as those of their coworkers accordingly. We can, then, conclude that an effective bureaucratic organization depends on both the organization of social relations along formal-rational lines as well as on ideas of community and shared norms of proper and improper conduct that coincide with organizational rules and thereby help to subordinate agents to bureaucratic regulation.

Along with an appropriate structure and culture of the state organization, the effectiveness of states also depends on their capacity to harness the participation of societal actors. In this way, state effectiveness is shaped by the ties between state and society and the impact of these ties on the mobilization of information and resources throughout society. James Scott (1998), for example, argues that state action is often ineffective because state and local actors do not collaborate for policy implementation and fail to share information and resources necessary for their success. Similarly, yet analyzing the opposite outcome, Milton Esman and

Norman Uphoff (1984) find that multiple ties between state and local actors are vital to the success of policy implementation because they allow the two-way transfer of knowledge and resources that make possible collaborative, positive-sum relations. State-society relations also allow societal actors to monitor state agents, thereby helping to ensure that they perform their duties adequately, and they provide a medium through which societal actors can make demands upon the state. In this way, ties between state and society not only increase the likelihood of the successful implementation of state policy in favor of public interests, but also help to prevent state structures from becoming unresponsive, ossified, repressive, and ineffective.

Given the importance of societal ties, state effectiveness undoubtedly depends on the characteristics of the societies in which states are embedded. The extent and type of economic production, for example, shapes state effectiveness. If a large portion of a national population is composed of subsistence farmers or of households with only semi-permanent residences, the state will have difficulty engaging societal actors, and the resources that the state receives from society will be minimal. The organization of social relations also affects state capacity. When societal relations are characterized by hierarchical relations of dependence and are dominated by a small number of patrimonial big men, the state must go through these intermediaries in order to engage the population, limiting the information and resources the state receives and forcing it to be heavily dependent on the intermediaries. Alternatively, as Robert Putnam (1993) finds in his study of democratic reform in Italy, larger numbers of individuals can be engaged in state-society relations when societal relations are more horizontally organized. Besides such structural aspects of society, commonly held norms and identities affect the state's ability to engage societal actors. State-society relations are undoubtedly shaped by views of legitimacy, which often depend on the belief that the state is serving the local community. When multiple and competing communal identities exist within a national society, legitimacy is often compromised if one or more communal groups are excluded from access to the state. State-society relations can then be severely limited.

While states need information and resources as well as cooperation from society, state-society relations must be structured in a certain way if developmental state action is to be maximized. The capacity of the state to act corporately, for one thing, is compromised if the boundaries of the state fade away. When this happens, the bureaucratic underpinnings and *esprit de corps* of the state organization begin to break down, and state agents become more difficult to coordinate and control. In addition, the range of potential state action may be severely limited if the state is dependent on powerful interest groups. An asymmetrical combination of state autonomy and state embeddedness within society is therefore optimal for effective state action (Evans 1995).

So, formal-rational organization, *esprit de corps*, and embeddedness are all needed for effective states. Yet, even if states have the capacity to pursue developmental policy, there is no guarantee that they actually will. States must choose to expend resources and effort to pursue national developmental strategies, and the reasons why they might do this are not so straightforward. Moreover, even if states do choose a developmental path, the policies leading to success are in no way self-evident.

Why Do States Become Handmaidens of Economic Growth?

In answering this question,[1] it may be useful to return again to the most distinctive feature of states—that they have a comparative advantage in the deployment of violence and aim for a monopoly of coercion in their domain. Charles Tilly (1985), possibly inspired by St. Augustine's fourth-century observation that if one takes away justice and the rule of law, states are not easily distinguished from large gangs of robbers (Augustinus 1984), made the coercive power of states the point of departure in his essay on "war making and state making as organized crime." Why should states develop institutions and policies easing economic transactions when they can acquire great treasure by coercive means? After all, one plausible explanation of the technological stagnation frequently found in large-scale agrarian societies points to "their highly exploitative social order in which . . . the rewards . . . were monopolized by a small, powerful, and wealthy elite that knew little about technology and cared less" (Lenski and Lenski 1974, pp. 87–88; see also Childe 1953; Veblen 1934).

The simplest—and the most common—answer to this question extrapolates from advanced modern states and argues that states benefit more from garnering a share in the expansion of economic production than from coercive extraction in stagnant economies. While helpful as a first orientation, this argument projects our current assumptions into history; and even for today's developing countries it assumes a long-term perspective of policy making that is not easily maintained in the pulls and pushes of political life. Rather than offering a causal account, it seeks to explain policy orientations by their long-term results. Unless we begin to identify the ways in which the long-term outcome is causally connected to the policy interest, this comes close to the fallacy of naïve functionalism.[2]

A realistic, even if stylized, account begins with the coalition building in which the elites of an emergent state are likely to engage, both with other power holders and with economically successful interests. S. N. Eisenstadt made this dual—and contradictory—engagement central to his analysis of *The Political System of Empires* (1963). While the one side of this involvement secures the support of patrimonial powers but adds little to the resources needed for building a more effective, proto-bureaucratic machinery of rule, the other can mobilize such resources but tends to undermine the patrimonial legitimacy on which the state still relies. Eisenstadt's comprehensive survey of premodern empires makes clear that this mutually constraining balance can last for very long periods of time and that the final outcome is by no means an assured victory of market-oriented merchants and a decline of patrimonialism. But under favorable circumstances state elites may be willing to refrain from discretionary "takings." And the power of the state may increasingly be made available to crush resistance to the market, to secure routes of transportation, to guarantee the legal decisions private parties make through contractual agreement, and to eliminate local and regional restraints on trade. In these developments, the impersonal rules used to rationalize the organization of the state begin to acquire a counterpart in the incipient rule of law governing state-society relations. The self-interest of state elites in greater economic returns is not an inevitable mechanism that leads to self-restraint of the state and to economic advance, but it does have the potential to set these developments in motion.

Even in the best of circumstances, this is likely to be a complex and halting process. The state elites' interest in being accepted and in securing advantageous cooperation is at first often limited to the most useful and powerful partners. And these may be more concerned to get direct preferential treatment than to secure self-restraint of the state and predictability through universalistic rule of law. Other interests, even those of potentially very productive groups, may be subjected to ruthless exploitation by the state and its elites.[3] Even if they did not focus on such direct modes of favoritism and exploitation by the state, Marx and Engels were not completely off the mark when they claimed in *The German Ideology* (1978) that the modern states of their time were "the form in which the individuals of a ruling class assert their common interests" (p. 187). A more comprehensive rule of law, especially one transcending class boundaries, was to await further historical transformations, critical among them the emergence of a democracy with real bite. The trajectory and the outcome of these developments are shaped primarily by the relative power of different groups and congeries of interest.

Even quite limited forms of the rule of law can, however, when coupled with policies promoting productivity, result in significant economic advance because they offer a measure of predictability to major economic actors. This was the case in Europe as well as later in East Asia. The creation of other institutions increasing predictability and productivity had other effects as well. They changed at the same time—in Kenya (Bates 1989) as well as in the earlier European cases—the structural conditions different groups found themselves in, and they transformed the power constellations among them. "Economy and polity thus interact, generating a process of change. . . . In this way, each society creates its own history" (Bates 1989, p. 154).

Historically, external pressure has been important for the balance of power between market and patrimonial interests. Indeed, international threats and pressure have often either given state actors leverage to shift policy or directly forced them to do so. In early modern Europe, for instance, rampant warfare and the increasing importance and accelerating costs of new military technologies made states more and more dependent on capitalists for loans and goods (Tilly 1992). Consequently, state elites chose to support capitalist interests because they were seen as vital to regime survival. Similarly, the state elites of later capitalist developers—mainly Germany, Russia, and Japan—found themselves in a competitive international environment dominated by industrialized Western Europe. In response, state elites embarked on extensive industrialization efforts in an attempt to reduce the threat that the industrialized countries posed. Along with war and competitive pressure, conquest provides an additional international dynamic influencing state economic policy. In South Korea and Taiwan, foreign conquest and occupation dramatically weakened patrimonial elites and initiated industrialization and market-based reforms (Shin 1998; Wade 1990). Colonial conquest in Africa, on the other hand, often strengthened patrimonialism: Indirect rule empowered local authorities by giving them executive, legislative, and judicial powers and left them with low levels of supervision, the combination of which allowed them to take personal control of local markets (Boone 1994; Mamdani 1996).

This brief examination of why states may come to serve economic growth demonstrates that the reasons are not as simple as they first appear. It also reaches a similar conclusion as our discussion of the characteristics that enable states to operate effectively: We see again that the interaction between state and society is of crucial importance. States become "handmaidens of economic development" in part because of their interest in domestic resources as well as because of domestic demands and international pressure, and they are kept to the task by interested groups monitoring them and pressing for suitable detail. We must remember, however, that what's suitable varies with different interests. And for major kinds of developmental state action—foremost among them being approximation to an impartial rule of law—the state needs a high degree of autonomy precisely from the most powerful and the most interested groups.

Which State Actions are Developmental?

Which state policies are effective means of furthering economic growth? The answer to this question is—though taken for granted by many—not at all obvious. The question is difficult to answer for several interrelated reasons. First, predictive knowledge about the outcomes of given policies, once implemented, is hard to come by; this was so in history and it is still the case today. Under which conditions does protecting infant industries from international competition eventually improve the terms of a country's comparative advantage and when does it simply constitute an unproductive subsidy to "rent seekers" who will remain uncompetitive in the long run? Equally difficult to anticipate are the chances of implementing policies. Land reform is notoriously difficult to achieve, and it often did not expand productivity; but there are also examples of successful land reform that improved both productivity and equity. Furthermore, there are quite a few factors other than state action that may affect economic advance and stagnation, among them the availability of technology appropriate to an economy's problems, access to capital, human skill development, the distribution of resources among different classes, population dynamics, physical conditions such as soil and temperature, or cultural differences encouraging or limiting entrepreneurship, to name just some that have been considered. And, the interaction among these factors as well as between them and state policies is less than fully understood. Finally, knowledge claims about social and economic policies are ineluctably intertwined with interests, and they are—because of the prevalent uncertainties—subject to fads and radical revisions as well as to the influence of overarching ideologies. Due to these uncertainties, it is instructive to look at and compare economic policy attempts of the early modern states in Europe and the two global waves of economic policy after World War II.

Mercantilist Policy and Economic Development

The broad label "mercantilism" covers the three centuries between the Middle Ages and the takeoff of capitalism. This also was the period of state formation in Europe, and it was a time fertile in attempts to engineer economic growth based on different theories.[4] Overall, 300 years of mercantilist policy attempts were not remarkably successful in engendering economic growth. They may, however, have laid the foundations for later developments. Throughout the period, policy relevant knowledge was contested.

The "mercantile system of political economy," to use the title of Adam Smith's analysis (1776), favored the interests of urban merchants and craftsmen. States often did so by granting monopolies and other direct favors. Robert Ekelund and Robert Tollison (1981) make this the center of their explanation of mercantilist policies: They were primarily the result of the pursuit of partial self-interest, the search for unproductive gain—"rents"—on the part of merchants and artisans. This fits our view about the halting development of the state's interest in serving economic advance, but it ignores that siding with "mercantile" interests against the proponents of "agricultural systems of political economy" (to use Adam Smith's terminology once more) represented a long-term policy choice of great consequence, even as it also served the interests of monarchs, their retainers, and favored urban groups. These policies were embedded in a broader conceptual change. They arose from views of development that centered around "the opposition of arts to nature and the belief in the unlimited possibilities of the development of the arts. Differences in levels of economic development—as of Europe when compared to America, or of the Netherlands or England when compared to Spain or Ireland—were [seen as] due to superiority in arts, not to natural conditions" (Herlitz 1993, p. 118).

One central policy goal of mercantilist policy was the economic unification of a state's territory, freeing trade from tolls on bridges, roads, and rivers, and from custom duties imposed at regional boundaries. In many countries, this met with only limited success. Much policy focused on improving crafts and manufacture to the relative neglect of agriculture. This raised and maintained standards of production even when it limited competition. Regulating production was also related to the issues of territorial integration of the economy because the urban guilds favored local market closure. France and England pursued divergent policies in the sixteenth and seventeenth centuries: A centralized regulation and institutionalization of local guilds that gave them a new lease of life in France contrasting with a system of regulation favoring neither town nor countryside in England. If Heckscher (1933) claims "this was probably one of the reasons why the industrial revolution began in England instead of France," it is clear that that was not an intended policy outcome (p. 335). Policies that were successful in their immediate goals had unforeseen and unintended consequences.

A common concern of mercantilist policies was external trade. They often favored export surpluses—protecting industries at home from competition and maximizing employment. Many theorists and policy makers came to see the accumulation of bullion as a mark of success. This was at the center of Adam Smith's critique of "the mercantile system," to which he devoted a large part of the *Wealth of Nations*. Hoarding foreign currency is clearly not in itself a reasonable goal of developmental policy. Yet, given the interest in cash generated by the needs of warfare, so common in the period, this was often perhaps less irrational than it seems, though the policy overlooked the inflationary consequences. Many authors and policy makers, however, avoided the fallacy of equating the accumulation of bullion with wealth. In fact, many considered the impact of gold imports on the Spanish economy as an example to be avoided: "A spectre haunted Europe in the mercantilist period: the fear of ending up like Spain, rich in gold, poor in production, and with a frighteningly unfavorable balance of trade" (Perrotta 1993, p. 18). On the other hand, we see among pre-classical writers an appreciation of the effect of aggregate demand on employment, which could be stimulated by export surpluses. These insights were virtually lost during the period of classical economics and rediscovered only in the twentieth century (Grampp 1993).

Recent Economic Policy Prescriptions: Statism and Neoliberalism

The two generations of development policy since the end of World War II offer similar evidence of uncertainty, divergent views, and radical shifts of policy opinion. The situation had of course changed radically. The capitalist revolution, which during the nineteenth century radiated from northwestern Europe, had created tremendous wealth. This opened new opportunities and ambitions across the globe, but it also transformed worldwide relations of power, of domination and dependence. Local and national economies saw themselves increasingly embedded in a globalizing economy. The transnational dimension was an essential characteristic of capitalism from the outset. While the relations between rich and poor countries were increasingly shaped by colonialism, the rich economies became more and more intertwined through trade and capital flows. This development reached an early apex before World War I. It was set back in the interwar period only to expand once again after World War II.

The Russian Revolution of 1917 challenged the advance of capitalism and suggested to some an alternative path toward industrialization and economic development. Partly because of that, and also for other important reasons, two paradigms of development vied with each other in the half century after World War II. On the one hand, states actively pursued development policy through multiyear plans and direct involvement in production; on the other, the state's role was minimized in an attempt to maximize the sphere in which the market mechanism could work. Neither the developmental state policies nor neoliberal policy prescriptions have been an unequivocal success, and the debate on adequate developmental policies continues.

The initial dominance of postwar statist policies is rooted in the global movement away from free trade during the Great Depression, centralized wartime production, and postwar reconstruction efforts. In actual practice, however, it began long before it became a dominant policy prescription. A central tenet was import-substitution industrialization (ISI), which was based on earlier state-led efforts to promote industrialization in Germany and Japan. The basic belief underpinning ISI was that the substitution of local manufactured goods for imported goods was necessary for industrialization and that nascent domestic industry required protection from foreign competitors. ISI prescriptions claimed that successful import substitution, in turn, depended on an interventionist state. Since nonindustrialized countries could not compete economically with the West, since indigenous capitalists were often lacking, and since industrialization was seen as central to development, states were needed not only to protect nascent industry through tariffs and quotas but also to assist, direct, and finance industrial production. Active state involvement provided infrastructure necessary for industrialization, helped overcome capital shortage and technical backwardness, and gave entrepreneurs confidence that their investments would pay off.

As the earlier mercantilist policy, this state involvement resulted in increased rent seeking and inefficiencies in many instances. In Latin America, which began ISI in the 1930s, preliminary attempts were moderately successful yet stagnated because producers were sheltered from competition for long periods of time and therefore were able to profit without increases in efficiency. The former Soviet Empire provides additional cases of rent seeking, stagnation, and collapse. In East Asia, however, ISI efforts were much more successful (Deyo 1987; Wade 1995). Like Latin America, several East Asian states pursued an ISI policy during the 1950s and 1960s that focused on protecting and financing new infant industry in low-technology areas. After an initial start-up period, production shifted from domestic consumption to foreign exports. This shift to export-oriented industrialization (EOI) forced local industry to compete with foreign producers and, therefore, limited the stagnation and rent-seeking that occurred in Latin America. And after low-tech industrial production became globally competitive, state policy in East Asia replicated the ISI-EOI cycle for higher technology industrial production as well, allowing countries such as Taiwan and South Korea to make the leap from nonindustrial to industrialized economies in a matter of decades and Japan to emerge from the rubble of World War II as a leading industrial powerhouse.

While ISI/EOI policy in Asia was generally implemented according to an overall strategy, unforeseen and fortuitous factors also promoted its success (Barrett and Chin 1987; Cumings 1987). The Cold War and wars in Korea and Vietnam caused large flows of capital into the region. Moreover, fears of communist proliferation caused the United States, among others, to offer beneficial terms of trade despite the fact that the Asian countries maintained strict import restrictions, giving them the best of both worlds (Koo 1987). Internal factors also promoted rapid industrialization in the Asian Newly Industrialized Countries (NICs). Intensive agriculture, for example, sustained and possibly helped discipline large populations, thereby making possible cheap yet efficient work forces.

Despite its industrial success, East Asian state-led development has also experienced serious trials. Since the early 1990s, the once unstoppable Japanese economy has faltered, and as of this writing there is no sign of recovery. Similarly, other East Asian NICs have experienced serious crises since the mid-1990s. Some suggest that the cause of the crisis is a combination of global overproduction, the globalization of financial services, and misguided assistance by the IMF and American Government, factors that are best addressed via effective state action (Houtzager 2003; Stiglitz 2002; Wade 2000). Others, however, claim either that the "new" era of globalization has made states much less relevant or that the Asian crisis is the result of "crony capitalism," of economic relations based on personal ties between state and economic actors, not market-based exchanges (Camdessus 1999). According to this latter view, interference has caused inefficiencies, since access to capital depends more on a firm's ties to the state than on economic potential. In South Korea, for example, firms depended on the state for capital, a dependence that once allowed the state to exert considerable control over firms. After a select number of huge firms controlled by powerful industrial families arose, however, the state became dependent on the firms for the country's economic well-being and could no longer use its control of credit markets to spur efficiency, resulting in economic stagnation and a decline in industrial competitiveness. This neoliberal view therefore suggests that economic recovery in East Asia requires a new state development policy characterized by state withdrawal and market competition.

Decades before the neoliberal critique of the East Asian economic crisis, free-market ideas of state development policy began to replace ISI/EOI as the dominant economic policy prescription. This perspective was promoted by powerful interests and institutions, among them the U.S. and British Governments as well as international organizations such as the IMF, World Bank, and OECD. Most basically, this policy is based on the belief that markets function best when state interference is minimized, since it only causes market distortions and inefficiencies. Influential studies by Robert Bates (1981) and neoliberal political economists emphasized how state interference promotes rent-seeking and therefore the nonproductive use of resources. Consequently, not only should the state refrain from direct involvement in production, but it should implement policy that makes possible free trade and free capital flows. With this, investment will go where it is most profitable, and countries will only produce goods for which they have a comparative advantage.

The neoliberal view has provided a needed critique of some of the more state-centered policies, demonstrating that state involvement can have negative effects on economic development. Yet, it has been severely criticized for placing too much faith in market mechanisms and not recognizing that all state interference is not the same. Alice Amsden, for example, has long maintained that the neoliberal mantra of "getting the prices right" is not only insufficient as advice but can also be profoundly misleading. With her recent study of late industrializing countries (2001), she has built a strong case for this contention, grounding it in a broadly comparative investigation. Her analysis focuses on the role of technology and knowledge that is largely specific to the context of firms and cultures as well as based on tacit, implicit, "local" ideas. Therefore, she claims, institutional patterns shaping and mobilizing this knowledge are of equal importance as the coordination mechanism of the market. She shows that the successful late industrializing countries developed systems of conditional subsidies and careful performance monitoring. These "reciprocal control mechanisms" allowed substantial government interventions—even interventions that significantly distort the workings of the market—without reaping the effects of rent-seeking and corruption.

In addition to such evidence that state involvement benefited economic growth, failures of neoliberal reforms also strengthen the case against unqualified "market fundamentalism." The adoption and implementation of neoliberal policy in Latin America during the 1970s, 1980s, and 1990s did little or nothing to relieve financial difficulties. Indeed, neoliberal programs throughout the world have rarely been overwhelming successes and have often caused increasing inequality and social hardship (Stiglitz 2002). And where they were relatively successful—such as in Mauritius' structural adjustment program in the mid-1980s—the state was central to the successful implementation of the reforms, struggled to maintain social welfare programs despite external pressure, and had laid the foundation for rapid economic growth in the late 1980s and early 1990s through state-led EOI policy in the early 1970s (Dabee and Greenaway 2001). Aside from such empirical objections, neoliberal policy prescriptions are increasingly under attack from normative concerns about human well-being: Global protests by environmentalists, unionists, and other activists and harsh critiques from former insiders, such as Joseph Stiglitz, portray neoliberalism as an inhumane, exploitative, and unsustainable means for the leading economic powers to protect their dominant positions.

As in the long period of mercantilism, no clear-cut consensus emerged on policies of economic development in the period after World War II. However, the extremes of a political command economy with little space for market exchange and a radically free market system that relegates state action to the fringes have lost credibility. And the mutual critiques of more statist and more market oriented policy proposals have led to a number of important partial agreements, resulting in a growing consensus over the need to combine market and state coordination mechanisms in mutually beneficial ways. Yet, our brief review also suggests that knowledge about development is still contested, that this knowledge is inevitably associated with interests and ideologies, that some outcomes are unforeseen and fortuitous, and that a number of factors such as the changing global context and domestic power relations undoubtedly shape the effectiveness of state policy.

Why Focus on Long-Term Social Change?

At various points in the preceding discussion, we saw that the impact of states on development involves slow, drawn-out processes. Both the internal development of state machineries and the development of synergistic interactions between state and society take time. This is the issue we explore in this volume. We investigate the long-term nature of developmental processes and state building, present evidence about some of the time scales involved, and explore the causal conditions that account for this long-term character of state building and economic development. We claim that an historical perspective is vital to the analysis of states and development for two general reasons: (1) For reasons yet to be fully understood, state building often seems to be a slow process, though occasional rapid processes are known as well; and (2) large institutions and their effects on developmental processes appear to persist over long historical periods.

State building appears to be a long-term process for three reasons: It involves the development of institutions and normative culture; it requires the coordination of many different actors and units; and it typically involves conflict and prolonged stalemates. As we have seen, state building does not only involve creating an effective administrative apparatus, but states also depend on the co-option and adaptation of preexisting social institutions, suggesting that state building is conditioned by the characteristics of the surrounding societies. In this way, society provides both material and organizational resources that states require, and considerable effort must therefore be made to establish productive relations with societal actors. This involves complex alignments of interests as well as the transformation of norms and ideas in different groups and strata. Furthermore, attempts by state elites to subordinate individuals and groups often cause varied and widespread resistance. The long ways to an eventual acceptance of state rule are littered with conflicts, stalemates, and compromises.

The rationale for analyzing development in a long-term perspective derives from the impact of states on other institutions and broad social processes. States and the continuous effects of relevant institutions can shape developmental trajectories for a long time. This is not just—and in the long run perhaps not primarily—a matter of developmental state policies. The structure of a state and its articulation with interests, institutions, and patterns of power in society have consequences that often remain stable in the long run. The contributions of this volume offer striking evidence of empirical linkages between the very existence of states as well as particular patterns of colonial rule and much later social and economic developments. The interpretation of these empirical linkages is partly suggested by the configurations in the historical evidence. Fortunately, it can build on a strong research tradition concerned with the comparative historical explanation of important trajectories over time (see, e.g., Mahoney and Rueschemeyer 2003; Tilly 1984); and it also benefits from recent analytic work on institutional transformations over time and path dependence (Mahoney 2000; Pierson 2000, 2004).

While understanding the historic roots of states and their long-term impact on social and economic development is of interest in itself, many may impatiently ask of what use such an inquiry is for today's pressing problems in the international scene. The implication that this is an "academic" enterprise of no practical value is, however, fundamentally mistaken. Hoping that structures whose creation does take long periods of time can materialize quickly, is to engage in wishful thinking. Identifying which points of leverage are not available for developmental action is as important as to determine those that are. At the same time, our inquiry into the long historical causes of state development and its effects on economy and society may also reveal certain aspects of state building that can be achieved more rapidly, and it can help to find conditions under which long lasting negative effects can be overcome.

The Contributions to This Volume

This volume is divided into three parts. Part I continues this chapter's theoretical discussion of the impact of states on development. Peter Evans sketches the different ways in which bureaucratic oversight, market functioning, and the assertion of democratic demands discipline state actions and contribute to state effectiveness. His argument emphasizes the interactions of these different modes of discipline. Next, Matthew Lange discusses the rule of law as a macro-institution making possible broad-based human development. The chapter takes off from the insights of Max Weber's sociology of law—arguably the core of his sociology—and claims that the rule of law not only contributes to economic growth but also to the self-organization of society and to democratic rule.

Part II investigates the long-lasting effects of states on development through comparative empirical analysis. Areendam Chanda and Louis Putterman analyze how the age of states affects economic growth. Using statistical methods, they find that the age of state organizations is positively related to economic growth yet not to the current quality of governance, suggesting that states have long-term effects on economic production through cultural, organizational, and human capital dimensions. James Mahoney and Matthias vom Hau analyze the long-term effects of colonial influence in Latin America. Building on Mahoney's finding that the ranking of Latin American countries in economic development has been remarkably stable during the last century and his hypothesis that colonial influence in Latin America is negatively related to economic growth, they examine comparative historical evidence on the legal and bureaucratic institutions of the colonial state for clues to a causal explanation. In the following chapter, Matthew Lange analyzes the impact of British colonialism on postcolonial developmental trajectories. He shows that British colonialism varied significantly in the degree of direct rule by Britain and, conversely, indirect reliance on local power holders. Measures of indirect rule correlate negatively with postcolonial governance and development. Theoretical argument and qualitative historical evidence suggest some ideas about causal mechanisms that may underlie this correlation.

Part III of the volume includes both theoretical and empirical analyses that investigate whether state building is inherently a long-term process. Dietrich Rueschemeyer opens the discussion with a theoretical contribution exploring why the institutional foundations of states and state-society relations are likely to be created over a considerable period of time, though the purposive and rapid creation of organizations seems possible under special conditions and becomes common within modern society. Combining power-resource and norm-theory perspectives, Rueschemeyer examines which aspects of state development are especially likely to be long-term in character and which can be subject to rapid development. In the following chapter, Thomas Ertman pursues the same questions from a comparative historical perspective. The chapter is based primarily on comparative historical analysis of state building in early-modern Europe. Next, Jaime Becker and Jack Goldstone analyze the impact of revolutions on state-building processes. Examining postrevolutionary developments offers a chance to test and sharpen insights from the two preceding chapters. Finally, Bruce Cumings provides a historical analysis of state building in South Korea. State development in South Korea after 1960 was relatively rapid and phenomenally successful in advancing economic growth. To what extent did this development build on Korea's previous history? Cumings offers an analysis of the Korean state before and after 1960 that further tests, qualifies, and refines the arguments developed in the two opening chapters of this section.

In the conclusion, the editors draw together insights derived from each thematic cluster—the pace of state building under different conditions and long-lasting effects of states on economic development. They also evaluate the relevance of the results of these analyses for current policy concerns: Identifying developments that are inherently long-term in character makes it easier to find the points of leverage that do have a chance of more immediate effects. It also makes it possible to warn against long-term negative outcomes of present actions.

Notes

The authors thank all of the contributors to this volume for their extremely helpful comments on an earlier version of this chapter.

1. This was Albert Hirschman's formulation of the question when he challenged the members of the Research Committee on States and Social Structures, which was working in the 1980s at the Social Science Research Council, not to take the answer for granted.

2. Barry Weingast (1993) observes tellingly that a "government strong enough to protect property rights is also strong enough to confiscate the wealth of its citizens" (p. 287).
3. Max Weber realized that his model of early capitalism—the interaction between universalist law, a bureaucratic but limited state, and competitive market exchange—ran into some difficulty when applied to England, a problem he never quite resolved. One of the alternatives he considered in explaining England's advance without a law approaching formally rational character was that "the English legal system offered a low degree of calculability but assisted capitalists by denying justice to the lower classes" (Trubek 1972, p. 747). An example of exploitation of weaker groups is described in the influential study by Bates (1981) that demonstrates how political manipulation of rural marketing boards in a number of African states yielded substantial resources that were used to build support for political elites and their policies. In the aggregate, this strategy was severely dysfunctional for economic development.
4. Heckscher's two volume monograph (1955) was for long the classic treatment of mercantilism. It is now the subject of revisionist treatments that insist on important differences between countries and time periods as well as on sharper distinctions between economic theories and policy proposals on the one hand and actual policies and the differential success on the other. Magnusson (1993) offers a good overview of the state of the discussion.

References

Amsden, Alice. 1989. *Asia's Next Giant: South Korea and Late Industrialization*. New York: Oxford University Press.

———. 2001. *The Rise of "the Rest": Challenges to the West from Late-Industrializing Economies*. New York: Oxford University Press.

Augustinus, Aurelius. 1984. *The City of God*. London: Penguin.

Barrett, Richard and Soomi Chin. 1987. "Export-Oriented Industrializing in the Capitalist World System: Similarities and Differences." In *The Political Economy of the New Asian Industrialism*, edited by F. Deyo. Ithaca, NY: Cornell University Press, 23–43.

Bates, Robert H. 1981. *Markets and States in Topical Africa: The Political Basis of Agricultural Policies*. Berkeley, CA: University of California Press.

———. 1989. *Beyond the Miracle of the Market: The Political Economy of Agrarian Development in Kenya*. New York: Cambridge University Press.

Boone, Catherine. 1994. "States and Ruling Classes in Postcolonial Africa: The Enduring Contradictions of Power." In *State Power and Social Forces: Domination and Transformation in the Third World*, edited by J. Migdal, A. Kohli, and V. Shue. New York: Cambridge University Press, 108–142.

Camdessus, Michel. 1999. "Governments and Economic Development in a Globalized World." Speech at *The 32nd International General Meeting of the Pacific Basin Economic Council*, Hong Kong, May 17.

Childe, V. Gordon. 1953. *Man Makes Himself*. New York: Mentor.

Cumings, Bruce. 1987. "The Origins and Development of the Northeast Asian Political Economy: Industrial Sectors, Product Cycles, and Political Consequences." In *The Political Economy of the New Asian Industrialism*, edited by F. Deyo. Ithaca, NY: Cornell University Press, 44–83.

Dabee, Rajen and David Greenaway (eds.). 2001. *The Mauritian Economy*. New York: Palgrave.

Deyo, Frederic (ed.). 1987. *The Political Economy of the New Asian Industrialism*. Ithaca, NY: Cornell University Press.

Eisenstadt, S. N. 1963. *The Political System of Empires*. New York: Free Press.

Ekelund, Robert and Robert Tollison. 1981. *Mercantilism as a Rent-Seeking Society*. College Station, TX: A&M University Press.

Esman, Milton and Norman Uphoff. 1984. *Local Organizations: Intermediaries in Local Development*. Ithaca, NY: Cornell University Press.

Evans, Peter B. 1979. *Dependent Development: The Alliance of Multinational, State, and Local Capital in Brazil*. Princeton, NJ: Princeton University Press.

———. 1995. *Embedded Autonomy: States and Industrial Transformation*. Princeton, NJ: Princeton University Press.

Gerschenkron, Alexander. 1962. *Economic Backwardness in Historical Perspective: A Book of Essays*. Cambridge: Harvard University Press.

Gorski, Philip. 1993. "The Protestant Ethic Revisited: Disciplinary Revolution and State Formation in Holland and Prussia." *American Journal of Sociology*, 99, 2: 265–316.

Grampp, William D. 1993. "An Appreciation of Mercantilism." In *Mercantilist Economics*, edited by L. Magnusson. Boston: Kluwer Academic Publishers, 59–85.

Hardin, R. 1982. *Collective Action*. Baltimore, MD: Johns Hopkins University Press.

Heckscher, Eli F. 1933. "Mercantilism." In *Encyclopaedia of the Social Sciences*, edited by E. R. A. Seligman and A. Johnson. New York: Macmillan, vol. 10, 333–339.

———. 1955. *Mercantilism*. London: George Allen & Uwin.

Herlitz, Lars. 1993. "Conceptions of History and Society in Mercantilism, 1650–1730." In *Mercantilist Economics*, edited by L. Magnusson. Boston: Kluwer Academic Publishers, 87–125.

Hirschman, Albert O. 1958. *The Strategy of Economic Development*. New Haven, CT: Yale University Press.

Houtzager, Peter. 2003. "Introduction: From Polycentrism to the Polity." In *Changing Paths: International Development and the New Politics of Inclusion*, edited by P. Houtzager and M. Moore. Ann Arbor: University of Michigan Press.

Johnson, Chalmers. 1982. *MITI and the Japanese Miracle: The Growth of Industrial Policy, 1925–1975*. Stanford: Stanford University Press.

Koo, Hagen. 1987. "The Interplay of State, Social Class, and World System in East Asian Development: The Cases of South Korea and Taiwan." In *The Political Economy of the New Asian Industrialism*, edited by F. Deyo. Ithaca, NY: Cornell University Press, 165–181.

Lenski, Gerhard and Jean Lenski. 1974. *Human Societies: An Introduction to Macrosociology*. New York: McGraw-Hill.

Magnusson, Lars (ed.). 1993. *Mercantilist Economics*. Boston: Kluwer Academic Publishers.

Mahoney, James. 2000. "Path Dependence in Historical Sociology." *Theory and Society*, 29: 507–548.

Mahoney, James and Dietrich Rueschemeyer (eds.). 2003. *Comparative Historical Analysis in the Social Sciences*. New York: Cambridge University Press.

Mamdani, Mahmood. 1996. *Citizen and Subject*. Princeton: Princeton University Press.

Marx, Karl and Friedrich Engels. 1978. "The German Ideology." In *The Marx-Engels Reader*, edited by R. Tucker. New York: Norton, 146–200.

North, Douglass. 1981. *Structure and Change in Economic History*. New York: Norton.

Olson, Mancur. 1965. *The Logic of Collective Action: Public Goods and the Theory of Groups*. Cambridge, MA: Harvard University Press.

Perrotta, Cosimo. 1993. "Early Spanish Mercantilism: The First Analysis of Underdevelopment." In *Mercantilist Economics*, edited by L. Magnusson. Boston: Kluwer Academic Publishers, 17–58.

Pierson, Paul. 2000. "Increasing Returns, Path Dependence, and the Study of Politics." *American Political Science Review*, 94, 2: 251–268.

———. 2004. *Politics in Time: History, Institutions, and Social Analysis*. New York: Cambridge University Press.

Polanyi, Karl. 1957. *The Great Transformation*. Boston: Beacon Press.

Putnam, Robert. 1993. *Making Democracy Work*. Princeton: Princeton University Press.

Rueschemeyer, Dietrich and Peter Evans. 1985. "The State and Economic Transformation: Toward an Analysis of the Conditions Underlying Effective Intervention." In *Bringing the State Back In*,

edited by P. Evans, D. Rueschemeyer, and T. Skocpol. New York: Cambridge University Press, 44–77.
Scott, James C. 1998. *Seeing Like A State: Why Certain Schemes to Improve the Human Condition Have Failed*. New Haven, CT: Yale University Press.
Shin, Gi-Wook. 1998. "Agrarian Conflict and the Origins of Korean Capitalism." *American Journal of Sociology*, 5: 1309–1351.
Smith, Adam. 1776. *An Inquiry into the Nature and Causes of the Wealth of Nations*. New York: Random House Modern Library.
Stiglitz, Joseph. 2002. *Globalization and Its Discontents*. New York: W.W. Norton.
Strayer, Joseph R. 1970. *On the Medieval Origins of the Modern State*. Princeton, NJ: Princeton University Press.
Taylor, M. 1987. *The Possibility of Cooperation*. New York: Cambridge University Press.
Tilly, Charles. 1984. *Big Structures, Large Processes, Huge Comparisons*. New York: Russell Sage Foundation.
———. 1985. "War Making and State Making as Organized Crime." In *Bringing the State Back In*, edited by P. B. Evans, D. Rueschemeyer, and T. Skocpol. New York: Cambridge University Press, 169–191.
———. 1992. *Coercion, Capital, and European States, AD 990–1990*. Cambridge: Basil Blackwell.
Trubek, David M. 1972. "Max Weber on Law and the Rise of Capitalism." *Wisconsin Law Review*, 3: 720–753.
Veblen, Thorstein. 1934. *The Theory of the Leisure Class*. New York: Modern Library.
Wade, Robert. 1990. *Governing the Market: Economic Theory and the Role of Government in Taiwan's Industrialization*. Princeton, NJ: Princeton University Press.
———. 1995. "Resolving the State-Market Dilemma in East Asia." In *The Role of the State in Economic Change*, edited by H. Chang and R. Rowthorn. Oxford: Clarendon Press, 114–136.
———. 2000. "Out of the Box: Rethinking the Governance of International Financial Markets." *Journal of Human Development*, 1, 1: 145–157.
Weber, Max. 1968. *Economy and Society*. New York: Bedminster Press.
Weingast, Barry R. 1993. "Constitutions as Government Structures—The Political Foundations of Secure Markets." *Journal of Institutional and Theoretical Economics*, 149, 1: 286–311.

CHAPTER TWO

Harnessing the State: Rebalancing Strategies for Monitoring and Motivation

PETER EVANS

Debating strategies for harnessing the state to the service of the common ends of its citizens is a perennial obligation of political theorists and practical politicians. On the one hand, societies must continually rethink ways of ensuring that the powers and legitimacy of state apparatuses are not appropriated for predatory purposes by private elites (and their allies within the apparatus itself). At the same time, societies must continually search for positive solutions to the problem of control—trying to find ways of making sure that those within the state apparatus have the information, capacity, and motivation required to implement societal goals.

The problem of disciplining and controlling the state has been conceptualized and politically contested in many different ways. Each era tries to selectively draw on prior historical lessons, while having its strategies shaped in unintended ways by the legacies of the past. Each national strategy is shaped by a country's place in the global political economy as well as its own history. My focus in this chapter is on the contemporary era, and on the ways in which the current theoretical and political context channels our efforts to harness the state.

Since the beginnings of modern public administration, three basic modes of control have been used to shape the effectiveness of state apparatuses. The imposition of professional norms, hierarchical authority structures, and standardized procedures are the classic modes of control. It is the development of bureaucratic structures that created the potential, albeit always far from fully realized, of making the exercise of power predictable rather than capricious and of orienting public institutions toward societal goals rather than the particular interests of the king or oligarchy.

From the beginning, market signals provided a powerful complement to bureaucratic structures. It is not just that markets defined the price parameters within which administrators must live. Indeed, while traditional administrative apparatuses may predate modern markets, markets were a central means of controlling state actors long before the development of modern bureaucracies. The intimate relations between the British Treasury and the private financial markets of the City of London were already going strong 300 years ago (Carruthers 1996). Conversely, as Mahoney (2002) documents, when conservative nineteenth-century oligarchs wanted to enhance the role of markets in their societies, they looked to strengthening state administrations as a means of generating more "market oriented" regimes. The recent rise of the East Asian Tigers is at the same time a story of the ability of bureaucrats to create market-oriented capitalist elites and a story of the ability of markets to keep state bureaucracies, which might have otherwise descended into a combination of militarism and predation, focused on developing and sustaining local productive capacity. In short, "hybridity" in the form of a combination of bureaucratic controls and market discipline has been an historical constant in the development of the modern state.

Democratic "bottom-up" control by the citizenry is the most recent, and (perhaps partially in consequence of this) the most fragile, of the three modes of controlling the state. Yet, if there is one pervasively hegemonic ideological principle with regard to harnessing the modern state, it is that democratic control is a *sine qua non*. There is an analytical sense to this rhetoric. Advocates of bureaucracy may wish to see this form of control as putting the state at the service of the common citizen; but the fact remains that bureaucracies are hierarchies, and it is very difficult to make hierarchies more responsive to those at the bottom than they are to commands from above. Likewise, while the more fervent proponents of the market like to see "bilateral voluntary exchange" as the ultimate form of democratic decision-making, the fact remains that "one person one vote" doesn't apply in markets. The right to "vote" in markets is proportionate to assets controlled, and no one would claim that market assets are distributed according to democratic principles.

In short, if harnessing the state means making sure that its actions reflect the common goals of ordinary citizens, there is no escaping the essential role of bottom-up democratic control. Nor is the role of democratic bottom-up control simply a question of political principles.

Markets and bureaucracy—even in combination—don't ensure transparency and accountability and some level of transparency and accountability is necessary for economic effectiveness. Consequently, some admixture of "bottom-up" control is likely to be a requisite for sustained developmental success. Mahoney's (2002) careful comparison of nineteenth-century Central American regimes is again a useful example. The "radical" liberal regimes that put markets and bureaucracy at the service of oligarchs were developmentally less effective in the long run than the "reformist" liberal regimes that were forced to respond to pressures from subordinate groups.

The problem, of course, is translating "democratic, bottom-up control" into concrete, observable institutional norms and structures. Eliding "democratic control" and "elections" won't do it. The problem is analogous to the difficulties of specifying the features of "real" (as opposed to fictitious) bureaucracy or defining what constitute useful and authentic "market signals," but evaluating the implications of different systems of political input for bottom-up control of the state is even more difficult.

Each of the three classic modes of harnessing the state has its strengths and weaknesses, but explicating the virtues and problems associated with each of these three modes of controlling the state is not the primary purpose of this essay. The argument here is that effective public administration, especially when development is the goal, requires the balanced, synergistic integration of all three modes of control—what I call "hybridity."

While this may seem an obvious and innocuous proposition, it becomes more interesting and controversial when set in the context of the evolution, over the last quarter of the twentieth century, of politics and policy with regard to how best to monitor and motivate state actors. During the past quarter century, the dominant mode of dealing with the problem has been framed in terms of "state reform" and the basic proposition of late-twentieth-century state reform has been that the solution to monitoring and motivating state actors is to shrink the role of bureaucratic controls and expand the role of "market signals."

This version of state reform might, of course, be quite consistent with the "hybridity." If one assumed that the balance between the different modes of control at the beginning of the period had become overreliant on bureaucratic control, increasing reliance on market signals could be considered an application of the "rebalancing" idea. The thrust of the late-twentieth-century state reform movement was, however, quite different. Its advocates rarely stressed the importance of strengthening a combination of different modes of control and often ignored the limits of using market signals alone.

This is not to say that late-twentieth-century state reform was without positive effects. Looking back over the results of a quarter century of state reform, there have been specific instances of gratifying success.[1] Nonetheless, the overall results leave a great deal to be desired. In both North and South, "trust in government" continues to decline, reflecting deep-seated convictions on the part of ordinary citizens that they do not control their states. In Latin America and Africa, trends in the conventional "bottom line"—that is, economic growth rates—show no signs of improving. Even more disturbing, the ability of states to deliver the basic public services and collective goods on which ordinary citizens rely remains precarious. In many cases, the capacity to deliver collective goods is deteriorating. Finally, the classic problem that was supposed to be brought under control by state reform—corruption—remains disturbingly prevalent. Some reconsideration of the conceptual underpinnings of late-twentieth-century strategies is clearly in order.

The proposition of this paper is, therefore, not just a general argument for conceptualizing control of the state in terms of hybridity, but a more context specific proposition that recent efforts to shift the mode of state control have gone overboard in the direction of an overemphasis on market signals and that, consequently, future improvements in state performance are likely to depend on recapturing a more balanced form of hybridity.

The discussion that follows is divided into four sections. The first briefly reiterates the basic propositions of the "hybridity model." The second argues that the value of the classic mode of control—bureaucratic capacity—has been systematically underestimated and that potentially effective strategies for improving state performance by means of improving bureaucratic capacity, most especially paying more attention to the power of intangible rewards, have been neglected. The third section argues that current tendencies to overestimate the potential role of "market signals" stem from at least two conceptual problems: first, the failure to take account of the limits that modern economic theory places on the efficacy of market signals in general and, second, using indicators that measure the preferences of powerful market-oriented elites as though they represented "market signals" understood as value-neutral indicators of efficacy. The fourth section reviews the obstacles to strengthening the "third leg" of the tripod of control—bottom-up democratic controls—and also argues for the potential returns to overcoming these obstacles. Finally, the conclusion reviews the overall argument and looks at the implications of the hybridity approach on future agendas of research and policy formation.

The Basic Hybridity Model

The hybridity perspective can be summarized in a set of three straightforward propositions. First and most basically, the effectiveness of public institutions depends on "hybridity," an integrated balance among three different (sometimes contradictory) modes of guiding administrative action. These are: (1) bureaucratic capacity built on meritocratic recruitment, professional norms, predictable, rewarding careers, and coordinated organizational structures, which enable states to pursue collective goals; (2) "market signals" that convey costs and benefits, facilitate the efficient allocation of resources, and provide "fiscal discipline" to make sure that goals remain consistent with available means; and (3) "bottom-up" democratic participation to ensure that the goals pursued by the state reflect the needs and desires of ordinary citizens. Each of the three helps ensure that administrative processes are transparent and accountable. Each represents a complementary means of preventing the state apparatus from being used for purposes of predation or individual rent-seeking. This tripartite combination can be conceived as a "Tripod Model" of state control that is portrayed graphically in figure 2.1.

The second proposition is that because late-twentieth-century state reform has focused excessively on escaping the perceived predominance

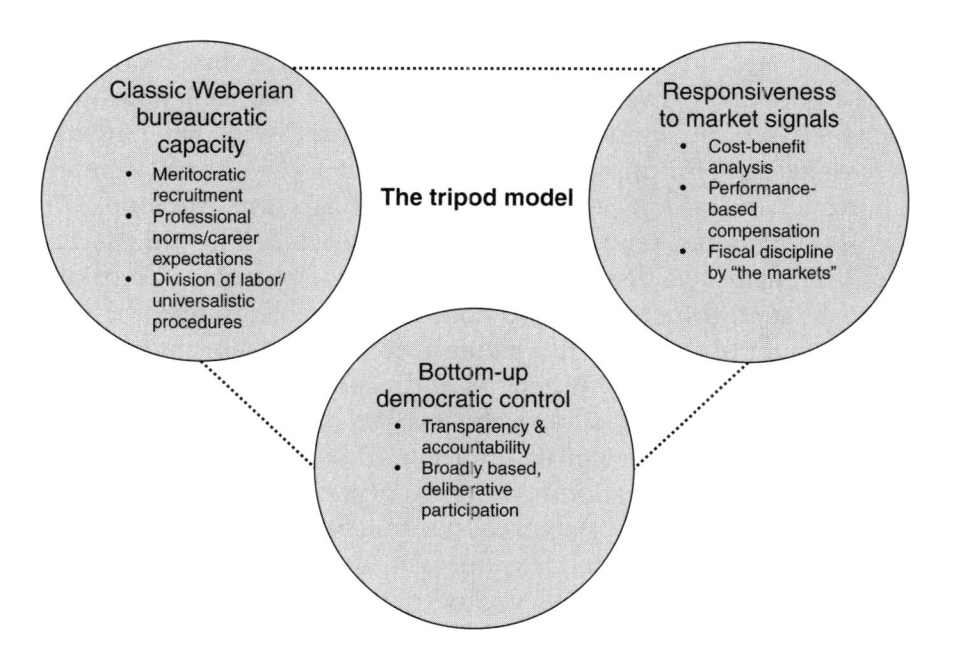

Figure 2.1 The tripod model of state control

of the first principle of control (classic bureaucratic capacity) by increasing reliance on the second principle of control (responsiveness to market signals), the balance necessary to maintain effective hybridity is being lost. Exaggerated efforts to substitute market signals for other indicators of performance or to make administration mimic markets, threaten to undermine bureaucratic capacity and carry their own intrinsic irrationalities and inefficiencies.

The move to "overweight" market signals is not hard to understand. Frequent and egregious failures on the part of traditional bureaucracies have validated both "neo-utilitarian" readings of conventional economic theory and the preferences of capitalist elites in support of focusing on market signals. State reformers have been urged to stop using public administrative apparatuses to perform tasks that might be done by private corporations. Even in the provision of core collective goods and public services, states have been encouraged to subject administrative organizations to disciplines based on performance measures that mimic markets.

The effect of these policy trends at the national level has been magnified by structural factors at the global level. The growing weight of international financial markets in determining national economic decisions and the emergence of global neoliberalism as the defining doctrine of international political economy result in powerful constraints for the trajectory of state reform, especially in the Global South. Administrators who want to experiment with reforms that emphasize anything other than ever greater reliance on markets fear being punished by "the markets" and, indeed, often are. The tendency of both global governance institutions, like the World Bank and the IMF, and private sources of global expertise, like the big consulting firms, to impose globally fashionable "blueprints" (which I have called elsewhere "institutional monocropping" [Evans 2004]) is a potent impediment to hybridity, especially to the development of the democratic leg of the tripod.

If increased reliance on markets were accompanied by an equally powerful expansion of democratic control, the problem might be less severe, but democratic control tends to be rhetorically honored rather than substantively instantiated. Election does not increase the range of policy options available to political leaders and the prerogative of electing leaders does not necessarily result in concrete democratic input into the policy making process. While there are encouraging instances of expanded democratic input, they are still not sufficiently generalized to challenge the overall tendency toward imbalance.

The final proposition of the hybridity approach follows directly from the first two. If imbalance is the problem, rebalancing the three modes of control is a likely means of securing performance from public institutions that will reduce corruption, improve the delivery of essential collective goods and generate increasing well-being for ordinary citizens. This entails more realistic assessments of the contribution of market signals, greater appreciation of the gains that can be realized from investing in traditional bureaucratic capacity, and a search for innovative ways of increasing the ability of ordinary citizens to enforce transparency and accountability. Reassessment of the actual and potential contributions of the classic mode of state control—bureaucratic capacity—is the place to start.

Underestimating the Value of Bureaucratic Capacity

Despite the arrogance and gross inefficiencies we have all seen flow from administrative hierarchies, it is important to remember what powerful instruments bureaucracies can be for achieving public ends. Indeed, most of the perverse consequences attributed to bureaucratic organization are in fact consequences of the absence of true bureaucratic norms and structures. Predatory states may perpetuate the superficial trappings of bureaucracy, but in practice they turn rules and offices into the opposite of bureaucracy—private marketable assets (Evans 1995).

A few years ago, Jim Rauch and I undertook a simple empirical exercise. Using a panel of experts, we collected estimates of the extent to which the core organizations of economic administration in a sample of developing countries, conformed to the basic features of true bureaucracies as originally identified by Max Weber: whether recruitment to public positions involved impersonal meritocratic criteria, whether those recruited into these organizations could expect long-term career rewards that approximated those available in the private sector, providing they preformed well, and so on. We found our "Weberianness" scale to be a strong predictor of economic growth (Evans and Rauch 1999). Controlling for initial GNP per capita and initial endowments of human capital, having higher levels of "Weberianness" turned out to be an impetus to the growth of GNP per capita, at least as powerful as any of the indicators used in traditional cross-country growth models. The results of our analysis are shown graphically in figure 2.2.

These results should not be interpreted as a defense of sclerotic administrative traditionalism. In most countries, increasing bureaucratic capacity is very likely to involve restructuring, that traditional bureaucrats will find quite traumatic. What these data do show is that simple organizational principles designed to increase the cohesion and

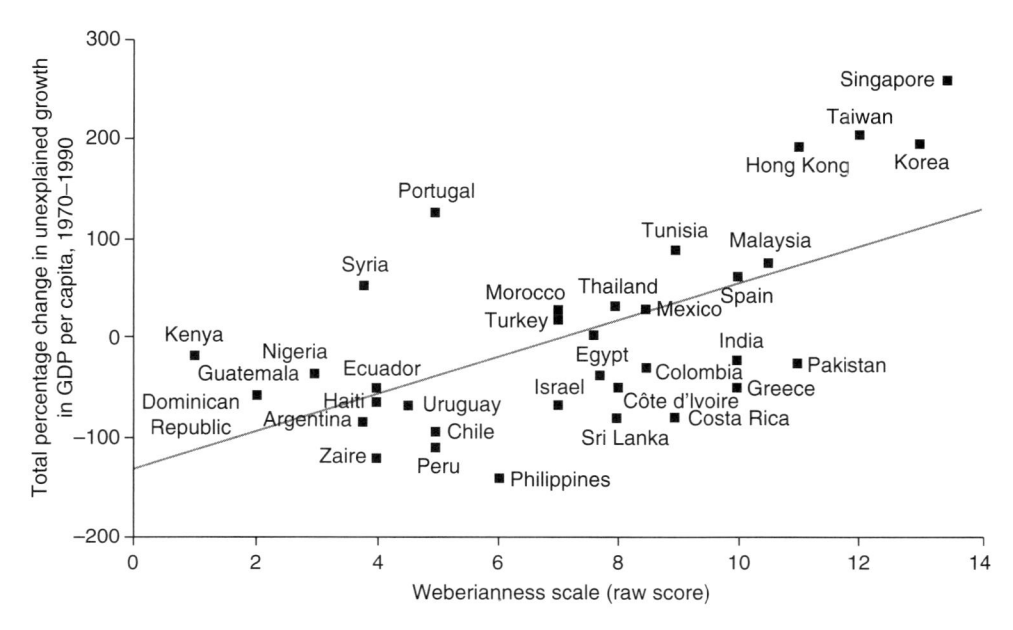

Figure 2.2 Total percent change in unexplained growth in per capita GDP (1970–1990) by "Weberianness" scale score
Source: Evans and Rauch (1999).

coherence of public institutions can pay large dividends in terms of standard economic goals.

In this sample of developing countries, the potential results from investments in improving bureaucratic capacity are very large. Roughly speaking, an increase of one half of a standard deviation in the Weberian score is worth a 26 percent increase in GDP from 1970 to 1990 (controlling for human capital and initial GDP per capita). Likewise, an increase of one standard deviation in the Weberian score is roughly equivalent to a shift in average years of education in 1965 from 3 years to 6 years (controlling for initial GDP per capita). In short, these results suggest that in most countries relatively modest improvement in bureaucratic capacity is worth as much as tens of billions of dollars if not hundreds of billions of dollars of investments in other areas.

The converse of the proposition that investments in bureaucratic capacity may have high returns relative to their costs is that *dis*investment in bureaucratic capacity may have higher costs than are generally acknowledged. This is particularly obvious when the institutional effects of disinvestment are taken into account. Internalization among administrators of the belief that they are collectively performing an invaluable service and that deviations from professional standards are morally unacceptable are essential to effective bureaucratic organization.

The construction of professional norms and career expectations, which underlie the commitments of individual office holders to honest, dedicated, and effective service, is an arduous task. While clever institutional innovations may occasionally allow rapid implantation of such norms in specific agencies or projects (as in the "health agents" example below), it takes a long time to construct generalized adherence to norms that permeates the state apparatus as a whole (see also Pelletier 2002). If general norms deteriorate or are undermined, they take an equally long time to reconstruct.

Such an institutional perspective puts policies that look at bureaucratic reform in simple fiscal terms in a different light. Austerity programs that undercut the expectation that public service can be the source of a rewarding career must be evaluated in terms of their institutional impact, not simply in terms of salary savings. Having first discovered that fiscal austerity rarely creates sufficient foundations for accelerated growth, the World Bank or IMF, returning in subsequent years to countries in which spending on public institutions has been radically cut, are likely to find corrupt and ineffectual public institutions whose downward spirals are difficult to reverse.

Missed opportunities for high return investments in the intangibles that make public services work are as important as losses from false economies. Without underestimating the role of career expectations that are rewarding in material terms, strategies of state reform must also take into account the powerful role of intangible rewards in building a professional public service. Recognition and public esteem can play a large role in the overall compensation "package" of public servants. Expanding this part of the package may cost very little in fiscal terms and have high returns in terms of performance. A brief example from the work of Judith Tendler will suffice to make the point.

Northeast Brazil is not renowned for its effective public institutions, or its developmental successes. Yet, in the late 1980s, the government of the state of Ceara instituted a public health program (Programa de Agentes de Saúde [PAS]) that eventually managed to reach 850,000 families and played a role in tripling the coverage of vaccinations and reducing infant mortality by 36 percent (see also Evans 1997b; Tendler 1997; Tendler and Freedheim 1994). The backbone of the program comprised roughly 7,000 unskilled "health agents" who were paid only the minimum wage. A good part of the secret of this program's success lay in its careful attention to the intangible aspects of building an effective public service.

Creating *esprit de corps* and a sense of "calling" among the health agents played a key role in eliciting high levels of performance. They were made to feel that they were valued professionals, whose vital contribution to the welfare of their communities was recognized both by elite officials and the public at large. The state government aggressively disseminated a positive image of the program in the popular media. Selection of the health agents involved trips to small communities and the honor involved in being selected was insistently stressed.

Those selected responded accordingly. As one health agent put it, "I was ready to look for a job in São Paulo. Now I love my job and I would never leave and abandon my community" (Tendler and Freedheim 1994, p. 1776). Their commitment translated into superior job performance and effective service delivery. Their communities' appreciation of their high level of performance further enhanced their status and increased their intangible compensation. In short, investment in intangibles generated a *virtuous* circle of increasing returns (as illustrated in figure 2.3).

From a fiscal point of view the ratio of investment to return in this program could hardly have been higher. The total cost of the program was only $2.00 per capita. Even if "returns" are defined in strictly economic terms, reductions in mortality and morbidity translate into

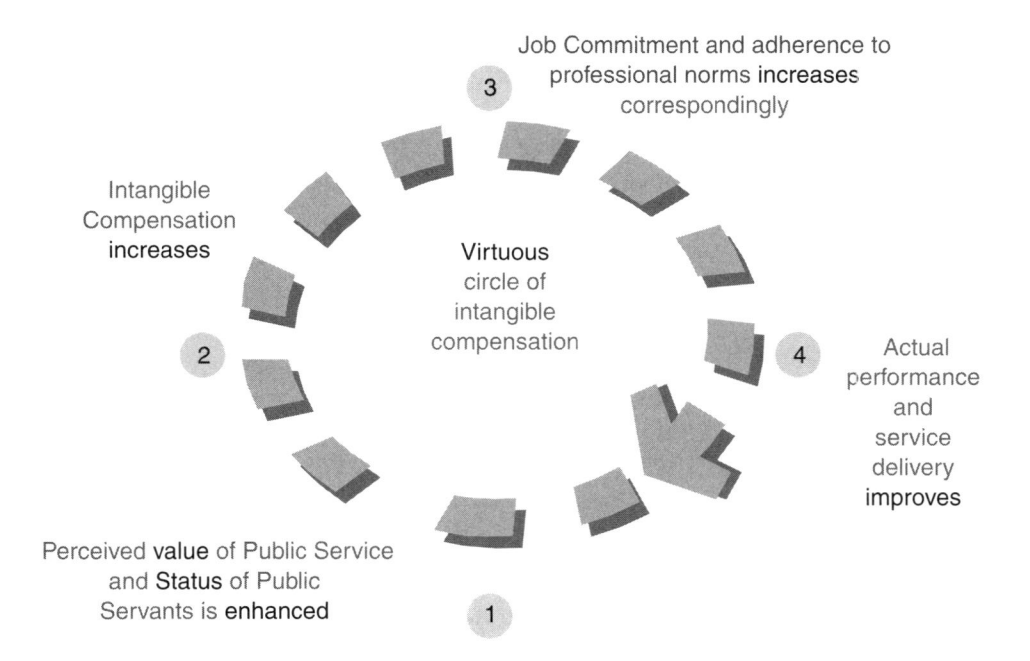

Figure 2.3 Virtuous circle of intangible compensation

increased capacity to engage in economically productive activities. If the total ratio of investment to increased local well-being from this program were systematically compared to schemes—always strongly endorsed by international lending agencies—that bestow hundreds of millions of dollars in subsidies on transnational firms in return for a few dozen local jobs, even the most conventional economic analysis would have a difficult time negating the value of investment in the intangible inputs to effective public service.

This example also points to a potential downside of current ideological insistence that the efforts of administrative officials almost inevitably produce results that are inferior to those that could be obtained via market mechanisms. If beliefs among the general citizenry in "public service" as a valuable, honored profession are a major component in the long-term career rewards of administrative personnel, then turning reliance on market signals into an ideological campaign can undercut the normative structures that underlie administrative effectiveness. It may even unintentionally legitimate corruption by implying that, as a general principle, individual maximization of material rewards should be valued over traditional norms of public service.

Once again, it is worth reiterating that none of these arguments should be taken as an excuse for the protection of bureaucracies that aren't delivering. Heaping praise on corrupt, ineffectual bureaucrats is not an investment in intangibles, protecting their long-term career rewards creates the wrong expectations among other administrators. Preserving rigid administrative rules that prevent effective delivery of collective goods is a disservice to would-be public servants, undermining their ability to secure the intangible rewards of community esteem.

Arguments for trying to increase bureaucratic capacity are arguments in favor of the positive agenda of the "new public management" that may threaten traditionalist sinecures within public administrations, but is, at its core, precisely an effort to increase bureaucratic capacity (see Barzelay 2001). In the end, building bureaucratic capacity is anything but a conservative strategy. It almost certainly requires more innovative thinking and imagination to build effective bureaucracies than does increasing the reliance on markets.

The Dangers of Overreliance on Market Signals

The tendencies toward imbalance that flow from underestimating the potential returns from enhancing traditional bureaucratic capacity are reinforced by the tendency to overestimate, or misunderstand, what reliance on market signals or market mimicking mechanisms can contribute to enhancing the effectiveness of public institutions. This overestimation stems from a variety of sources, but I will focus my attention on two of them.

First, policy makers often have an outmoded understanding of how markets work. The complexities of modern theories of how markets work, and the implications of those complexities for development policy, are largely ignored (Easterly 2001). The work of Stiglitz on the one hand and North, on the other hand, provides powerful reminders of how essential it is to start from modern economic theory rather than a simplistic, archaic version when attempting to formulate policies for state reform.

Second, what is portrayed as giving weight to "market signals" is often not that at all. Instead, it amounts to simply giving greater weight to the self-interested preferences of powerful market actors at the expense of the interests of other citizens who have a more difficult time portraying their preferences as "market signals." The "ICRG" (International Country Risk Guide) data, which are widely used to judge the comparative performance of states in the Global South, will provide an interesting illustration of this problem.

Perhaps the biggest problem with using market signals to control states is that it requires a much more sophisticated understanding of markets than the one found in most contemporary policy debates. Modern economic theory leaves the easy optimal equilibriums of earlier, simpler models behind. Coordination failures are a central concern. Equilibria are multiple, and simple linear solutions can end up being seriously suboptimal (see Hoff 2000; Hoff and Stiglitz 2001). This is true even in markets for conventional commodities and is much more telling in the case of collective goods or those that involve significant externalities, as do most of the goods provided through the core functions of states.

The skepticism of modern economics with regard to markets has been amply validated in practice as well as in theory. The recent sad experience of the state of California is a good example. Those in charge of replacing administrative controls with market signals in the provision of electric power apparently believed that for a homogeneous commodity like electricity, the construction of a market that would provide efficient, cost-minimizing allocation was an easy task that could be accomplished quickly with relatively little oversight. As the citizens of California discovered to their chagrin, nothing could have been farther from the reality. Simple parameters such as how much capacity was available proved prone to manipulation by suppliers, generating huge profits for them and correspondingly huge losses for consumers. With their state in debt billions of dollars to power companies and their own electrical bills soaring, Californians appreciated, even if they did not fully understand, the complexities of trying to construct a market as well as the dangers of ignoring those complexities.[2]

The insights of Douglass North's "new institutionalism" go even further. North's historical analysis makes it clear that the way in which markets operate depends on the broader institutional context in which they are embedded.[3] In a Northian perspective, public institutions and markets are Siamese twins. North foregrounds a simple proposition that was central to Adam Smith and remained a fundamental (but too often implicit) assumption in subsequent neoclassical analysis. Markets require a combination of formal and informal disciplining institutions; otherwise, they don't function. Each needs the vibrancy of the other in order to prosper.

Northian institutionalism is also amply justified by recent practical experience. Simplistic expectations that markets would deliver allocative efficiency and incentives for increased output and productivity in the former Soviet Union, regardless of the character of the institutional context, proved to be a cruel hoax (King 2002). Even in the United States, the institutional framework that allowed markets to operate effectively required more explicit attention than most had assumed. The economically costly scandals of firms like Enron and WorldCom forced even the market-oriented United States to recognize the perverse outcomes that can result when informal norms erode and public institutions fail to discipline powerful market actors, at least to the extent of monitoring the quality of the information they offer other market actors. Emphasis on the role of market signals in constraining public institutions must be accompanied by equal emphasis on the role of public institutions in disciplining private market actors.[4]

Taking into account the theoretical problems posed by the ways in which modern economics understands markets—and the practical reflections of these problems—is a fundamental problem for strategies that ground their hopes for better control of the state exclusively on greater use of market signals. The empirical challenge of deciding what constitutes a valid "market signal" is simpler but also crucial. The crux of the problem is being able to distinguish the preferences of the powerful from "objective" indicators of relative resources' scarcities and productive performance.

Allowing the self-interested preferences of powerful market actors to be defined as proxies for market signals may be more a political than a theoretical problem but it is still symptomatic of the dangers of allowing market signals to become the exclusive arbiter of administrative decisions. The "ICRG" data, which are widely used to judge the comparative performance of states in the Global South, provide an interesting illustration.[5] ICRG ratings purport to be an objective indicator of whether public institutions are providing the kind of institutional foundations that a Northian institutional analysis would suggest is necessary for the efficient operation of markets. They can also, however, be interpreted as a "beauty contest" that allows international business consultants (who appear to provide most of the ratings solicited by the PRS group in constructing the ICRG) to indicate which countries are trying hardest to conform to policy preferences of the firms who are the clients of these consultants.

The findings of recent research by Mick Moore and his collaborators at IDS support this latter interpretation (Houtzager and Moore 2003; Moore et al. 1999). Moore and his collaborators were interested in the relative ability of poor countries to deliver increased welfare for its citizens by controlling the constraints imposed by income levels. They calculated each country's performance in delivering welfare as measured by the UNDP's Human Development Index (HDI) controlling the GDP per capita, and called their indicator "RICE" (Relative Income Conversion Efficiency). To their surprise, they found that better ratings on ICRG indicators were *negatively* correlated with RICE (see figure 2.4). What this suggests is that countries that tried harder to conform to the preferences of the ICRG's raters were less able to construct the institutions necessary to speak to the needs of their poorer citizens. If ICRG indicators might reflect "market signals," they reflect a particular version of such "signals" that corresponds to one set of interests at the expense of other interests.

In the end, the problem is not whether public administrations should pay attention to "market signals"—of course they should. The problem is that "market signals" are a deceptively complex set of indicators. As long as paying attention to "market signals" is defined as building institutional structures that connect the delivery of collective goods with the preferences of citizens and users on the one hand, and the relative scarcity of different kinds of resources on the other, then paying attention to market resources is an excellent strategy for improving the performance of public institutions. Excellent examples of the gains that can be achieved by paying attention to "market signals" in this sense can be found by looking at the bus systems of the Brazilian cities of Curitiba and Porto Alegre.[6] Both systems are prizewinning models of efficiency that deliver a superior level of collective transport. Both systems are operated by

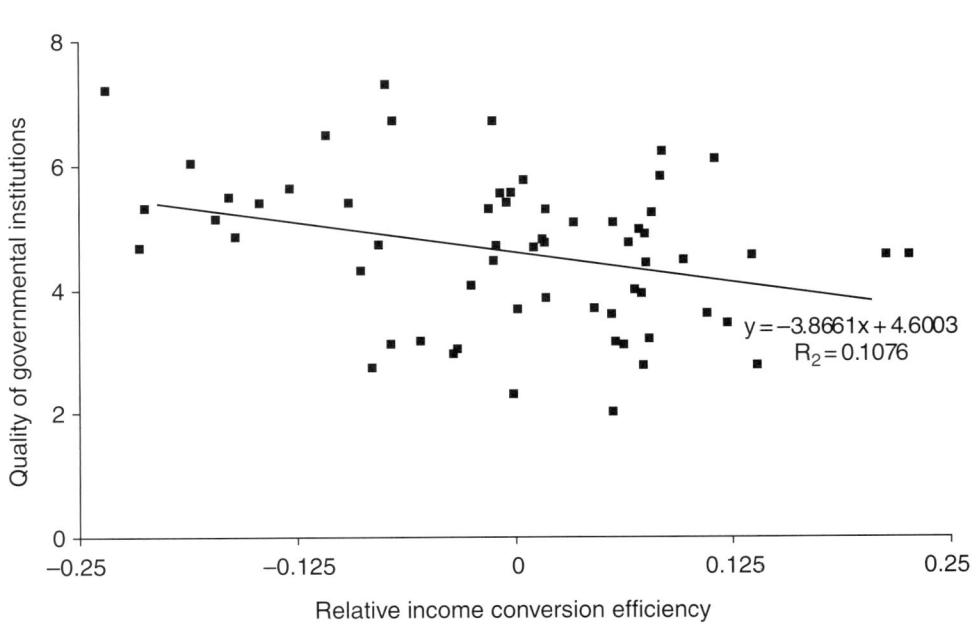

Figure 2.4 Quality of government institutions (ICRG) by relative income conversion efficiency (RICE)

private profit making companies. However, both cases also involve carefully constructed institutional frameworks aimed at aligning the incentives of the operating companies with the long-term needs and interests of the consumers they serve.

Like bureaucratic capacity, market signals are an essential element in controlling and directing the activities of the administrative machinery of the state. And, like bureaucratic capacity, the effectiveness of market signals depends on the institutional framework in which they are embedded. However, neither bureaucratic capacity nor market signals can deliver real state reform in the absence of the third element of hybrid administrative forms—effective bottom-up democratic control.

The Challenges of Building a Democratic "Third Leg" to the Tripod

Optimistic assessments of the "Third Wave" of democratization would suggest that we can take the strengthening of the "third leg" of hybridity for granted (see Huntington 1991, 1997). Elections are increasingly seen as the only internationally legitimate way of transferring political power, and non-electoral regimes are becoming correspondingly scarcer. At the same time, the concept of "participation" has become part of the mantra of even organizations like the IMF and the World Bank.[7] There is, indeed, much to be applauded in the recent evolution of political institutions. Elections and civil rights are essential elements in the institutional foundations of effective bottom-up control and the fact that even technocratic institutions recognize the value of participation opens up additional possibilities for a balanced hybridity. Nonetheless, it would be dangerously premature to assume that bottom-up democratic control was firmly ensconced as an effective element in controlling contemporary states. To the contrary, the hopeful spread of elections as the principal means of validating political authority has been paralleled by a discouraging disillusionment regarding the contribution of democratic rule to harnessing the state to societal goals.

Even as electoral transfers of power have become the norm in a widening set of countries, it has become increasingly clear that holding regular elections and maintaining at least nominal protection for civil rights is not sufficient to generate public discussion that has real bearing on the weighting of developmental goals or the allocation of collective resources (see also Bertucci 2002). The increasing tendency toward a "hollowed out" version of democracy in the South argues for a more substantial institutional response (Yusuf and Stiglitz 2001, p. 249). An aphorism attributed to Adam Przeworski sums up the problem: "People are allowed to vote but they aren't allowed to make choices."

As elections spread and the limitations on their political consequences become clearer, the question is whether disillusionment can be transformed into a quest for more effective forms of democratic control. As Heller (2000) points out, democracy should not be treated as a yes/no dummy variable. "Thin" democracy in the form of elections without a surrounding carapace of supportive institutions may well be insufficient to reshape state action, but this does not mean that "thicker" forms of democratic control cannot succeed.

In the relatively rare cases where "thicker" forms of bottom-up democratic control have been successfully instantiated, the results have been promising. Experiments with forms of "participatory budgeting," which in some cases (e.g., Kerala, India) have shifted responsibility for as much as 40 percent of planned budget, have shown that democratic mechanisms can be effective in improving the quality of resource allocation. These experiments are not only efficient in the sense of increasing the extent to which public expenditures actually correspond to the felt needs of the citizenry; they have also forced increased transparency and accountability. In view of the dismal record of all other anti-corruption devices attempted to date, democratically deliberative procedures of resource allocation may turn out to be the best and most practical way of confronting the ubiquitous problem of corruption.

There are two other important benefits of strengthening the democratic leg of the tripod. First, democratic engagement is likely to have positive normative spillovers. Increasing citizens' sense that they have some real control over the allocation of public resources increases identification with public institutions and valorizes the notion of "public service." Indeed, deliberative democratic control may be the only way to generate "ownership" of public institutions and programs sufficient to legitimate the increased levels of taxation necessary to escape the fiscal crises that currently plague all public institutions (North and South). Second, insistence on bottom up democratic control is probably the best insurance against efforts to increase bureaucratic capacity that inadvertently result in the reenthronement of innovation-stifling bureaucratic rule-following.

Some will worry that a movement to rebalance the agenda of state reform by increasing democratic, bottom-up control will lead to dangerous neglect of basic rules of efficiency, that fiscal prudence and questions of cost-effectiveness could be swept aside by populist pandering. In fact, the structural constraints of the new global political economy make this highly unlikely.

Barring the collapse of international financial markets, the power of the market signals/market mimicking leg of the tripod of modern public administration is very secure. Both the ideological hegemony (inside public administrations and outside of them) of the idea that markets are efficient and the irreducible power of international financial markets ensure the continued prominence of the market signals side of the triumvirate. The recent ascension of Lula (Luiz Inácio da Silva) to the Brazilian Presidency offers an excellent case in point. Lula's Workers' Party not only prides itself on being a champion of democratic, bottom-up control, but also has its origins, at least in part, in Marxist, "anti-imperialist" ideological propensities. Nonetheless, the new administration was clear that it had no choice but to embrace traditional fiscal prudence. The Workers' Party government pursued fiscal prudence with a zeal that won admiration from the IMF and put to shame more powerful governments supposedly sensitive to market signals—most obviously the United States.

If there is a large upside and small downside to "thickening" democratic control, what are the obstacles to thickening? First of all, "thick" democracy is much less amenable than either of the other two modes of control to implementation based solely on changes in the formal rules governing public institutions. Effective bottom-up control must be broadly rooted in "civil society." It requires mobilization and engagement on the part of a significant segment of the citizenry and consequently represents a much more ambitious project of institutional change than programs designed to enhance the role of markets or strengthen the bureaucracy.

The most potent and specific source of resistance to such ambitious programs of institutional change is elites with a vested interest in current strategies of controlling the state. Privileged private elites, who have no trouble gaining access to public decision-makers independently of standard democratic procedures, have little to gain from the institutionalization of robust, inclusive, deliberative democracy. To the contrary, they are likely to oppose deliberative procedures, simply because effective bottom-up democracy increases the possibility that public institutions will address the interests of ordinary citizens, which are inevitably at least in partial competition with particular interests of elites.[8]

In terms of the present discussion of state reform, however, the responses of state officials themselves are more interesting than those of private elites. On the one hand, strengthening democracy may be the only way of preserving allocation of resources to the public institutions on which they depend for their livelihoods (Evans 1997a). On the other hand, state officials are hardly immune from elitism, if only because of their penchant for technocratic decision-making. Amartya Sen (1999) perceptively notes that "a democratic search for agreement or a consensus can be extremely messy and many technocrats are sufficiently disgusted by its messiness to pine for some wonderful formula that would simply give us ready-made weights that are 'just right' ." (p. 79). In the end, the state bureaucracy itself could end up playing a key role in tipping the balance in favor of strengthening the democratic leg of the tripod (or in failing to do so).

Conclusion: The Difficulties and Promise of Recapturing Hybridity

The "bottom line" of this essay is hardly nuanced. A better balanced hybridity must be a central part of moving beyond the twentieth-century agenda of state reform to a twenty-first-century version of this agenda (see also Mayntz 2002). Without a better balance among bureaucratic capacity, democratic engagement, and market signals, state administrations, particularly in the Global South, are unlikely to be able to surmount the daunting challenges that they now face.

Those persuaded by this analytically simple proposition may also be lulled into the assumption that the research and policy agendas implied by accepting the hybridity perspective are equally straightforward. Unfortunately, research and policy implications are anything but straightforward. While it is not difficult to criticize late-twentieth-century state reform as one-dimensional and theoretically naïve, endowing the hybridity alternative with the conceptual elegance and programmatic clarity that made late-twentieth-century state reform such a powerful intellectual and policy movement is a prodigiously hard goal to attain.

To begin with, the methodological and data requirements of developing hybridity arguments are formidable. Even simple comparative data over time on bureaucratic structures, the prevalence of meritocratic recruitment, and so on are painfully difficult to put together. And, the difficulty of such a project pales in comparison to the prospect of trying to compile systematic comparative estimates of intangible rewards and the consequences of their cross-national distribution for state performance that will convince skeptics. The same methodological difficulties apply to the comparative analysis of what constitutes "thick" democracy and what its consequences are to state performance.

Theorizing the complex interactions among modes of control implied by the hybridity proposition is certainly no easier than collecting the necessary empirical evidence. In the end, the most effective method of pursuing the hybridity agenda may be the one that I have employed in this paper—using the perspective as a sensitizing lens that illuminates the broader significance of concrete strategies for harnessing the state. The way in which the hybridity approach highlights the potential returns to investments in intangible rewards to public servants is a good example. This piecemeal and pragmatic method of moving forward also has the additional advantage of being intellectually compatible with the alliances between actors within the state and those within civil societies, alliances that must be central to any effective rebalancing.

Efforts to rebalance the agenda of state reform will depend on the practical imaginations and determination of those who confront the dilemmas of state reform "on the ground." It will depend equally on the intellectual imagination of more detached students of market, bureaucracy, and democratic politics. Extracting analytical lessons from myriad historical examples of "effective and defective states" and translating them into institutional proposals that are lucid and compelling is the continuing challenge of those who claim to be experts on the state, and it is a challenge that has rarely been more urgently relevant to ongoing political debates.

Notes

This paper is an effort to reframe in a more theoretical and historical perspective my earlier paper, "Hybridity as an Administrative Strategy: Combining Bureaucratic Capacity with Market Signals and Deliberative Democracy," *Revista del CLAD: Reforma y Democracia*, 25(2003): 7–33.

1. Particularly noteworthy are the efforts of Luis Carlos Bresser Pereira in Brazil (see Gaetani 2002).
2. For a very accessible, nontechnical account of the economics of California's energy crisis, see chapter 12 of Krugman (2003).
3. North's (1990) "institutional frameworks" are analogous to what sociologists might call "a normative order" (p. 107). They explicitly include informal norms and customs as well as formal rules and procedures. Their scope of reach goes far beyond guaranteeing property rights by punishing force and fraud. See also North 1981, 1986.
4. Even cases touted as successes, dramatic increases in "marketizing" administrative functions have not necessarily overcome Northian problems. For example, in New Zealand, where a massive governmental overhaul in the mid-1980s to the early 1990s privatized many state enterprises and deregulated the economy, Hazeldine (1996) argues that one outcome was *increased* transaction costs and that macroeconomic results were mixed (Hazeldine 1997). There are, of course, a number of more optimistic assessments, e.g. Scott (2001).
5. ICRG scores are produced by the Political Risk Services (PRS) group (http://www.prsgroup.com/icrg/icrg.html). See Moore et al. (1999) for a description of methods used to calculate a composite score from five ICRG measures.
6. For a synopsis of the institutional framework in the case of Curitiba, see Evans (2000).
7. According to Kanbur and Squire (2001), "Development practitioners have come to a consensus that participation by the intended beneficiaries improves project performance" (p. 215). Even at the more aggregate level of loan performance," 'ownership' has been shown to be a key factor in the success or failure of structural adjustment loans" (Kanbur and Squire 2001, p. 215).
8. It should be noted that one plausible obstacle that does *not* seem to be supported by the empirical evidence is the unwillingness of ordinary citizens to devote their time to democratic deliberation once credible institutions have been put in place. (On this point see Abers 2000; Baiocchi 2001; Fung and Wright 2003; Isaac 2000; Isaac and Heller 2003.)

References

Abers, Rebecca. 2000. *Inventing Local Democracy: Grassroots Politics in Brazil*. Boulder, CO: Lynne Rienner.

Baiocchi, Gianpaolo. 2001. "Participation, Activism, and Politics: The Porto Alegre Experiment and Deliberative Democratic Theory." *Politics and Society*, 29, 1: 43–72.

Barzelay, Michael. 2001. *The New Public Management: Improving Research and Policy Dialogue*. Berkeley, CA: University of California Press.

Bertucci, Guido. 2002. *The Role of Decentralized Governance in Fostering the Participation of Minorities*. VII International Congress of CLAD on State Reform and Administrative Development, Lisbon, Portugal.

Carruthers, Bruce. 1996. *City of Capital: Politics and Markets in the English Financial Revolution*. Princeton, NJ: Princeton University Press.

Easterly, William. 2001. *The Elusive Quest for Growth: Economists' Adventures and Misadventures in the Tropics*. Cambridge, MA: MIT Press.

Evans, Peter. 1995. *Embedded Autonomy: States and Industrial Transformation*. Princeton, NJ: Princeton University Press.

———. 1997a. "The Eclipse of the State? Reflections on Stateness in an Era of Globalization." *World Politics*, 50, 1: 62–87.

Evans, Peter. (ed.). 1997b. *State-Society Synergy: Government Action and Social Capital in Development.* Berkeley, CA: UC Berkeley International and Area Studies Publications [Research Series, no 94]. [Also published as a special section of *World Development* 24, 6: 1033–1132. June 1996.]

———. 2000. "Sustainability, Degradation and Livelihood in Third World Cities: Possibilities for State-Society Synergy." In *The United Nations and the Global Environment in the 21st Century: From Common Challenges to Shared Responsibilities*, edited by P. Chasek. Tokyo: United Nations University Press.

———. 2004. "Development as Institutional Change: The Pitfalls of Monocropping and Potentials of Deliberation." *Studies in Comparative International Development*, 38, 4: 30–52.

Evans, Peter and James Rauch. 1999. "Bureaucracy and Growth: A Cross-National Analysis of the Effects of Weberian State Structures on Economic Growth." *American Sociological Review*, 64: 748–765.

Fung, Archon and Erik Wright. 2003. *Deepening Democracy: Institutional Innovations in Empowered Participatory Governance.* London: Verso.

Gaetani, Francisco. 2002. *Public Management Policy Change in Brazil: 1995–1998.* VII International Congress of CLAD on State Reform and Administrative Development, Lisbon, Portugal.

Hazeldine, Tim. 1996. "The New Zealand Economic Revolution after 10 Years." Auckland, NZ, Department of Economics, Auckland Business School, the University of Auckland. Working Paper No. 161.

Hazeldine, Tim. 1997. "Is there an Alternative Approach?" In *Business Reporting: A New Zealand Guide to Financial Journalism*, edited by A. Lee. Wellington, NZ: Journalists Training Organisation.

Heller, Patrick. 2000. "Degrees of Democracy: Some Comparative Lessons from India." *World Politics*, 52: 484–519.

Hoff, Karla. 2000. *Beyond Rosenstein-Rodan: The Modern Theory of Coordination Problems in Development.* Annual World Bank Conference on Development Economics, The World Bank.

Hoff, Karla and Joseph Stiglitz. 2001. "Modern Economic Theory and Development." In *Frontiers of Development Economics: The Future in Perspective*, edited by G. Meier and J. Stiglitz. New York: Oxford University Press, 389–460.

Houtzager, Peter and Mick Moore (eds.). 2003. *Changing Paths: The New Politics of Inclusion.* Ann Arbor, MI: University of Michigan Press.

Huntington, Samuel. 1991. *The Third Wave: Democratization in the Late Twentieth Century.* Norman, OK: University of Oklahoma Press.

Huntington, Samuel. 1997. "After Twenty Years: The Future of the Third Wave." *Journal of Democracy*, 8, 4: 3–12.

Isaac, Thomas and Richard Franke. 2000. *Local Democracy and Development: People's Campaign for Decentralized Planning in Kerala.* New Delhi: Left Word Books.

Isaac, Thomas and Patrick Heller. 2003. "Decentralization, Democracy and Development: The People's Campaign for Decentralized Planning in Kerala." In *Deepening Democracy: Institutional Innovations in Empowered Participatory Governance*, edited by A. Fung and E. Wright. London: Verso, 86–118.

Kanbur, Ravi and Lyn Squire. 2001. "The Evolution of Thinking about Poverty: Exploring the Interactions." In *Frontiers of Development Economics*, edited by G. Meier and J. Stiglitz. New York: Oxford University Press, 183–226.

King, Lawrence. 2002. "The Emperor Exposed: Neoliberal Theory and De-modernization in Postcommunist Society." Unpublished manuscript. December 6.

Krugman, Paul. 2003. *The Great Unraveling. Losing our Way in the New Century.* New York: W.W. Norton and Co.

Mahoney, James. 2002. *The Legacies of Liberalism: Path Dependence and Political Regimes in Central America.* Baltimore, MD: Johns Hopkins University Press.

Mayntz, Renate. 2002. *National States and Global Governance*. VII International Congress of CLAD on State Reform and Administrative Development, Lisbon, Portugal.

Moore, Mick et al. 1999. *Polity Qualities: How Governance Affects Poverty*. Washington, DC: The World Bank. http://www.worldbank.org/poverty/wdrpoverty/dfid/moore.pdf

North, Douglass. 1981. *Structure and Change in Economic History*. New York: Norton.

———. 1986. "The New Institutional Economics." *Journal of Institutional and Theoretical Economics*, 142: 230–237.

———. 1990. *Institutions, Institutional Change, and Economic Performance*. Cambridge: Cambridge University Press.

Pelletier, Jacques. 2002. *The Impact of Values: A Human Resources Perspective*. VII International Congress of CLAD on State Reform and Administrative Development, Lisbon, Portugal.

Scott, Graham. 2001. "Managing Governments for Better Performance and Results." Workshop on Financial Management and Accountability, United Nations Department of Economic and Social Affairs, Villa Lubin, Rome, Italy.

Sen, Amartya. 1999. *Development as Freedom*. New York: Alfred A. Knopf.

Tendler, Judith. 1997. *Good Government in the Tropics*. Baltimore: Johns Hopkins University Press.

Tendler, Judith and Sara Freedheim. 1994. "Bringing Hirschman Back In: A Case of Bad Government Turned Good." *World Development*, 22, 12: 1771–1791.

Yusuf, Shahid and Joseph Stiglitz. 2001. "Development Issues: Settled and Open." In *Frontiers in Development Economics: The Future in Perspective*, edited by G. Meier and J. Stiglitz. New York: Oxford University Press.

CHAPTER THREE

The Rule of Law and Development: A Weberian Framework of States and State-Society Relations

Matthew Lange

This chapter provides a general theoretical framework on states and development that is based on Max Weber's sociology of law, which is arguably the "core" of Weber's substantive sociology and "an essential key to the understanding of his analysis of political and economic phenomena" (Parsons 1971, pp. 40, 41).[1] To do so, it is divided into two sections. The first section claims that negative-sum social relations characterized by one-sided domination have negative effects on development and that positive-sum social relations characterized by multilateral collaboration have positive effects on it. Next, the section describes how associations, bureaucracy, and markets make possible positive-sum relations on a large scale but recognizes that each coordination structure has a tendency to personalize power and thereby limit the extent of positive-sum relations. As such, large-scale coordination problems must be seen as major developmental obstacles.

The second section of the chapter claims that institutions—and in particular states—affect how power is organized in society and therefore shape the functioning of coordination structures. When states are organized to promote personal rule by elite officials, they create hierarchical relations of dependence that promote zero-sum relations and thereby obstruct broad-based social coordination. Alternatively, state rule through an impersonal legalism makes possible broad-based coordination within three social spheres: within the state, within society, and between state and society. In doing so, a state-enforced rule of law creates an institutional environment that promotes effective associational, bureaucratic, and market structures; their synergies; and thereby broad-based development.

Social Coordination and Development

In his acclaimed discussion of *Development as Freedom*, Amartya Sen (1999) conceptualizes human development as the capacity of individuals to pursue their well-being. As such, economic opportunities, democracy, education, health, and self-esteem are all developmental. Alternatively, discrimination, violent coercion, and exploitation are examples of "unfreedoms" that can impede individual capabilities.

Although focusing on the individual, Sen does not suggest that development is strictly an individual-level phenomenon. Instead, he recognizes that the capacity of individuals to pursue their well-being depends on their social relations in two important ways. First, social relations can impede development when they prevent individuals from pursuing their personal well-being. A lower-caste Indian's configuration of social relations, for instance, might impede development as freedom due to the negative effects it has on self-esteem, economic opportunity, and access to public goods. Sen, therefore, proposes that development as freedom is maximized when individuals are free from social relations that are characterized by one-sided domination. Alternatively, social relations can enhance development when they allow individuals to combine their resources and pursue their well-being collaboratively. This might take the form of community development projects providing public goods to large numbers of individuals or, as Patrick Heller (1999) finds in his analysis of democratization in Kerala, sustained collective mobilization to free subordinate groups from unequal social relations. Thus, social relations have important effects on development as freedom, and a fundamental difference between developmental and antidevelopmental social relations is the extent to which relations are either positive-sum, zero-sum, or negative-sum.[2]

At the most basic level, positive-sum relations require information and resource exchanges among individuals in order to coordinate their actions for mutual gain. On a small scale, these coordinated exchanges can occur through informal interaction among a small number of actors (Ostrom 1990; Portes 1995; Saxenian 1996). With larger groups, however, more formal structures are necessary to coordinate the greater number of actors. Milton Esman and Norman Uphoff (1984) recognize that

Table 3.1 Four coordination structure ideal types

	Bureaucratic structures	Associational structures	Market structures	Clientelist structures
Main actor	States and other formal orgs.	Voluntary groups	Economic actors	Patrons, clients
Principal mechanism	Regulation	Association	Exchange	Mutual, though asymmetric, dependence
Locus of power	Rules on force and capital	Group opinion	Supply and demand	Control of goods and services
Guides for behavior	Rules	Agreement	Price signals	Status and power
Strengths	Central coordinaion, permanency	Adaptable, low resource requirements, active engagement	Active engagement, individual initiative	Low resource requirements, adaptable
Weaknesses	Rigid, resource intensive	Impermanent, decision-making problems	Low collective control	Limited potential for collective action

a number of different formal structures can coordinate action among large groups of individuals yet describe three ideal-type structures—bureaucracy, association, and market—and suggest that all three provide the basic building blocks for large-scale social coordination. Table 3.1 summarizes the key characteristics of the three types of social coordination as well as a fourth, clientelist structure.

Bureaucratic structures use rules as formal guides to social relations and depend on a high degree of power concentration and the sanctioning of members through set procedures. These structures have the advantage of a clear chain of command and formal rules governing individual action, both of which facilitate corporate action, predictability, and a degree of permanence; yet due to these characteristics, bureaucratic structures are rigid, difficult to organize, and resource intensive. *Associational structures* are similar to bureaucratic organizations in that they create corporate groups. They differ, however, since their coordination mechanism depends on individual participation and the agreement of members. Sanctions are applied by members through social pressure, and the mode of operation is bottom-up rather than top-down. Because associations lack a rigid chain of command, extensive formal rules, and paid employment, they are less permanent and less centrally coordinated than bureaucratic organizations. Faced with complex problems, they also have difficulty arriving at speedy decisions. However, they have the advantage of being dynamic, engaging large numbers of individuals, and requiring few resources.

Market structures differ from bureaucratic and associational structures since they do not require formal membership and are neither plagued by nor oriented to the solution of collective action problems. Instead, self-interested producers, consumers, and investors follow price signals to exchange goods and services in attempts to maximize individual utility. Market structures are able to engage more individuals and to utilize their personal initiative and knowledge to a greater extent than the other coordination structures. The structure is severely disadvantaged for many activities, however, since its dependence on selective incentives impedes collective control over individual action. As a result, many collective action problems are simply sidestepped. Finally, *clientelist structures* are hierarchical networks linking a patron to multiple clients. Although exchange is a vital component of both market and clientelist structures, clientelism differs in that prices do not guide relations. Instead, mutual dependence is the main mechanism underlying a coordinated action. The exchanges also differ from those within markets in that they are inherently unequal due to the patron's greater status and power. Clientelist structures require only moderate resources and are easily constructed, yet their asymmetric character places severe limits on the potential range of coordinated action.

All four structures make social coordination possible through different mechanisms: rules (bureaucracy), group opinion (associations), supply and demand (markets), or mutually dependent relationships (clientelism). In doing so, each allows a number of individuals to collaborate in order to accomplish tasks that could not be completed individually. In this way, all are developmental. Clientelist structures, however, are quite prone to being captured by individuals, thereby endowing actors with great personal power and limiting the extent to which relations are positive-sum. Indeed, clientelist structures facilitate asymmetric power relations since they prevent clients from (a) gaining leverage against patrons due to the absence of formal rules and patron control of resources and information; (b) organizing to limit the power of individual patrons; and (c) switching allegiance to another patron who offers more equitable exchange relations (Burt 1992; Mamdani 1996; Scott 1972).

Although personal control is less common in the other coordination structures, it is far from absent. Charles Perrow (1979) recognizes that bureaucracy often places power in individual hands and thereby allows elites to use the structure for personal benefit, and Talcott Parsons (1964) notes that the top of a bureaucracy is not itself bureaucratic in character. Similarly, associations can be captured by powerful individuals or groups who use them to pursue their own interests, such as Nazi capture and control of civil associations in Germany (Berman 1997; Birnbaum 1988). Finally, both monopolistic and monopsonistic control of markets enable individuals and firms to exercise considerable power over exchange relations, thereby distorting market mechanisms.

As these examples demonstrate, particular structures are not sufficient for positive-sum relations on a large scale: they must be combined with constraints that limit the personal power of actors. According to Peter Evans's analysis in this volume (chapter two), one way of doing this is by combining bureaucracy, markets, and democracy in order to utilize the different disciplining mechanisms of each. In this way, the structures provide different checks on the concentration of power and thereby help to minimize it.

Authority systems and institutions are additional means of safeguarding the functioning of coordination structures. Weber (1968), for example, recognized that the coordination of social relations at meso- and macro-levels requires normative and cognitive guides to the exercise of power (see also Gorski 1993, 2003). He found that clientelist structures often depend on ideas of traditional authority, which provide clients with some checks on patron abuses and deter clients from rebelling. Alternatively, he described in considerable depth how rational-legal authority promotes discipline within bureaucracies by shaping ideas of proper and improper action. Thus, Weber stressed that authority systems shape how power can be exercised in social relations and recognized that they can take different forms. The next section investigates how different state-enforced authority systems affect the possibility of coordinated social action at the macro-level and thereby development.

State Authority Systems: Personal and Legal Rule

According to Weber, the action-orientations of individuals are important determinants of the overall structure of social relations (see Kalberg 1994; Weber 1968). By this, he meant that shared principles can guide the individual actions of many people, promote particular patterns of social relations, and thereby become important social carriers shaping the overall structure of society. Traditional and rational-legal authority are two ideal-typical action-orientations that Weber discussed extensively and believed had important effects on social relations. Given their effects on how power can be exercised, these authority-based action-orientations are integral aspects of political institutions. States, in fact, are important instruments that spread and enforce particular action-orientations throughout society, thereby constructing a macro-social order affecting power relations. Analyses of such systems of rule must therefore focus on state structures and the action-orientations of its officials.

Weber recognized several types of traditional authority but focused on patriarchal and patrimonial authority. Individuals in a system of patriarchal authority act according to traditional principles concerning personal ownership and rights that are based on the patrilineal family (Weber 1968, p. 1010). Patrimonialism is a subtype of patriarchalism that occurs when political control extends beyond a certain territorial limit and requires a permanent staff that governs local subjects according to patriarchal principles. Patrimonialism therefore decentralizes power by placing it in the hands of a dispersed political elite who are under certain obligatory constraints to look after the well-being of their subjects (Weber 1968, pp. 1011–1012). Despite these traditional constraints, the elite often have considerable discretion to use their economic and coercive resources to act as they choose. Weber, for instance, noted that patrimonialism's concentration of power in individual hands often transforms group rights into personal rights (1968, pp. 231–232). As a result, patrimonial authorities generally have considerable powers over their subjects, and patrimonialism therefore promotes hierarchical social relations characterized by clientelism and one-sided dependence.

At its extreme, the concentration of power under patrimonial systems frees the elite from institutional constraints and results in a new type of authority based on personal might, something Weber referred to as sultanism. Here, the underlying principle is not some traditional idea but is simply brute force. The unchecked violence and open threats of mafiosi approach this ideal type. When given a territorial basis, personal rule results in what Arthur Stinchcombe (1999) calls *caudillismo*, or a "personalized pyramidal network" that is organized simply to control and extract resources from the population (p. 70). Examples include early-modern European states—that Charles Tilly (1985) finds were ruled by mob-like groups offering "protection"—and modern Somalia and the Democratic Republic of Congo. Similar to patrimonial states, *caudillo* states often create hierarchical relations of dependence based on a system of clientelism between central and local actors. They differ, however, in that unadulterated power and dependence shorn from any idea of legitimate authority underlie social relations. In addition, the inherent struggles for power within the *caudillo* state, which are caused by the absence of any form of traditional authority and the premium placed on personal power, make it much less stable than the patrimonial state.

Legal rule is an ideal type that is diametrically opposed to personal rule in that the power of individuals is always subordinate to set rules.

This system of rule depends on the institutionalization of rational-legal authority, and the basic action-orientation of rational-legal authority is rules—not patrimonial rights or personal might. These rules are not controlled by any individual or group and dictate how one should act in a given situation.

According to Weber, legal rule is dependent on the combination of formal and rational organization. Formality refers to the autonomy of state actors from such other social orders as those grounded in religion, ethnicity, class, or political party. It entails a corporate structure that separates official members from nonmembers and subordinates the officials to rules governing duties and the chain of command. As such, formality promotes both internal coherence and distinct group boundaries with society.

Rationality is defined as the degree to which the organization is capable of formulating, promulgating, and applying universal rules. As such, rational rules can be applied systematically to all situations, at all times, under all circumstances. At its extreme, rationality suggests that the actions of individuals are guided by four principles:

(1) that every decision of a concrete case consists in the "application" of an abstract rule of law to concrete fact situation;
(2) that by means of legal logic the abstract rules of the positive law can be made to yield the decisions for every concrete fact situation;
(3) that, consequently, the positive law constitutes a "gapless" system of rules, which are at least latently contained in it, or that the law is at least to be treated for purposes of legal practice as if it were such a gapless system;
(4) that every instance of social conduct can and must be conceived as constituting either obedience to, or violation, or application, of rules of law (Weber 1968, p. xliii).

Unlike personal and patrimonial rule, legal rule does not promote clientelistic and hierarchical social relations. Instead, legal rule makes possible corporate state organization and, through regulation, more horizontal social relations. Legal rule therefore is much more advantageous to broad-based social coordination, something the next section now discusses.

★ ★ ★

So far, this chapter has suggested that development as freedom involves the maximization of positive-sum relations, described coordination structures that promote positive-sum relations on a large scale, and recognized the tendency of the various coordination structures to personalize power and thereby diminish their developmental potential. Next, it proposed that institutional orders that regulate power relations might affect the functioning of coordination structures and described two such systems: personal rule and legal rule. The final section combines insight from the previous section and provides a theoretical framework proposing that the different state-enforced systems of rule have very important effects on macro-coordination structures and thereby development. When enforced by state institutions, legal rule improves state regulative and administrative effectiveness while personal rule impedes both. In doing so, legal rule enhances (1) the state provisioning of public goods; (2) the functioning of markets and associations; and (3) state-society synergy. In these three ways, legal rule is therefore much more conducive to broad-based development than personal rule.

Legal Rule and Effective State Administration

Both rule-based power and personalized power affect social relations within the state organization itself and thereby have an impact on the capacity of state agents to act corporately. Despite its bad reputation in the public, many recognize that a bureaucratically organized administrative institution prevents actors from pursuing their individual self-interests and therefore provides an effective coordination mechanism that makes possible corporate state action.[3] And, rules are the fundamental mechanism enforcing bureaucratic coordination since they provide "definitions of the powers of office, the terms of access to it, and the line dividing proper from improper pressure or influence" (Parsons 1964, p. 350). As Weber (1968) recognized long ago, meritocracy, salary-based compensation, full-time employment, a set hierarchical chain of command, and rule-based procedures—when combined with rational-legal authority systems—all interact to remove power from individuals and societal groups and place it within rules.

On the other hand, when legal rule is absent, states lack effective mechanisms for the control of large numbers of state actors. This, in turn, promotes rampant rent-seeking and unstable hierarchies of power dominated by individuals. Such personal rule frees state actors to use their coercive power to indiscriminately prey on others for personal gain and aggrandizement (Evans 1995). Unless held in check by personal loyalties, something that is very difficult to accomplish for long periods of time once states reach a certain size, these tendencies impede corporate action and thereby state implementation of development projects. Most basically, therefore, a bureaucratic state promotes human development by preventing state actors from abusing their positions for personal gain.

Bureaucracy also promotes social development in a more constructive fashion, by making possible corporate action necessary for the provision of public goods. The administrative capacity of states, for example, affects their abilities to provide physical infrastructure allowing individuals to pursue their well-being. Transportation, communication, water, and electrical networks all provide individuals with resources that assist the pursuit of material well-being. Yet, such infrastructure is expensive to construct and maintain, is difficult to organize, and is hampered by collective action problems and a tendency toward monopolization. Historically, bureaucratically organized states have proved themselves capable of overcoming such difficulties.

Besides physical infrastructure, the administrative capacity of states promotes development by expanding human capital. One public good that states often provide is education, which increases individual access to information, expands job opportunities, promotes critical thinking and problem solving, and thereby empowers individuals to pursue their well-being. States are also the primary providers of health care and therefore help individuals to maintain the most basic element of development as freedom: individual health. Finally, states promote human capital by protecting individuals from extreme hardship. This often takes the form of poor relief, unemployment insurance, and retirement benefits.

Corporate state action can also promote development by making possible national markets: State efforts to construct, monitor, and steer the national economy provide a public good affecting economic production and depend on an effective, bureaucratically organized state. Most basically, capitalist production requires an integrated, national market, something that Karl Polanyi (1957) recognizes depends on state coercion and administration. And, once constructed, national markets continue to depend on state administration. As emphasized by economists, macro-economic factors—such as the balance of trade, foreign reserves, and exchange and interest rates—shape incentives to economic production within the national economy, and effective state management of such factors therefore promotes economic development (Rodrik 1997; Smith 1993; Stiglitz 2002). In particular, states must limit extreme fluctuations that destabilize incentives, increase risk, and thereby deter economic production and investment. To prevent this, state officials must have the information necessary for sound, long-term economic policy; the autonomy to disregard short-term interests and pressure from powerful actors that would obstruct optimal economic management; and the personnel with the proper training and infrastructural capabilities for the implementation and adjustment of the economy in accord with the changing economic and social environment. Notably, all three of these characteristics depend on high levels of administrative capacity and therefore bureaucratic organization.

Besides simply allowing the state to act as a handmaiden or midwife to economic development, effective state administration also makes possible the role of an economic demiurge, or developmental state (Amsden 1989; Evans 1995; Johnson 1982; Wade 1990). In late developers such as Germany, Japan, and South Korea, the state took a very active role in economic production in an attempt to spur industrialization. This more constructive role was necessary in order to provide the capital and initiative necessary for successful industrialization when (1) industrial powers already exist and/or (2) local entrepreneurs are absent. Effective state administration, in turn, is absolutely necessary for a developmental state since it limits the ability of state actors to exploit the numerous rent-seeking opportunities made possible by state involvement in the economy and allows state actors to gather the information and resources necessary for efficient production.

Legal Rule and Effective State Regulation

Along with state administration, legal and personal rule also affect state regulation of societal relations. With personal rule, state officials regulate societal relations according to their own interests and whims, and a functioning legal framework is therefore either nonexistent or under the personal control of elite interests. This, in turn, creates social relations in which personalized power is unrestrained and enforces informal social hierarchies characterized by dependence and predation. Indeed, "systems of local power which tend to reach extremes of violent, personalistic rule" result when "the effectiveness of a national order embodied in the law and the authority of the state fades off" (O'Donnell 1993, p. 1358). And several scholars note that regional power brokers often prevent local populations from cooperating with one another and creating collective coordination structures due to vertical relations of dependency: relations in which power is concentrated within a single individual, which enables that individual to obstruct developmental processes threatening his or her power (Granovetter 1995; Heller 1999; Mamdani 1996; Putnam 1993). Finally, even if legal institutions are rational but controlled by elite groups (apartheid South Africa being a notable example), they become an instrument through which privileged groups are able to dominate and exploit others.

Legal rule, on the other hand, promotes human development by regulating societal power relations. With rule-based power, a legal framework governs relations among societal actors and thereby prevents extreme power asymmetries from arising. As Georg Simmel (1955) describes,

> Legal conflict rests on a broad basis of unities and agreements between enemies. The reason is that both parties are equally subordinated to the law; they mutually recognize that the decision is to be made only according to the objective weight of their claims; they observe the forms which are unbreakably valid for both; and they are conscious that they are surrounded in their whole enterprise by a social power which alone gives meaning and certainty to their undertaking. (p. 37)

Within this institutional environment, legal rule limits the personal power of societal actors and provides the stability and protection needed for the organization of complex coordination structures such as markets, bureaucratic organizations, and associations.

While state administrative capacity is necessary for the construction and maintenance of national markets, rule-based state regulation—as institution-oriented economists increasingly stress—is necessary for their functioning (North 1981). Market structures promote development by creating opportunities for individuals to pursue material gain through exchange, and legal regulation of property rights and contracts is the most basic requirement for functioning national markets. Weber (1968) noted that the formality and rationality of law promoted capitalist development in Western Europe by increasing the relative calculability of law[4]: when the law and its application are understood, individuals are able to make productive investments without inordinate risks. The protection of property rights is quite possibly the most basic type of social regulation necessary for market production and expansion. In addition, legal regulation makes possible freedom of contract, which is also a basic necessity of functioning markets since the exchange of goods and information is needed for price equilibriums derived from supply and demand (Weber 1968, p. 668).

While the development literature increasingly emphasizes that state regulation is necessary for the functioning of market structures, few recognize that the rule of law also promotes development by promoting the formation and functioning of societal associations and formal organizations. Here, instead of empowering individuals to participate within markets, legal rule enhances the ability of individuals to pursue their well-being by breaking down hierarchical relations of dependence and exploitation and thereby expanding opportunities to organize collective coordination structures for the pursuit of group interests. Associations, for example, allow individuals to pursue activities that are more easily accomplished through collective action and promote development by optimizing efficiency, equity, and empowerment of social groups. This, in turn, allows individuals to manage their affairs, participate in activities affecting their economic productivity and quality of life, and influence public decisions.[5] And legal regulation promotes their formation since it empowers less privileged groups to free themselves from elite domination and to organize themselves based on bottom–up decision-making processes (Evans 1996; Lange 2003; Mendez, O'Donnell, and Pinheiro 1999).

Legal Rule and State-Society Synergy

Along with state-centered analysis focusing on state capacity to administrate and regulate, state-society synergy has become a major focus of development studies over the past decade, with numerous insightful analyses describing the positive-sum relations that can exist between state and society.[6] Indeed, even the most enlightened and organized state cannot be an omnipotent demiurge independently constructing paths of national development because states require social embeddedness to harness the participation, initiative, and know-how of societal groups (Esman and Uphoff 1984; Evans 1995). Yet, state-society relations can be anything but synergistic, often resulting in the mutual destruction of state and society or the despotic control of one by the other.[7] While the former tends to occur when rule-based state institutions exist, the latter predominates when the state is characterized by personal rule.

Legal-rule promotes synergistic relations between state and society in two ways. First, legal rule shapes the coordination capacity of both state and society. Synergy involves collaborative relations that allow groups to combine their resources and effort for mutual benefit and therefore depends on the mobilizational capacity of state and societal actors. Because bureaucratic organization enhances the possibility of coordinated state action, and because rule-based regulation of societal relations improves the functioning of markets, formal organizations, and associations within society, legal rule improves the possibility of state-society synergy.

Next, legal rule directly affects state-society synergy by formalizing relations and enforcing norms of interaction that extend beyond particularistic, local communities. When the state is governed by rules and its relations with society are dictated by set procedures and laws, the potential for arbitrary action by either state officials or societal actors is reduced, opening a space for formal relations between the two. In this way, ties between state and society provide "institutionalized channels for the continual negotiation and renegotiation of goals and policies" (Evans 1995, p. 12) and promote cooperative relations by creating mutual respect, trust, and norms of reciprocity (Putnam 1993). And legal rule institutionalizes norms of interpersonal conduct that are based on general rules, not particularistic ideas of community, something that facilitates collaborative relations among distant and diverse groups.

Active relations between state and society, in turn, allow societal actors to continually place demands on the state, something that promotes state responsiveness and helps to prevent the iron law of oligarchy from setting in (Heller 2001; Lipset, Trow, and Coleman 1956). Thus, while legal rule promotes state-society relations, the latter also helps to maintain state effectiveness. Equally important, collaborative relations between state and society also affect developmental processes by allowing diverse actors to combine information and resources and act collectively. In doing so, they make possible the exploitation of comparative coordination advantages for mutual benefit. That is, through collaboration and the transfer of information and resources, state and societal actors are able to benefit from the advantages of more than one coordination structure. As shown in figure 3.1, three distinct types of structural synergies exist: market–bureaucratic, bureaucratic–associational, and associational–market.

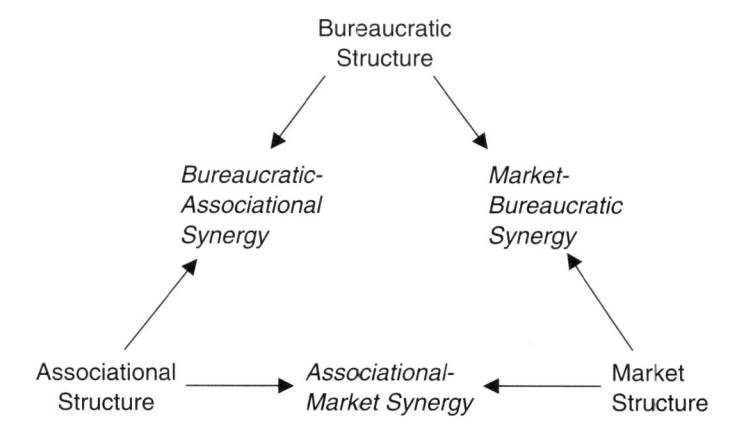

Figure 3.1 Three types of structural synergy

Market-Bureaucratic Synergy

Positive-sum relations between state and economic actors promote development by exploiting the state's central control and permanence to guide economic production and the market's ability to discipline production and engage a large number of individuals. A growing body of work recognizes that economic development depends on the combination of the bureaucratic and market structures (Amsden 1989; Evans 1995; Stiglitz 2002; Wade 1990). As Ziya Onis (1991) writes:

> Key to rapid industrialization is a strong and autonomous state, providing directional thrust to the operation of market mechanisms. The market is guided by a conception of long-term national rationality of investment formulated by government officials. It is the "synergy" between state and market which provides the basis for outstanding development experience. (p. 110)

Peter Evans (1995) notes that states can promote national development by adjusting prices through market regulation and subsidies, an interference that endows the state with considerable control over producers. State autonomy, in turn, enables it to guide otherwise short-sighted and risk-averse capitalists to pursue productive activities with the greatest potential to expand the national economy over the long run. State-led development, however, also depends on embeddedness, or network ties between state actors and economic producers, which allows both state and economic actors to benefit from the information, participation, and resources of the other in their collaborative attempt to expand economic production.

Bureaucratic-Assocational Synergy

Next, positive-sum relations between the state and local associations increases resource and information exchanges to optimize the centralization, resources, and permanence of the state and the adaptability, participation, and low maintenance costs of local groups. Several analyses of state-society synergy recognize that network relations between states and local associations expand local-level development.[8] For example, in a study of 16 developing countries, local associations are vital intermediaries enabling relations between state and society that exploit the comparative advantages of each. Uphoff and Esman (1979) find that upward and downward linkages between the state, associations, and local populations are positively correlated with agricultural productivity, educational attainment, nutrition levels, and life expectancy.

And, while associations increase state capacity to implement developmental policy, Theda Skocpol (1997) recognizes that states can also create an "opportunity structure" that nourishes, encourages, and rewards voluntary associations (p. 472). In colonial Mauritius, for example, the rapid expansion of state ties to subordinate classes during the 1940s and 1950s sparked an explosion of societal associations: the number of co-ops, labor unions, and registered associations increased from 284 to 971 in little more than a decade (Lange 2003, p. 416). These associations, in turn, were a vital component of state-led development efforts.

Associational-Market Synergy

Finally, rule-based legal institutions also promote development by making possible the synergy of market and associational structures. Markets and associations often derive positive-sum benefits from one another by exploiting the ability of associations/organizations to collectively monitor and direct the actions of members as well as the capacity of markets to enhance production efficiency. Both of these, in turn, increase stability and resource mobilization in order to improve the functioning of markets. Several analyses of market development in the Third World note that markets rely on associational and bureaucratic structures for the pooling of resources and mutual monitoring. For example, Robert Bates (1989) notes that both the state and local organizations were necessary for the creation of agricultural markets in Kenya. He writes that "organizations do not necessarily stand in opposition to markets. Rather they are often put in place in an effort to underpin and to unleash market forces. Kenya's capacity to secure the benefits attainable from exchanges in the market has largely been based on its capacity to create organizations" (p. 150). Focusing on common-pool resources, Elinore Ostrom (1990) suggests that associations may correct market failures caused by free-riders. She finds that associations enable groups to exploit collective goods most efficiently since they make possible constant supervision of members, which is necessary to prevent the destruction of collective goods through the short-term maximization of self-interest.

Conclusion

This chapter provides a theoretical framework based on Weber's sociology of law and suggests that legal rule promotes social development by increasing the general coordination capacity of society. Reviewing much of the development literature, it shows that coordination structures such as associations, bureaucracies, and markets make possible positive-sum exchanges among actors within the state, within society, and between state and society, yet depend on the extent to which power is derived from formal and rational rules, not individual capabilities. As the primary enforcers of legal rule, states contribute to the self-organization of complex societies and are therefore important determinants of broad-based, human development.

Notes

Special thanks is given to Jim Mahoney, Dietrich Rueschemeyer, and Matthias vom Hau for their extensive and extremely insightful comments on earlier drafts of this paper.

1. See also Kalberg 1994; Kronman 1983; Rheinstein 1967.
2. Many social relations are zero-sum in character, with some people receiving absolute benefits, others absolute costs. Robbery is a prime example. In competitive situations such as violent conflict in which no victor emerges, all participants might incur absolute losses, something known as negative-sum relations. While both zero- and negative-sum relations prevent many individuals from pursuing their well-being, positive-sum relations allow all actors to receive an absolute benefit from participation. Notably, although development as freedom therefore appears to be maximized when negative- and zero-sum relations are absent, a society with only positive-sum relations is not necessarily more developmental than one with some combination, as conflict often promotes more equitable distributions of societal resources, prevents the iron law of oligarchy from setting in, and sparks innonation. See Coser 1956 for a classic sociological analysis of beneficial effects of conflict.
3. See Evans 1995; Evans and Rauch 1999; Goldsmith 1999; Gorski 1993; Jackson and Rosberg 1984; Rueschemeyer and Evans 1985; Rueschemeyer 1986.
4. See also Trubek 1972.
5. Also see Heller 1999; Ostrom 1990; Putnam 1993; Tendler 1993; Uphoff 1992; Woolcock 1998.
6. See Evans 1995, 1996; Heller 1999; Onis 1991; Tendler 1993; Tendler and Freedheim 1994; Uphoff 1992; Wang 1999.
7. See Callaghy 1984; Mamdani 1996; Migdal 1988.
8. See Hadenius and Uggla 1996; Heller 1999, 2001; Ostrom 1990; Tendler 1993; Tendler and Freedheim 1994.

References

Amsden, Alice. 1989. *Asia's Next Giant: South Korea and Asian Industrialization*. New York: Oxford University Press.
Bates, Robert. 1989. *Beyond the Miracle of the Market*. New York: Cambridge University Press.
Berman, Sheri. 1997. "Civil Society and the Collapse of the Weimar Republic." *World Politics*, 49, 3: 401–429.
Birnbaum, Pierre. 1988. *States and Collective Action: The European Experience*. New York: Cambridge University Press.
Burt, Ronald. 1992. *Structural Holes: The Social Structure of Competition*. Cambridge, MA: Harvard University Press.
Callaghy, Thomas. 1984. *The State-Society Struggle: Zaire in Comparative Perspective*. New York: Columbia University Press.

Coser, Lewis. 1956. *The Functions of Social Conflict*. London: Free Press.
Esman, Milton and Norman Uphoff. 1984. *Local Organizations: Intermediaries in Local Development*. Ithaca, NY: Cornell University Press.
Evans, Peter. 1995. *Embedded Autonomy: States and Industrial Transformation*. Princeton: Princeton University Press.
———. 1996. "Government Action, Social Capital and Development: Reviewing the Evidence on Synergy." *World Development*, 24, 6: 1119–1132.
Evans, Peter and James Rauch. 1999. "Analysis of 'Weberian' State Structures and Economic Growth." *American Sociological Review*, 64, 5: 748–765.
Goldsmith, Arthur. 1999. "Africa's Overgrown State Reconsidered: Bureaucracy and Economic Growth." *World Politics*, 51, 7: 520–546.
Gorski, Philip. 1993. "The Protestant Ethic Revisited: Disciplinary Revolution and State Formation in Holland and Prussia." *American Journal of Sociology*, 99, 2: 265–316.
———. 2003. *The Disciplinary Revolution: Calvinism and the Rise of the State in Early Modern Europe*. Chicago: Chicago University Press.
Granovetter, Mark. 1995. "The Economic Sociology of Firms and Entrepreneurs." In *The Economic Sociology of Immigration*, edited by A. Portes. New York: Russell Sage, 128–165.
Hadenius, Axel and Frederick Uggla. 1996. "Making Civil Society Work, Promoting Democratic Development: What Can States and Donors Do?" *World Development*, 24: 1621–1639.
Heller, Patrick. 1999. *The Labor of Development*. Ithaca, NY: Cornell University Press.
———. 2001. "Moving the State: The Politics of Democratic Decentralization in Kerala, South Africa, and Porto Alegre." *Politics and Society* 29, 1: 121–163.
Jackson, Robert and Carl Rosberg. 1984. "Personal Rule: Theory and Practice in Africa." *Comparative Politics*, 16, 4: 421–444.
Johnson, Chalmers. 1982. *MITI and the Japanese Miracle: The Growth of Industrial Policy*, 1925–1975. Stanford: Stanford University Press.
Kalberg, Stephen. 1994. *Max Weber's Comparative-Historical Sociology*. Chicago: University Press of Chicago.
Kronman, Anthony. 1983. *Max Weber*. Stanford: Stanford University Press.
Lange, Matthew. 2003. "Embedding the Colonial State: A Comparative-Historical Analysis of State Building and Broad-Based Development in Mauritius." *Social Science History*, 27, 3: 397–423.
Lipset, Seymour Martin, Martin Trow, and James Coleman. 1956. *Union Democracy: The Inside Politics of the International Typographical Union*. New York: Free Press.
Mamdani, Mahmood. 1996. *Citizen and Subject*. Princeton: Princeton University Press.
Mendez, Juan, Guillermo O'Donnell, and Paul Pinheiro (eds.). 1999. *The (Un)Rule of Law and the Underprivileged in Latin America*. Notre Dame, IN: University of Notre Dame Press.
Migdal, Joel. 1988. *Strong Societies and Weak States: State-Society Relations and State Capabilities in the Third World*. Princeton: Princeton University Press.
North, Douglass. 1981. *Structure and Change in Economic History*. New York: Norton.
O'Donnell, Guillermo. 1993. "On the State, Democratization and Some Conceptual Problems." *World Development*, 21, 8: 1355–1369.
Onis, Ziya. 1991. "The Logic of the Developmental State." *Comparative Politics*, 24, 1: 109–126.
Ostrom, Elinore. 1990. *Governing the Commons*. New York: Cambridge University Press.
Parsons, Talcott. 1964. "Evolutionary Principles in Society." *American Sociological Review*, 29: 339–357.
———. 1971. "Value-Freedom and Objectivity." In *Max Weber and Sociology Today*, edited by O. Stammer. Oxford: Blackwell.
Perrow, Charles. 1979. *Complex Organizations*. Glenview, IL: Scott, Foresman.
Polanyi, Karl. 1957. *The Great Transformation: The Political and Economic Origins of Our Time*. Boston: Beacon.

Portes, Alejandro. 1995. "Economic Sociology and the Sociology of Immigration: An Overview." In *The Economic Sociology of Immigration*, edited by A. Portes. New York: Russell Sage, 1–41.

Putnam, Robert. 1993. *Making Democracy Work*. Princeton: Princeton University Press.

Rheinstein, Max. 1967. *Max Weber on Law in Economy and Society*. New York: Simon and Schuster.

Rodrik, Dani. 1997. "The 'Paradoxes' of the Successful State." *European Economic Review*, 41: 411–442.

Rueschemeyer, Dietrich. 1986. *Power and the Division of Labour*. Stanford: Stanford University Press.

Rueschemeyer, Dietrich and Peter Evans. 1985. "The State and Economic Transformation: Toward an Analysis of the Conditions Underlying Effective Intervention." In *Bringing the State Back In*, edited by P. Evans, D. Rueschemeyer, T. Skocpol. New York: Cambridge University Press, 44–77.

Saxenian, Annalee. 1996. *Regional Advantage: Culture and Competition in Silicon Valley and Route 128*. Cambridge, MA: Harvard University Press.

Scott, James. 1972. "The Erosion of Patron-Client Bonds and Social Change in Rural Southeast Asia." *Journal of Asian Studies*, 31, 1: 5–37.

Sen, Amartya. 1999. *Development as Freedom*. New York: Knopf.

Simmel, Georg. 1955. *Conflict and the Web of Group Affiliation*. New York: Free Press.

Skocpol, Theda. 1997. "The Tocqueville Problem: Civic Engagement in American Democracy." *Social Science History*, 21, 4: 455–479.

Smith, Adam. 1993. *Wealth of Nations*. New York: Oxford University Press.

Stiglitz, Joseph. 2002. *Globalization and Its Discontents*. New York: W.W. Norton.

Stinchcombe, Arthur. 1999. "Ending Revolutions and Building New Governments." *Annual Review of Political Science*, 2: 49–73.

Tendler, Judith. 1993. "Tales of Dissemination in Small-Farm Agriculture: Lessons for Institution Builders." *World Development*, 21, 10: 1567–1582.

Tendler, Judith and Sara Freedheim. 1994. "Trust in a Rent-Seeking World: Health and Government Transformed in Northeast Brazil." *World Development*, 22, 12: 1771–1791.

Tilly, Charles. 1985. "War Making and State Making as Organized Crime." In *Bringing the State Back In*, edited by P. Evans, D. Rueschemeyer, T. Skocpol. New York: Cambridge University Press, 169–191.

Trubek, David. 1972. "Max Weber on Law and the Rise of Capitalism." *Wisconsin Law Review*, 3: 720–753.

Uphoff, Norman. 1992. *Learning from Gal Oya*. Ithaca, NY: Cornell University Press.

Uphoff, Norman and Milton Esman. 1979. *Local Organization for Rural Development: Analysis of Asian Experience*. Ithaca, NY: Cornell University.

Wade, Robert. 1990. *Governing the Market*. Princeton: Princeton University Press.

Wang, Xu. 1999. "Mutual Empowerment of State and Society: Its Nature, Conditions, Mechanisms, and Limits." *Comparative Politics*, 31, 2: 231–249.

Weber, Max. 1968. *Economy and Society*. New York: Bedminster Press.

Woolcock, Michael. 1998. "Social Capital and Economic Development." *Theory and Society*, 27: 151–208.

PART II

Long-Lasting Effects of States on Development

CHAPTER FOUR

State Effectiveness, Economic Growth, and the Age of States

AREENDAM CHANDA AND
LOUIS PUTTERMAN

In the late twentieth century, makers of maps and atlases faced the challenge of keeping up with numerous changes in countries' names and borders. One thing remained a constant, however: find a piece of inhabited territory, and it was certain to belong to some country or other—a country with a government, a flag, an army, and all of the other trappings of the modern nation state. For a country to lack a central government, as, for example, Somalia did during most of the 1990s, was a noteworthy and exceptional fact.

The nation-state is not an entirely new development on the world stage, as it was preceded by empires and kingdoms that in parts of the world have existed for more than three thousand years. Yet many of today's nations stand in places where there was no political entity above the band or tribe level until a few hundred—in some cases not much more than one hundred—years ago. One might wonder whether a society's experience with national cohesion and with operating a state has any relationship to its success in doing so and to the economic outcomes that are often ascribed to the policies and competencies of governments. It seems that no one had taken up this question systematically until we began researching it a few years ago. In this chapter, we discuss our investigation and the results.

The Very Long Run

Our research was motivated by noting major differences among regions of the developing world that appear to result from very long-term historical experience. Although countries in East Asia and sub-Saharan Africa, for example, had rather similar per capita income levels in the decade or two following World War II, the 1980s and 1990s saw several East Asian nations shoot up to middle- and even high-income status, while many sub-Saharan African (SSA) countries experienced very low or negative economic growth. The first impulse of conventionally trained economists is to credit different economic policies for such differences: the scarcity-reflecting prices and exchange rates, the high rates of investment in physical and human capital versus the over-valued exchange rates, monopoly marketing boards, and "white elephant" investment projects. Upon further reflection, few would rule out the possibility that institutional and social differences could be more fundamental than differences in policies, or that institutional factors might largely account for policy. Evidence was found to support the ideas that the slower growing countries had more corrupt governments, more political instability, more ethnically heterogeneous populations, and so on. However, these institutional and social differences, too, might reflect something of a deeper and longer-term nature.

Nations like China, Japan, and Korea were politically united with common national languages for many centuries, whereas countries like Nigeria, the Congo, and Uganda were united neither politically nor linguistically before their colonization a little over a century ago. Other countries can be similarly compared: India and Thailand are relatively old countries; the Philippines and New Guinea relatively new; and Brazil, Chile, and Argentina fall in between. Some countries, like Indonesia, Mali, and Mexico, include very old kingdoms or principalities, but incorporate these and other areas into larger entities that had no existence before the colonial era.

There are some fairly well understood reasons why nations formed at very different times in different parts of the world. The trend in history was for political entities to become larger, as larger and more concentrated populations coalesced in a region. This development frequently followed the advent and intensification of agriculture, often coupled with reliance on irrigation. States did not arise simultaneously everywhere because agriculture did not arise simultaneously in all parts of the world: it arose earliest in West Asia, Egypt, the Indus Valley and China, a little later in Mexico, Peru, and West Africa, and not at all in precolonial Australia and in the far north of the Americas and Eurasia. Biologist turned geographer and historian Jared Diamond pulls together evidence from many fields in his influential book *Guns, Germs and Steel* (1998).

He argues that a few geographic and "biogeographic" factors explain the differences in early agricultural development—and thereby in later technological development—among the world's regions. Chief among those factors are the conditions for diffusion of agricultural techniques among areas of similar latitude and the presence of potentially domesticable seed-bearing grasses and animals among the native flora and fauna that survived the arrival of humans to a region.

Economists Douglas Hibbs and Ola Olsson (2004) have recently carried out statistical tests that show that the geographic and biogeographic factors identified by Diamond can almost perfectly account for the dates of the onset of agriculture in different regions. They find that the date of the onset of agriculture that is predicted by those factors (in a world model calibrated by the handful of known inventions of agriculture) can single-handedly explain 53 percent of the variation of per capita incomes among 112 countries in 1997. When the date of agriculture's onset is joined by an index of "institutional quality" (see later) and by a geographic measure in a multivariate regression for the same 112 countries, the three variables together account for 80 percent of the variance in 1997 per capita incomes, without any reference to such conventional economic variables as investment levels, trade-openness, or government deficits. Moreover, a separate regression equation shows that 38 percent of the difference in the quality of institutions measure is itself explained by the date of onset of agriculture.

Not all early states were directly agricultural in origin. Where large agricultural populations grew, pastoralists organized to prey upon and sometimes conquer the agricultural states. In a neighborhood of kingdoms and states, there were both pressures and incentives to either have a state or be incorporated into one. Such opportunities and pressures help make sense of history's Huns, Mongols, and Turks. But given ancient methods of transportation and communication, these influences did not extend outward indefinitely, as they do today. On the eve of Rome's sacking by the Visigoths in 410 CE, the peoples of the Mediterranean had no idea what lay south of the Sahara or across the Atlantic, nor did they have any clue that Australia, New Guinea, or the Pacific Ocean and its numerous islands existed. Rome was in turn unknown to those living in these regions.

Expansion of technologically successful peoples happened many times in history, as exemplified by the spread of Han Chinese people and culture from north to south China and of Bantu languages and crops from west to central and east Africa. However, the isolation of world regions from one another fully ended only with the overseas expansion of western European countries between the sixteenth and the nineteenth centuries.

States and Development

In an ongoing project, we have been formally testing the conjecture that differences in early development might account for differences not so much in *levels* of income (as in Hibbs and Olsson's study) but in *rates* of economic growth during recent decades. We find that early development did not account for differences in countries' levels of development at the mid-point of the twentieth century, but that greater preindustrial development does seem to have bestowed advantages in subsequent decades, during which the now decolonized countries of Asia and Africa, the already independent nations of Latin America, and other less developed countries strove to achieve economic development in an environment of growing world trade and transmission of technological and institutional know-how. In the first formal investigation, Burkett, Humblet, and Putterman (1999) and Putterman (2000) estimated growth regression equations with data for 58 less developed countries. Each equation included the growth rate of real GDP per capita as its dependent variable and four conventional explanatory factors—initial per capita income, the investment to GDP ratio, the secondary school enrollment ratio, and the current population growth rate—as core explanatory variables. The authors then added to the equation, one at a time, each of three demographic and agricultural intensity measures that can be viewed as proxies for early development: population density, farmers per cultivated hectare, and the proportion of cultivated land that is irrigated.[1] They found that all three factors were highly correlated with growth rates for 1960–1990, that their inclusion raised by 15–21 percent the proportion of the variance in growth rates that the equation explained, and that they remained significant predictors of the rate of economic growth even when institutional and geographic variables suggested by other economists—for example, ethno-linguistic heterogeneity (Easterly and Levine 1997) and the trade openness, landlocked and tropics variables suggested by Sachs and Warner (1997)—were added to the equation.

In this chapter, we present tests of whether an early appearance and subsequent maintenance of state-level organization is a good predictor of recent rates of economic growth or of current levels of income. From one point of view, such tests simply substitute one more measure of early development (state experience) for the early agriculture variable of

Hibbs and Olsson, and the population density and agricultural intensification measures of Burkett et al. The historic presence of states may be just one more indicator of early development, as also would be, for example, the early use of writing.

However, there is reason to take an interest in the early state over and above the rationale for studying those other variables. Many observers believe that states have played a major part in promoting economic and social well-being in modern times. Some, to be sure, take the view that "that government which governs least governs best" and that the best way for states to facilitate economic growth is to "get out of the way" of the market. However, the majority of economists agree that, at the very least, governments play crucial roles in providing a stable currency, rule of law, and physical infrastructures like ports and highways. Many, though not all, would also go so far as to endorse the World Bank pronouncement that "development requires an effective state, one that plays a catalytic, facilitating role, encouraging and complementing the activities of private businesses and individuals" (World Bank 1997, p. iii). This makes it pertinent to investigate whether not just early development, but also early experience with states, in particular, has facilitated recent economic growth through the specific channel of superior state performance.

Early state experience could affect current measures of state effectiveness and stability for at least three different kinds of reason. First, the experience of operating state-level institutions might improve state capacity through some sort of learning-by-doing or trial-and-error process. Second, it is possible that early economic and social development more generally, for which an early state is merely one proxy, increases the likelihood of having a well functioning state today. Possible reasons include (1) that dense populations lead to complexity of social organization, including weakening of the family or clan as the main seat of loyalty, which is conducive to better state functioning and less clientelism and corruption; (2) that early development leads to increases in literacy and other skills helpful for operation of an effective state; and (3) that early development leads to formation of a common ethnic and linguistic identity, which makes it easier to operate a state effectively. Third and finally, part of the relationship between income and a well functioning state could run from income to state, instead of the other way around. If so, and if early development, including an early state, is directly favorable to income growth, then an early state may be associated with a state of better quality through the channel of economic development.

Measuring State Experience

"Statehist" Version 1

In order to gauge quantitatively the effect of state experience, we need a measure of that experience. Although there are numerous country data sets covering economic and political variables, no such measure could be identified for use in our project. Therefore, Bockstette, Chanda, and Putterman (2002) found it necessary to construct a measure of state antiquity. We first explain the way in which their index was defined, describe the source and method of compilation, and provide some descriptive statistics. Recently, additional research was conducted to increase the index's reliability. We discuss that exercise as well, and put the new version of the index to its first use.

Both versions of the index were constructed as follows. We began by dividing the period from 1 to 1950 CE into 39 half centuries. Years before 1 CE were ignored on grounds that the experience of more than 2,000 years ago would be unlikely to have much effect today, so the required research effort with incomplete data would not be justified. For each period of 50 years, we asked 3 questions (and allocated points) as follows: (1) Is there a government above the tribal level? (1 point if yes, 0 points if no); (2) Is this government foreign or locally based? (1 point if locally based, 0.5 points if foreign [i.e., the country is a colony], 0.75 if in between [e.g., a local government with substantial foreign oversight]); (3) How much of the territory of the modern country was ruled by this government? (1 point if over 50 percent, 0.75 points if between 25 and 50 percent, 0.5 points if between 10 and 25 percent, 0.3 points if less than 10 percent.) Answers were extracted from the historical accounts on each of 119 countries in the *Encyclopedia Britannica*. The scores on the three questions were multiplied by one another and by 50, so that for a given 50-year period, what is today a country was given a score of 50 if it was an autonomous nation, 0 if it had no government above the tribal level, 25 if the entire territory was ruled by another country, and so on.

To combine the data of the 39 periods, Bockstette et al. tried alternative rates for discounting the influence of the past, ranging from 0 to a discount of 50 percent for each half century. At a 50 percent discount rate, for example, the contribution to the state antiquity index of having had an autonomous state over the whole territory from 1850 to 1900 is $50 \times (1.5)^{-1} = 33.33$, that from 1801 to 1850 is $50 \times (1.5)^{-2} = 22.22$, and so on. The bulk of the analysis in the paper used *statehist05*, which has a discount rate of 5 percent (i.e., 0.05).[2] To make the series easier to interpret, the sum of the discounted series for each country was divided by the maximum possible value the series could take given the same discount rate. Thus, the index was normalized to take values ranging from 0 to 1.

Statehistn05

By their own admission, the research on which the index used in Bockstette et al. was based, was far from definitive. The initial results in Bockstette et al. are intriguing and are leading other economists to explore that paper's "statehist" series in their own studies. Recognizing both the utility of the series and the weakness of the index's treatment of some countries, we decided to check and improve the quality of the information going into it. For this reason, a new version of the index was prepared late in 2002 and will be used for the first time in this chapter. Like the original effort, the new research relied mainly on the *Encyclopedia Britannica*, but unlike the original, more attention was paid to the region-based *Macropedia* articles, which provide more early historical detail than the country entries. Special attention was devoted to countries like Mexico, Mali, and Indonesia, where states have been present for long periods but have historically covered only a portion of the present-day country.

The history of every country previously studied was revisited and in almost all cases there were at least minor revisions made. With both the old *statehist05* and the new version, called *statehistn05*, normalized to lie between 0 and 1, values increased by 0.1 or more for 20 countries, and declined by 0.1 or more for 9 countries.[3] Despite the seeming imbalance in these numbers, the sum of increases nearly equaled the sum of decreases, so that the average of the revisions in *statehistn05* for 104 countries is only 0.019. Looking at the absolute values of the changes, the average country's value of *statehist05* (*statehistn05*) changed by 0.084. The correlation between *statehistn05* and *statehist05* is 0.8957, indicating a high degree of overall consistency even though there were substantial revisions for a few countries (6 countries' values changed by 0.3 or more). An appendix indicating the main historical facts that lie behind each country's index values, and the new index and constituent values for each 50-year subperiod, are available for inspection and use.[4] Average values for major regions, weighted by country population, appear in table 4.1.

Statehist1500

A new departure of this paper is to investigate the effects of early statehood by considering the historic presence of states up to the year 1500 but not beyond, a year that has become a common point of departure in the

Table 4.1 Regional averages of *statehistn05* and *statehist1500* (weighted by 1960 population)

	Statehistn05	Statehist1500
East-Asia and Pacific	0.83	0.79
Latin America/Caribbean	0.36	0.15
Middle East & North Africa	0.71	0.69
North America[a]	0.20	0.00
South Asia	0.69	0.67
Sub-Saharan Africa	0.41	0.29
Western Europe	0.75	0.67
Total	0.67	0.60

[a] North America is defined as Canada and the United States only.

historical growth literature due to its association with the discovery and colonization of the Americas.[5] *Statehist1500* is calculated from the revised state history data in the same manner as *statehistn05*, except that only the 30 half centuries ending in 1500 are taken into account and the discounting of the past takes 1500 as its starting point. Average values of *statehist1500* by region, again weighted by population, are also included in table 4.1.

State Antiquity, Per Capita Income, and Growth

Table 4.2 presents bivariate correlations between *statehistn05* and *statehist1500*, on the one hand, and real per capita GDP in 1960, 1970, 1980, 1990, and 1995, as well as the rate of growth of per capita GDP from 1960 to 1995. Notice that per capita income was not significantly

Table 4.2 Income levels and growth: correlations with *statehistn05* and *statehist1500*

	GDP pc 1960		GDP pc 1970		GDP pc 1980	
Correlation	0.02	−0.01	0.10	0.06	0.14	0.10
Sample size	95	95	95	95	95	95

	GDP pc 1990		GDP pc 1995		GDP growth 1960–1995	
Correlation	0.23*	0.20+	0.24*	0.21*	0.44**	0.44**
Sample size	95	95	94	94	95	95

Note: GDP levels are in logs.
In each column, the numbers on the left are correlations with *statehistn05*, those on the right are correlations with *statehist1500*.
**$p < 0.01$ level; *$p < 0.05$; +$p < 0.10$.

related to either full state history (*statehistn05*) or pre-Columbian state history (*statehist1500*) in the years 1960, 1970, and 1980. Only in 1990 does the relationship with the income level become significantly positive, at the 10 percent level for *statehist1500* and at the 5 percent level for *statehistn05*. However, both state antiquity measures are significantly correlated with per capita income of 1995 at the 5 percent level, and both are correlated with the growth rate of per capita income during 1960–1995 at the far more significant 0.01 percent level. Thus, until rather recently, countries' experiences of statehood were poor predictors of their levels of development, but during the 35 years since 1960, such experience looks like a good predictor of growth—a conclusion we soon check by controlling for other influences.

Why was early development—of the state in particular and also of other aspects of economic and social organization[6]—not a good predictor of income until recently? We suspect that the answer has something to do with the era of European expansion, industrialization, and colonization that lasted roughly from 1500 until the early 1960s. Acemoglu, Johnson, and Robinson (2002) show that colonized regions that were more urbanized, and by extension more economically developed, in 1500, experienced a "reversal of fortune," becoming poorer than were the originally less urbanized regions by 1990. Acemoglu et al. attribute this to different exploitative strategies of the colonizing powers: policies that erected extractive institutions not conducive to economic dynamism in the previously advanced countries, but institutions favorable to new investment and settlement in the once sparsely populated countries. Whatever the exact cause, having been ahead (from the standpoint of technology, commerce, and large-scale political institutions) in 1500 did not impart advantages during the long era in which European powers extended their reaches overseas. During that long epoch, almost no country outside of Europe and the "neo-Europes" of North America, Australia, and New Zealand was able to successfully join the industrial revolution that began in Northwest Europe in the late eighteenth century.

After decolonization in Asia and Africa, in a process that accelerated with the adoption of more growth-favoring policies in China and India in the 1980s, countries with different historical backgrounds began to diverge economically in what can perhaps be seen as a kind of reversal of the reversal identified by Acemoglu et al. South Korea, Taiwan, China, Thailand, Indonesia, India, and other Asian countries experienced rapid economic growth, while sub-Saharan countries that had had similar per capita incomes in the early 1960s saw growth sputter out and turn negative. The successful Asian countries appeared to build on linguistic and cultural unity, prior urban and commercial foundations, and relatively strong state capacities, while their African counterparts were relatively disadvantaged along these same lines. Latin American countries fell some place in between, their national coherence in little doubt after what was already more than a century of independence, but with deep social divisions born of troubled racial and class histories, often including large marginalized populations. Although several of these countries achieved a degree of industrialization before 1950, their social problems contributed to the maintenance of counter-productive economic policies and to the existence of unstable and self-protective states (Ranis 1992).

How are Early Statehood and State Quality Related?

Table 4.3 shows correlations between *statehistn05* and *statehist1500*, on the one hand, and five measures of political stability and "state quality," on the other. These are the risk of government repudiation of contracts, the risk of government expropriation of property, the degree of corruption in government, the quality of the bureaucracy, and a measure of the rule of law.[7] To define all measures so that higher values are "better," the first three measures are inverted—that is, they are to be understood as "lack of risk of repudiation," "lack of risk of expropriation," and "lack of corruption." Correlations for the average of the five measures, dubbed "institutional quality," are also shown.

Statehistn05 is seen to be positively associated with all five variables, at levels of significance that range from 10 percent for the corruption and

Table 4.3 Political, institutional, demographic and geographical variables: correlations with *statehistn05* and *statehist1500*

	Institutional quality		Lack of corruption		Lack of govt. repudiation of contracts	
Correlation	0.22*	0.18+	0.18+	0.13	0.27**	0.24*
Sample size	93	93	93	93	93	93

	Lack of expropriative risk		Rule of law		Bureaucratic quality	
Correlation	0.25*	0.23*	0.19**	0.14	0.18**	0.16
Sample size	93	93	93	93	93	93

Note: In each column, the numbers on the left are correlations with *statehistn05*, those on the right are correlations with *statehist1500*.
**$p < 0.01$ level; *$p < 0.05$ level; +$p < 0.10$ level.

bureaucracy measures to 5 percent for rule of law and 1 percent for repudiation and expropriation. For the combined "institutional quality" variable, the correlation is significant at the 5 percent level. *Statehist1500* is also positively associated with all six measures, but only the repudiation and expropriation measures reach significance at the 5 percent level, with the bureaucracy measure approaching significance at the 10 percent level and the corruption and rule of law measures being decidedly insignificant. *Statehist1500*'s correlation with combined institutional quality is significant at the 10 percent level. The correlations for *statehistn05* are consistent with the possibility that state quality may be directly influenced by state experience. The fact that *statehist1500*, which fails to take into account the experience of statehood during 1501–1950, is less significantly associated with these measures than is *statehist05*, which does so, may speak for such causality as well. It is improbable that the experience of many centuries ago would have much *direct* impact on state capacity if interrupted by centuries of statelessness (how much influence can Maya experience with governance have on the capacity of the contemporary Guatemalan state?).

Growth Regressions

To learn more about the relationships between early state experience, economic growth, and state capability, we need to control for the simultaneous influences of other variables. In this section, we report the estimates of multiple regression equations to explain differences in growth rates. We focus on growth, rather than levels of income, given the evidence of a more direct connection, as seen in table 4.2.

Table 4.4 shows a set of regressions in which the average 1960–1995 growth rate of per capita GDP is the dependent variable. All specifications include the same four core explanatory variables used by Burkett et al. (1999), which are also common to many other growth studies (see Levine and Renelt 1992 ; Barro 1991). Per capita GDP in 1960 is included because income is expected to grow more slowly the higher the income already attained, other things being equal. The average share of investment in GDP in 1960–1995 is expected to be positively correlated with the growth rate. Initial education, proxied by the 1960 secondary school enrollment ratio, controls for the possible impact of human capital on growth. And the average population growth rate during 1960–1995 is included because growth of per capita income may be smaller—for given levels of investment—when it is spread over more heads, including a large number of children not yet in the labor force. The simple correlations of

Table 4.4 Regressions with per capita GDP growth rate (1960–1995) as dependent variable

	Model 1	Model 2	Model 3	Model 4	Model 5	Model 6	Model 7
Constant	0.049**	0.025	0.029	0.021	0.028	0.054*	0.064**
	(2.69)	(1.22)	(1.41)	(1.05)	(1.51)	(2.30)	(2.83)
Log of per capita GDP (1960)	−0.011**	−0.008**	−0.008**	−0.01**	−0.009**	−0.013**	−0.014**
	(−4.24)	(−2.98)	(−2.81)	(−3.57)	(−3.30)	(−4.14)	(−4.4)
Secondary schooling	0.033*	0.03*	0.03*	0.08**	0.029**	0.006	0.007
	(2.56)	(2.53)	(2.43)	(1.71)	(2.62)	(0.5)	(0.6)
Log of population growth rate (1960–1995)	−0.001	0.001	0.001	0.006**	0.001	0.001	0.001
	(0.48)	(0.57)	(0.55)	(2.14)	(0.56)	(0.32)	(0.4)
Log of investment rate (1960–1995)	0.017**	0.015**	0.015**	0.012**	0.014**	0.007*	0.007*
	(5.85)	(5.79)	(5.42)	(5.23)	(5.87)	(2.50)	(2.22)
Statehistn05		0.022**		0.025**	0.018**	0.017**	
		(3.52)		(4.62)	(3.54)	(2.66)	
Statehist1500			0.017**				0.013*
			(3.46)				(2.57)
Institutional quality				0.004**		0.004**	0.005**
				(4.12)		(3.5)	(3.66)
Population density (1960)					0.001**	0.001**	0.001**
					(9.51)	(4.65)	(4.46)
East-Asia/Pacific						0.008*	0.007+
						(2.24)	(1.81)
Latin America						0.004	0.003
						(1.02)	(0.87)
Middle East and North Africa						0.006+	0.004
						(1.81)	(1.33)
North America						0.007	0.006
						(1.36)	(1.08)
South Asia						0.0005	−0.002
						(0.09)	(−0.41)
Sub-Saharan Africa						−0.009	−0.011*
						(−1.51)	(−1.96)
Western Europe						0.001	0.001
						(0.18)	(0.13)
Observations	88	88	88	79	87	78	78
R-Square	0.47	0.56	0.56	0.67	0.66	0.79	0.79

Note: Numbers in parentheses are t statistics (calculated from heteroscedastic consistent standard errors). Secondary schooling refers to secondary school enrollment ratio in 1960. Institutional quality is as measured by the ICRG index.
**p < 0.01; *p < 0.05; +p < 0.10.

these variables with *statehistn05* and *statehist1500* are reported in Table A of the appendix. In the initial specification in which only these four variables are included, shown in column (1), all have the predicted sign, and three of the four are highly significant, the exception being the population growth rate.

In column (2), *statehistn05* is added to the set of explanatory variables, and has a positive partial correlation with the growth rate, significant at the 1 percent level. Indeed the significance level of the coefficient on the state antiquity measure exceeds that of all the other coefficients apart from the investment share. Column (3) repeats the exercise but substitutes *statehist1500* for *statehistn05*. Strikingly, the extent of statehood on the territories of present-day nations prior to Europe's Age of Exploration is almost as strong a predictor of recent economic growth as is the version of the state antiquity measure that includes 1500–1950 experience, with a similar level of statistical significance.

It remains possible that state experience merely *appears* to influence recent economic growth because it is proxying for important variables that are omitted from specifications (2) and (3). First, state experience is associated with state quality, as seen in table 4.3, and may therefore be proxying for that in equations (2) and (3) of table 4.4. In column (4) we add to the specification of column (2) the combined institutional quality measure considered in table 4.3. Institutional quality does appear to positively affect growth, according to the column (4) estimate, but its inclusion only strengthens the significance of *statehistn05*.[8] In fact, when the institutional quality variable is added to the column (3) specification, which uses *statehist1500* in place of *statehistn05*, the coefficient on *statehist1500* also becomes significant at the 0.1 percent level. (This specification is not shown, to conserve space.) So it appears that a long history of statehood has been conducive to recent economic growth for reasons above and beyond those of the quality of the state today, or due to impacts on state capacity that fail to be captured by the ICRG measure of institutional quality.

Another possibility is that high values of the state variable are associated with high growth rates because of general advantages of early development that may work through channels other than state capacity (Burkett et al. and Putterman 1999, 2000). That is, *statehistn05* could be functioning in equations (1) to (4) as a proxy for early development, which has been found to perform similarly in such equations when proxied by variables such as population density. Column (6) adds 1960 population density to the specification of column (2). Population density does have a highly significant positive coefficient in this equation, but its inclusion does not diminish the significance, and only slightly lowers the coefficient estimate of *statehistn05*. The same applies when using *statehist1500* in place of the latter (not shown).

A third possibility is that state experience is proxying for region of the world, which influences growth for some other reason. Quite a few proposed explanatory variables have been added to growth regressions and found to be significant in the absence of controls for region yet insignificant when such controls are added. In column (7), we add dummy variables controlling for the seven regions used in table 4.1: East Asia and Pacific, Latin America, Middle East and North Africa, North America, South Asia, Sub-Saharan Africa, and Western Europe. Fully 79 percent of the variation in growth rates is explained by this specification. *Statehistn05*, population density, and institutional quality remain positive predictors of the growth rate, all of them significant at the 1 percent level. The final column shows that *statehist1500* can be substituted for *statehistn05* in this specification of the growth equation with only a small diminution in statistical significance: at the 5 percent significance level, a country is predicted to have grown more rapidly during 1960–1995 if it had substantial experience of state-level organization before 1500.

Between 1960 and 1995, the average growth rate of the industrialized countries was almost twice as fast as that of the developing countries. Since most industrialized countries—those of Europe and Japan—had long state histories, perhaps our results are sensitive to their inclusion in our sample.[9] It is important to ask, that is, whether a longer history of statehood has been advantageous to growth among today's *developing countries* in particular. One can find sets of cases that seem likely to fit this pattern—compare China, India, and South Korea in recent decades with Haiti, Kenya, and the Philippines—but there are also numerous exceptions: for example, Ethiopia has one of the longest records of continuous statehood in the developing world, but a poor record for economic growth. We visit the question formally by estimating regressions paralleling those of table 4.4 for the set of non-OECD member countries only.[10] The results, shown in table 4.5, are qualitatively the same as those in table 4.4. Even with the full set of explanatory variables, including the applicable region dummies, *statehistn05* and *statehist1500* are positive predictors of the rate of growth and are significant at the 1 percent level.

Before completing our discussion of the relationship between early statehood and recent growth, a related connection, that with social and economic "modernization," may be worth mentioning. A study by Temple and Johnson (1998) shows that countries with higher values of a mid-1960s modernization index based on research by Adelman and Morris (1967) experienced faster economic growth in the period from 1960 to 1985. Were "old countries" also ahead with respect to modernization in the 1960s? Bockstette et al. show that *statehist05* and Temple and Johnson's index are positively and significantly correlated but only if Latin America is excluded.[11] In an early version of their paper, they also

Table 4.5 Regressions with per capita GDP growth rate (1960–1995) as dependent variable, developing country sample only

	Model 1	Model 2	Model 3	Model 4	Model 5	Model 6	Model 7
Constant	0.043*	0.023	0.027	0.005	0.029	0.029	0.038+
	(2.17)	(0.95)	(1.19)	(0.26)	(1.36)	(1.38)	(1.88)
Log of per capita GDP (1960)	−0.010**	−0.008*	−0.008*	−0.008**	−0.009**	−0.010**	−0.011**
	(−3.67)	(−2.36)	(−2.36)	(−3.26)	(−2.86)	(−3.22)	(−3.53)
Secondary schooling	0.067**	0.054*	0.057*	0.042**	0.049*	0.033*	0.035*
	(3.14)	(2.38)	(2.39)	(2.69)	(2.26)	(2.12)	(2.01)
Log of population growth rate (1960–1995)	0.003	0.001	0.002	0.003	0.002	0.006	0.006
	(0.66)	(0.13)	(0.37)	(0.72)	(0.41)	(1.41)	(1.6)
Log of Investment rate (1960–1995)	0.013**	0.013**	0.013**	0.008**	0.013**	0.004	0.004
	(4.49)	(4.67)	(4.36)	(2.97)	(4.59)	(1.44)	(1.14)
Statehistn05		0.023**		0.029**	0.019**	0.020**	
		(3.1)		(5.49)	(2.95)	(2.96)	
Statehist1500			0.017**				0.014**
			(3.00)				(2.75)
Institutional quality				0.006**		0.006**	0.006**
				(5.49)		(4.03)	(4.04)
Population density (1960)					0.001**	0.001**	0.001**
					(9.69)	(2.79)	(2.93)
East-Asia/Pacific						0.009	0.011
						(1.3)	(1.43)
Latin America						0.003	0.005
						(0.49)	(0.73)
Middle East and North Africa						0.002	0.003
						(0.35)	(0.48)
Sub-Saharan Africa						−0.007	−0.007
						(−1.01)	(−0.88)
Western Europe						0.013+	0.013+
						(1.79)	(1.85)
Observations	70	70	70	61	69	60	60
R-Square	0.46	0.55	0.55	0.75	0.65	0.82	0.82

Note: Numbers in parentheses are *t* statistics (calculated from heteroscedastic consistent standard errors). Schooling refers to secondary school enrollment ratio in 1960. Institutional quality is as measured by the ICRG index.
**p < 0.01; *p < 0.05; +p < 0.10.

reported that inclusion of the index in a growth equation did not alter the significant relationship between the growth rate and *statehistn05*.[12] The conclusion is that there may be some connection between mid-twentieth century modernization and early development and statehood but that the latter is a stronger predictor of recent growth than the former is.

Early States and Income Levels:
A Less Robust Relationship

Although table 4.2 shows that there is no significant correlation between early statehood and income *level* before 1990, income levels of 1995 are significantly related to *statehistn05*, leaving open the possibility that early statehood might be almost as good a predictor of recent income *level* as it is of recent income *growth*. The series of regression exercises shown in table 4.6 make it clear that that is not the case. In columns (1) and (2), *statehistn05* and *statehist1500*, respectively, are made the sole explanatory variables. Each has a positive coefficient, significant at the 1 percent level, but can explain only 8 or 9 percent of the variance in (the logarithm of) 1995 income. In column (3), only non-OECD countries are included, and *statehistn05* is no longer significantly related to income level. There is less agreement on which variables to include when predicting the level of income than when predicting income growth. What is clear is that we should not predict income using measures of education, health, population growth, or even investment, which are likely to be as much influenced by income as they are determinants of it. We select as plausible exogenous determinants of income to explore in multivariate regressions (1) access, which measures a country's access to ports (i.e., whether a country is landlocked or not);[13] (2) 1960 population density, a demographic inheritance that might influence but is unlikely to be influenced by 1995 income; (3) absolute latitude, or distance from the equator, found strongly predictive of income in a number of studies; and (4) the region dummies that were used in the regressions of tables 4.4 and 4.5. Adding the access and population density variables only, in column (4), does no harm to *statehistn05*'s apparent influence on income in the full world sample—its coefficient remains positive and significant at the 1 percent level. Population density also shows a positive but slightly less significant influence, access has an unexpectedly negative and significant effect, and the explained variance jumps from 9 percent to 24 percent. When either latitude, the region dummies, or both are added (in models 5 through 7), however, the sign on the coefficient of *statehistn05* turns negative, and the negative coefficient is even significant at the 10 percent level in the last equation. The results (not shown here) are even worse when non-OECD countries only are considered. When enough additional variables are controlled for, then, an early state predicts *faster development*, but not higher *achieved development* as of 1995. It seems that the advantage conferred by an early state has not been operative for long enough to translate it into an advantage with respect to the level of income thus far achieved.[14]

Table 4.6 Regressions using log of per capita GDP (1995) as dependent variable

	Model 1	Model 2	Model 3[a]	Model 4	Model 5	Model 6	Model 7
Constant	7.37**	7.65**	7.35**	7.61**	7.09**	8.72**	7.701**
	(37.04)	(51.35)	(37.20)	(36.7)	(44.43)	(13.05)	(11.23)
Statehistn05	1.35**		0.468	1.04**	−0.44	−0.52	−0.530+
	(3.24)		(1.05)	(2.64)	(−1.40)	(−1.62)	(−1.80)
Statehist1500		1.01**					
		(3.00)					
Access				−9.17**	−7.46**	−0.31+	−0.338*
				(−3.43)	(−3.90)	(−1.85)	(−2.12)
Population density				0.061*	0.08**	0.05**	0.06**
(1960)				(2.45)	(4.81)	(3.2)	(3.87)
Absolute value of					0.05**		0.03**
latitude					(9.7)		(3.69)
East-Asia/Pacific						0.03	0.512
						(0.05)	(0.83)
Latin America						−0.54	0.069
						(−0.85)	(0.11)
Middle East and						−0.06	0.097
North Africa						(−0.10)	(0.16)
North America						1.17	1.219+
						(1.52)	(1.7)
South Asia						−0.98	−0.538
						(−1.48)	(−0.85)
Sub Saharan						−1.65*	−0.925
Africa						(−2.55)	(−1.45)
Western Europe						1.13+	0.840
						(1.79)	(1.41)
Observations	103	103	80	101	101	101	101
R-Square	0.09	0.08	0.01	0.24	0.61	0.75	0.78

Note: Numbers in parentheses are t statistics (calculated from heteroscedastic consistent standard errors). Access is an indicator of whether a country is landlocked.
[a] Developing country sample.
**$p < 0.01$; *$p < 0.05$; +$p < 0.10$.

Early States and State Quality: More Mixed News

One of the more intriguing aspects of the finding that countries with earlier states have been achieving more rapid economic growth in recent decades is the intuitively appealing possibility that this might be due to the translation of state experience into state capacity and of state capacity into economic success. Many attribute the economic successes of Japan, South Korea, Taiwan, and more recently China to the efficacy of strong states. Might not the strength of state capability in these cases itself result from their long traditions of state administration? And might not the comparative failures and middling performances of the

Philippines, Indonesia, Mexico, and India be attributed to the relative absence of a state tradition in the first and the more fragmented and discontinuous histories of statehood in the others? The bivariate correlations between the institutional quality measures and state history in table 4.3, and the significant correlation between institutional quality and growth in several specifications in tables 4.4 and 4.5 lend some support to this conjecture. However, the performance of the state history variables as predictors of state quality in multivariate regressions turns out to be disappointing.

Table 4.7 illustrates results found for the individual state quality measures by means of a series of regressions using the combined measure of institutional quality as dependent variable. In columns (1) and (2), we see that *statehistn05* and *statehist1500* are significant positive predictors of current institutional quality when entered alone, although together with constant terms each explains only about 4 percent of the dependent variable's variation. Column (3) shows that when OECD countries are dropped, the coefficient on *statehistn05* is no longer either positive or significant. Columns (4)–(7) report specifications in which various combinations of control variables are introduced: the population density, latitude, and region dummies used in table 4.6, and the ethnic heterogeneity variable used by Easterly and Levine (1997), and a number of subsequent studies. Similar to the results for income level in table 4.6, we find that whenever either latitude, the region dummies, or both are included in the regression, the coefficient of *statehistn05* has the "wrong" sign, being negative and significant at the 5 percent level in the specification with ethnic heterogeneity, population density, and latitude. When only ethnic heterogeneity and population density are included (still using a world sample), *statehistn05* remains positive and is significant at the 10 percent level. Column (8) shows that the coefficient on *statehistn05* is negative and insignificant for non-OECD countries in the full specification paralleling column (7).

To check the possibility that the failure of the state history variables to be robust predictors of state quality might be due to peculiarities of the ICRG's institutional quality measures, we also looked at the governance indicators constructed by Daniel Kaufmann, Aart Kraay, and Pablo Zoido-Lobaton (2002). In addition to rule of law and corruption, which appear in the ICRG data, they include measures of voice and accountability, political stability and absence of violence, government effectiveness, and regulatory quality. Their data are for the late 1990s and 2002 and thus somewhat more recent than the ICRG variables, but most of the variation among countries is presumably similar to what it was

Table 4.7 Regressions using institutional quality (1982–1995) as dependent variable

	Model 1	Model 2	Model 3[a]	Model 4	Model 5	Model 6	Model 7	Model 8[a]
Constant	5.25**	5.72**	5.21**	6.35**	3.66**	6.98**	4.52**	5.36**
	(11.76)	(18.39)	(16.08)	(10.85)	(7.49)	(5.25)	(3.21)	(4.95)
Statehistn05	1.87*		−0.188	1.44+	−1.42*	−0.93	−1.03	−1.37
	(2.22)		(−0.28)	(1.66)	(−2.13)	(−1.34)	(−1.59)	(−1.66)
Statehist1500		1.20+						
		(1.82)						
Ethno-linguistic fractionalization				−2.16**	0.83	−1.68*	−0.65	−0.43
				(−2.92)	(1.40)	(−2.59)	(−0.99)	(−0.53)
Population density (1960)				0.07	0.15**	0.04	0.07*	0.09*
				(1.47)	(4.36)	(1.22)	(2.13)	(2.47)
Absolute value of latitude					0.11**		0.06**	0.03+
					(9.68)		(3.64)	(1.83)
East-Asia/ Pacific						1.28	2.09+	1.05
						(1.00)	(1.71)	(1.23)
Latin America						−1.41	−0.10	−0.55
						(−1.12)	(−0.08)	(−0.67)
Middle East and North Africa						−0.37	0.03	−0.30
						(−0.3)	(0.02)	(−0.35)
North America						3.87*	3.54*	
						(2.52)	(2.47)	
South Asia						−0.34	0.31	
						(−0.25)	(0.24)	
Sub-Saharan Africa						−0.54	0.61	−0.05
						(−0.41)	(0.49)	(−0.07)
Western Europe						3.17*	2.63*	1.38
						(2.60)	(2.29)	(1.03)
Observations	93	93	69	87	87	87	87	63
R-Square	0.05	0.03	0.001	0.18	0.62	0.73	0.77	0.39

Note: Numbers in parentheses are *t* statistics (calculated from heteroscedastic consistent standard errors).
**p < 0.01; *p < 0.05; +p < 0.10.
[a] Developing country sample.

a decade earlier. The results of calculating bivariate correlations and multivariate regressions like those above using the variables in Kaufmann et al. are qualitatively quite similar to those using the ICRG measures. The Kaufmann et al. measures are positively and generally significantly correlated with *statehistn05* in bivariate correlation or single variable regressions for a world sample; but significance, positive sign, or both usually disappear when other variables—especially latitude or region dummies—are added or when the OECD countries are dropped from the sample.[15]

Conclusion

In recent decades, "old countries"—countries that gave rise to early states, kingdoms, and empires and those that maintained forms of political organization above the tribal level for large parts of the last two millennia—have been recording more rapid economic growth, on average, than have "new countries." This result is remarkably robust, standing up in multivariate regressions for both world samples and samples including developing countries only. This chapter shows that it also stands after an extensive revision and, hopefully, improvement in the quality of our data series on the antiquity of the state. By 1995, old countries also had higher incomes than new countries, but that result was not as robust. During the turbulent period from about 1500 to around 1960, the moderately old countries of northwestern and western Europe and their new off-shoots in North America, Australia, and New Zealand leapfrogged ahead of similarly aged countries in the Americas and Africa and older countries in Asia, leading to a situation in which old and new countries were on a roughly similar footing. After 1960, however, advantages of oldness associated with population density, an old state, and perhaps additional as yet unstudied factors permitted old countries to grow faster than new ones.

It is tempting to speculate that the state itself is a key to this faster recent growth. Some old countries, like Japan, China, and Korea, have had strong states and strong economic growth in recent decades; some new countries, like Haiti, Kenya, and the Philippines, have had weaker states and slower economic growth. Faster growth is statistically associated with both older states and higher values of institutional quality measures. However, we were unable to confirm a robust relationship between the age of the state and its capability or performance. Only in full world samples without controls for other factors is the relationship between the age of the state and the quality of state institutions positive and significant, as the conjecture would imply. Among developing countries alone, and when other factors are controlled for, the relationship is usually insignificant and often negative. And even statistically significant negative relationships are found in some multivariate regressions.

We are thus left with the question of *why* older countries have been growing more rapidly of late. According to the evolutionary hypothesis advanced by Burkett et al. and Putterman, there may be a set of capabilities and propensities—for example, to operate large-scale organizations, to master mechanical and engineering skills, to engage in trade, to balance family against larger social spheres, to value education—that develop in concert with the evolution of society from the foraging band to the agrarian state to the modern industrial state. Those further along this spectrum of development may have an easier time taking the next step than do those further behind, a fact that may, however, have been put on hold by Europe's successive conquests in the non-European world.

Despite the statistical weakness of the relationship in the exercises above, state effectiveness may yet turn out to be one of the relative advantages conferred by early development. The relationship may simply be too complex to be picked up by our exercises. Some strong states, like China in the late 1950s, may guide their countries into directions not conducive to economic growth. Some countries that had states for many centuries—Guatemala, Mali, and Ethiopia, for example—may not have developed capable modern states for various reasons: the lack of continuity between ancient state structures and the colonial and postcolonial structures that replaced them, ethnic clashes stemming from related population movements, or less advantageous principles of state organization. Some old states may have been resistant or unreceptive to modernization. And some countries—China again comes to mind—may have states capable of fostering modernization but not of scoring well on measures of rule of law, voice, or absence of corruption. Perhaps, with additional controls, or with measures of state capacity less focused on investor and citizen rights and more focused on state administrative capacity,[16] a more robust positive relationship between the age of the state and its contemporary capacity will yet be uncovered.

Appendix

Table A Additional correlations

	Statehistn05	Statehist1500
Statehistn05	1	0.95**
Statehist1500	0.95**	1
Secondary schooling	0.15	0.13
Log of investment rate (1960–1995)	0.19+	0.21+
Log of population growth (1960–1995)	−0.30**	−0.25*
Institutional quality	0.20+	0.16
Population density (1960)	0.19+	0.17
Absolute latitude	0.41**	0.36**
Ethno-linguistic fractionalization	−0.18	−0.10

**$p < 0.01$; *$p < 0.05$; +$p < 0.10$.

Notes

1. Use of these variables as indicators of stage of development follows the focus on similar factors in the developmental stage theory of Boserup (1965). Because good data was not easily located for earlier years, measures of the three variables were taken for 1960 on the assumption that these still reflected earlier conditions.
2. At the 5% rate, the period 1000–1950 CE would receive 71% of the overall weight in the index, versus 29% for the millennium 1–1000 CE, if each half century had on average the same score prior to discounting.
3. The increases were for Angola, Ethiopia, Ghana, Mali, Mauritania, Nigeria, Rwanda, Senegal, Uganda, Morocco, Tunisia, Bolivia, Guatemala, Mexico, Peru, Indonesia, Sri Lanka, South Korea, Belgium, and Turkey. The decreases were for Central African Republic, Gabon, Republic of Congo, Zimbabwe, Fiji, Papua New Guinea, Italy, Norway, and Sweden.
4. At present, they can be downloaded from links to http://www.econ.brown.edu/fac/Louis%5FPutterman/
5. See, e.g., Acemoglu, Johnson, and Robinson (2002).
6. Similar findings of lower correlation with income before 1990 are found not only for *statehist05* by Bockstette et al., but also for the preindustrial development variables studied by Burkett et al.
7. These measures were introduced into the growth literature by Knack and Keefer (1995). They are released annually in the International Country Risk Guide (ICRG). *Rule of Law* measures the existence of established peaceful mechanisms for adjudicating disputes. Along with *Risk of Expropriation*, they are likely to capture the security of property and contract rights. *Repudiation of Contract by the Government* is another indicator of contract enforcement and government credibility. The remaining two variables, *Corruption in Government* and *Quality of Bureaucracy* have been regarded as proxies for the general efficiency with which government services are provided. See Knack and Keefer (1995) for further details.
8. The value of the coefficient on *statehistn05* also increases slightly. The effect of faster population growth becomes positive and significant, but this does not persist in the remaining specifications.
9. On the other hand, it is worth noting that in the cases of the United States, Canada, Australia, and New Zealand, dubbed by some economic historians as the "neo-Europes," we made no special adjustments for the low values of *statehist*. Hibbs and Olsson, by contrast, assign Western European "biogeography" to the neo-Europes on the grounds that the "crop suite" of Western Europe was transferred wholesale to them.
10. OECD countries here are to be understood as those countries belonging to the OECD by the 1980s—Western Europe, North America, Japan, New Zealand, and Australia. Given the nature of the study, newer members such as Mexico and Korea are not considered OECD countries for purposes of this analysis.
11. Latin American countries with longer histories of statehood, such as Mexico, Peru, and Bolivia, were less modernized than some with shorter state histories, such as Argentina, Chile, and Brazil.
12. The result was left out of the published version for reasons of space only.
13. This variable was taken from Bloom and Williamson (1998).
14. China and India are now growing rapidly but have a long way to go to catch up with the world's high-income countries.
15. We also checked the bivariate correlations between the "Weberianness of the state" (Web) index of Evans and Rauch (1999) and our *statehist* variables. For the 34 countries on which observations are available, the correlation between Web and *statehistn05* is 0.4191 and that between Web and *statehist1500* is 0.3580. Both correlations are significant at the 5% level. We did not estimate regressions with Web due to its smaller sample size.
16. Citing the negative correlation between Moore, Leavy, Houtzager, and White's (1999) RICE variable and the ICRG institutional quality index, Peter Evans asks in his contribution to this

volume whether the ICRG's index may be measuring qualities favored by foreign investors, as opposed to state capacity per se.

References

Acemoglu, Daron, Simon Johnson, and James Robinson. 2002. "Reversal of Fortune: Geography and Institutions in the Making of the Modern World Income Distribution." *Quarterly Journal of Economics*, 117, 4: 1231–1294.

Adelman, Irma and Cynthia T. Morris. 1967. *Society, Politics and Economic Development*. Baltimore, MD: Johns Hopkins University Press.

Barro, Robert. 1991. "Economic Growth in a Cross-Section of Countries." *Quarterly Journal of Economics*, 106: 407–444.

Bloom, David E. and Jeffrey G. Williamson. 1998. "Demographic Transitions and Economic Miracles in Emerging Asia." *World Bank Economic Review*, 12, 3: 419–455.

Bockstette, Valerie, Areendam Chanda, and Louis Putterman. 2002. "States and Markets: The Advantage of an Early Start." *Journal of Economic Growth*, 7: 347–369.

Boserup, Ester. 1965. *Conditions of Agricultural Growth: The Economics of Agricultural Change Under Population Pressure*. New York: Aldine.

Burkett, John P., Catherine Humblet, and Louis Putterman. 1999. "Pre-Industrial and Post-War Economic Development: Is There a Link?" *Economic Development and Cultural Change*, 47, 3: 471–495.

Diamond, Jared. 1998. *Guns, Germs and Steel: The Fates of Human Societies*. New York: W.W. Norton.

Easterly, William and Ross Levine. 1997. "Africa's Growth Tragedy: Policies and Ethnic Divisions." *Quarterly Journal of Economics*, 112: 1203–1246.

Evans, Peter and James Rauch. 1999. "Bureaucracy and Growth: A Cross-National Analysis of the Effects of 'Weberian' State Structures on Economic Growth." *American Sociological Review*, 64: 748–765.

Hibbs, Douglas A. and Ola Olsson. 2004. "Geography, Biogeography and Why Some Countries Are Rich and Others Are Poor." *Proceedings of the National Academy of Sciences*, 101: 3715–3720.

Kaufmann, Daniel, Aart Kraay, and Pablo Zoido-Lobaton. 2002. "Governance Matters II: Updated Indicators for 2000–01." Unpublished paper, The World Bank.

Knack, Stephen and Philip Keefer. 1995. "Institutions and Economic Performance: Cross Country Tests Using Alternative Institutional Measures." *Economics and Politics*, November 7, 3: 207–227.

Levine, Ross and David Renelt. 1992. "A Sensitivity Analysis of Cross-Country Growth Regressions." *American Economic Review*, 82: 942–963.

Moore, Mick, Jennifer Leavy, Peter Houtzager, and Howard White. 1999. "Polity Qualities: How Governance Affects Poverty." Institute of Development Studies, University of Sussex.

Putterman, Louis. 2000. "Can an Evolutionary Approach to Development Predict Post-War Economic Growth?" *Journal of Development Studies*, 36, 3: 1–30.

Ranis, Gustav. 1992. "The Role of Governments and Markets: Comparative Development Experience." In *State and Market in Development: Synergy or Rivalry?*, edited by L. Putterman and D. Rueschemeyer. Boulder, CO: Lynne Rienner.

Sachs, Jeffrey and Andrew Warner. 1997. "Sources of Slow Growth in African Economies." *Journal of African Economies*, 6, 3: 335–376.

Temple, Jonathan and Paul A. Johnson. 1998. "Social Capability and Economic Growth." *Quarterly Journal of Economics*, 113, 3: 965–990.

World Bank. 1997. *World Development Report 1997: The State in a Changing World*. Washington: World Bank.

CHAPTER FIVE

Colonial States and Economic Development in Spanish America

JAMES MAHONEY AND MATTHIAS VOM HAU

Recent research on Latin America argues that Spanish colonialism caused a reversal of development trajectories in the region (Mahoney 2003; see also Acemoglu, Johnson, and Robinson 2001, 2002; Engerman and Sokoloff 2002). During the late colonial and the early postindependence periods—roughly between 1750 and 1850—the wealthy colonial centers tended to fall behind and turned into the least economically prosperous areas in Spanish America. By contrast, poor colonial backwaters often experienced impressive growth and became the wealthiest territories. To a large extent, the regional development hierarchy established during this critical historical epoch is still found today.

In this chapter, we argue that state formation was one major process through which colonialism affected long-run development in Spanish America. Spanish colonizers did not create a single type of state structure throughout the entire empire; rather, they developed dramatically different state apparatuses across regions. In the centers of the Spanish Colonial Empire, such as New Spain and Peru, *mercantilist states*[1] were created to oversee the central administrative tasks of tax collection, public works, defense, and support for the Church. These states also helped coordinate the Spanish colonial economy, which was oriented toward the extraction of precious minerals through the use of a dependent labor force. Among other things, mercantilist states were marked by rent seeking, conservative elite control, and substantial dependence on external authorities in Spain.

By contrast, in peripheral colonial regions such as Argentina, Uruguay, and Costa Rica, state formation was basically absent during most of the colonial period and only gained momentum in the late colonial period and after independence from Spain. During these times, *minimal states* became prevalent in peripheral areas. These states correspond roughly with the "nightwatchman" state advocated by Adam Smith, a kind of state that developed because these regions were largely outside of the Spanish mercantilist economy. Though less corrupt and more autonomous from colonial control than mercantilist states, minimal states nevertheless lacked autonomy from important elite actors of the peripheries—export merchants, urban notables, and bourgeois lawyers and intellectuals.

During the critical 1750–1850 period, colonial peripheries that developed minimal states were more successful at achieving development than the colonial centers with mercantilist states. Minimal states were better able to capitalize on the new free trade policies and the opening of local markets that began with the Bourbon Reforms of the eighteenth century and continued into the nineteenth century when the Latin American region was gradually incorporated into the global capitalist economy. Whereas mercantilist states were burdened by guilds, monopolies, and rent seeking, minimal states were better positioned to coordinate economic activities in ways that promoted international trade and domestic markets. While having advantages over mercantilist states, minimal states nevertheless possessed their own fundamental limitations, starting with the fact that these states lacked autonomy from elite economic actors necessary to oversee broad-based development projects that could sustain high levels of growth over the long run. Similarly, their limited organizational capacities prevented minimal states from establishing the infrastructure necessary for industrial production. At best, then, Spanish colonialism left behind state apparatuses that could achieve only moderate and distorted forms of development.

Defining Mercantilist and Minimal States

The effects of state action on development vary dramatically depending on the internal structure of the state and its ties to non-state actors. Here we use three dimensions—internal organization, autonomy from domestic groups, and colonial dependence—to distinguish between two ideal types of colonial states: *mercantilist* and *minimal*.

Internal State Organization

Our first dimension concerns the internal organization of states. Max Weber famously distinguished between *patrimonial* and *rational-bureaucratic* states.

Rational-bureaucratic states exhibit a coherent administrative and coercive apparatus that operates on the basis of a set of formal, rational rules. The bureaucratic practices of these states are kept separate from private life; state agencies rely on hierarchy, written records, and the delegation of authority in order to fulfill highly specific tasks. Administrators and civil servants working within such bureaucratic structures tend to display a distinct corporate identity, propelled and maintained through merit-based promotion and lifelong career trajectories in public service. Weber argues that a rational-bureaucratic state is a crucial prerequisite for development. Only this type of state is able to provide economic actors with a secure and predictable environment for commercial transactions, and to extract and mobilize resources for long-term investments in state-led development projects (Weber 1972, pp. 551–562, 815).

By contrast, patrimonial states are harmful for development as they lack bureaucracy. These states are controlled by a small group of personally interconnected elites whose authority is based on traditional law without explicit, written rules. Bureaucratic practices often overlap with private interest; rent seeking and the sale of office figure prominently in patrimonial states. Likewise, specialized education and merit-based career trajectories for civil servants are absent. Patrimonial states are also associated with publicly created monopolies, arbitrary taxation, and a general lack of financial calculability that hinders investment by economic actors such as business elites. Moreover, the lack of bureaucratic organization negatively affects the capacity of states to engage in broad-based development projects themselves (Weber 1972, pp. 138–139, 642–643).

During the colonial period in Spanish America, all states probably came closest to Weber's patrimonial type. Traditional authority was important, and a fully rationalized bureaucratic structure was largely absent. Nevertheless, the extent of patrimonialism varied, with some states being so little developed that neither an efficient bureaucracy nor burdensome corruption and monopolistic closure were pervasive. These minimal states exhibited laissez-faire apparatuses with a limited reach, and they could be found most commonly in the peripheral regions of the colonial empire, where the Spanish did not lay down enduring mercantilist institutions.

As an ideal type, a minimal state corresponds with the "nightwatchman" state advocated by neo-utilitarian theorists and many free market economists. It features an administrative apparatus whose central functions are restricted to protecting individual liberties, upholding property rights, and ensuring law and order. Thus, minimal states display certain legal, administrative, and coercive organizations that provide an institutional framework for the basic functioning of trade and market exchange.

At the same time, the internal organization of these states lacks the reach to actively pursue broad-based economic development projects or to set up the infrastructure necessary for industrial production. Minimal states are marked by the relative absence of a bureaucratic apparatus endowed with the capacities to effectively intervene into the marketplace, generate revenues, and invest in mass schooling or public infrastructure.

In point of fact, of course, Latin America never featured states that perfectly correspond to this ideal type. For example, states in the region have always placed at least some restrictions on trade, featured important pockets of rent seeking, advanced some infrastructural measures, and sometimes actively intervened in the market to stimulate production. However, we suggest that beginning in the late-colonial period, the incipient states in Argentina, Uruguay, and Costa Rica approximated the ideal-typical laissez-faire organization of a minimal state in important respects.

Autonomy from Domestic Elites

A large literature explores the importance of state autonomy for economic development (for overviews see Evans, Rueschemeyer, and Skocpol 1985; Migdal, Kohli, and Shue 1994). Among the most distinguished works in this context is Peter Evans's *Embedded Autonomy* (1995). Evans's argument builds on Weberian insights about the importance of rational bureaucracy, but it also takes into consideration the configuration of state-society linkages. He specifically argues that "underlying differences in state structures and state-society relations" define different types of states, which in turn shape developmental prospects (p. 44).

Evans differentiates between *predatory* and *developmental states*. With respect to internal structure, predatory states are patrimonial in orientation, much like the mercantilist states we discussed above. Yet, predatory states are also defined by their ties to domestic actors. These states have substantial autonomy from society in the specific sense that no organized domestic group can be said to control them. Instead of being captured by domestic forces, predatory states are composed of highly autonomous officeholders who "prey" on society to serve their own narrow goals (Evans 1995, pp. 45–47).

By contrast, developmental states exhibit "embedded autonomy." These states possess the corporate coherence to maintain autonomy from societal groups. Yet, unlike what Weber advocates, developmental states are not completely insulated from society. Rather, they are embedded in a dense set of social ties with key domestic groups, especially capitalists.[2]

These dense connections allow state agents to effectively design and coordinate economic policy in close consultation with economic elites (Evans 1995, pp. 12, 48–50).

In late-colonial and early-independence Spanish America, state-society relationships were quite different from either of Evans's predatory and developmental states. Both types are states in which governing and bureaucratic elites exhibit autonomy from major societal groups. By contrast, mercantilist and minimal states display the relative absence of state autonomy; a distinguishing feature of these states is that they are largely captured by domestic elites. The substantial economic weight of these groupings vis-à-vis the state shaped official decisions and policies. Local elites also established more direct forms of control over the state apparatus, for instance by purchasing important administrative offices, or by forming kinship ties between elite members and state officials (see Andrien 1982; Kicza 1983). In this sense, the early Spanish American state types correspond more closely to Marxian formulations of the "instrumental state," or a state that serves as a tool of domination for dominant classes (see Carnoy 1984).

Thus, mercantilist states have an internal organization similar to predatory states, marked by patrimonial relationships and the absence of fully rationalized bureaucratic procedures. At the same time, mercantilist states found in colonial Spanish America work on behalf of a specific domestic group, not simply a small clique of ruling elites. As a result, mercantilist states are more prone to promote developmental projects than predatory states, even if these developmental projects serve the interests of only the dominant class. Indeed, the relative absence of full-blown predatory states in late-colonial and early-independence Latin America may have helped the region avoid the severe levels of poverty and economic underdevelopment that characterize parts of Africa.[3]

A key difference between minimal states and mercantilist states concerns the specific domestic group that has captured the state. With minimal states, this group corresponds with liberal elites, who find their social base among bourgeois merchants, urban elites, and intellectuals. Liberal elites and their interest organizations are characterized by the advocacy of free markets, the protection of private property, and a more expanded role of the state in trade promotion and the creation of infrastructure. By contrast, with mercantilist states, this controlling group is composed of colonial and conservative elites who benefit from state regulation of markets and special corporate benefits. During the colonial period, this dominant class especially included merchants protected by state monopolies, church officials, and agrarian elites with dependent labor forces.

After independence from Spain, conservative elites largely continued to recruit themselves from these social groupings. The most important difference from the colonial period is that immigrants from Spain, who often became powerful guild merchants, played a less dominant role in the demographic make-up of conservative elites (Brading 1971; Gootenberg 1996; Halperín Donghi 1988).

These differing groups reflect the different economies present in former colonial centers and former colonial peripheries. In the colonial centers, the mercantilist orientation of the economy empowered conservative colonial elites, whereas in the colonial peripheries the relative absence of mercantilist institutions allowed for stronger liberal factions.

The fact that contrasting economic structures shaped the kind of elite that controlled mercantilist and minimal states raises the broader question of whether these states were simply reflections of different modes of production, exercising little autonomous causal force on their own. Our view is that mercantilist and minimal states are best seen as intervening variables that stand between the organization of the colonial economy and long-run development outcomes in the postcolonial period. These states are, in part, a reflection of the organization of the colonial economy, but the specific ways in which dominant class actors exercise authority is not a mechanical outgrowth of the economy. For example, the mercantilist state of New Spain became somewhat more liberal toward indigenous labor policy than the mercantilist state of Peru, and this outcome cannot be easily understood as a reflection of differences in the two economies. Moreover, the causal relationship between elite interests and state policy is not unidirectional. By providing the basic legal framework for economic activity, states, even instrumental states, shape the very economic structures and collective actors that constitute them, such that the distinction between cause and effect becomes blurred.

Colonial Dependence

The literature on states has been centrally concerned with mapping distinct configurations of state-society relations and their potential effects on development. Much of the focus here is the problem just discussed of "internal autonomy," or the relationship between states and domestic actors. Although major states theorists usually note the important effects of global context in shaping the ability of states to pursue development, they nevertheless maintain a strict analytic separation between the state and this "external"—or international—environment (e.g., Rueschemeyer and Evans 1985; Migdal 1988). However, we argue that in the context of colonialism and its immediate aftermath, this strict distinction is not appropriate. Rather, the external relationship between the state and a colonizing power is a basic defining dimension of a colonial state that needs to be built into a typology that seeks to explain development prospects. Indeed, we suggest that the different modes of international dependency that characterize nearly all postcolonial states constitute essential defining features of these states and merit explicit examination.

By definition, a colonial state is subservient to another state; colonial states are not sovereign entities. Clearly, this situation of extreme dependence fundamentally shapes the goals and actions of these states. Colonial states are ultimately controlled by state agents who are direct representatives of the colonizing power and who are charged with making policy to support that external nation. Policies such as tariffs or taxes, and also infrastructural measures of the colonial state, are ultimately oriented toward the interests of the colonizing power. The development prospects of the colonial state and the interests of different local elite factions are of secondary importance. This distinguishes colonial dependence from other forms of international domination. For instance, states engaged in economic imperialism still need to appeal—at least to a certain extent—to local interests.

On this basis we suggest that in a situation of colonial dependence, the economic organization of the colonizing power can have dramatic effects on the structure and orientation of the colonial state. In Latin America, the Spanish mercantilist model was designed to ensure favorable trade balances through the accumulation of precious metals (Andrien 1985; Walker 1979). Accordingly, Spain established mercantilist states in precisely those territories where gold and silver were located, and where a substantial indigenous labor force could be harnessed to work the mines and provide labor for plantations to feed the settler population. By contrast, the Spanish Crown chose to ignore areas where minerals and indigenous people were sparse, leaving them virtually "stateless" for much of the colonial period.

In the mid-eighteenth century, the mercantilist orientation of Spain began to give way to more liberal economic arrangements. Between 1713 and 1762, the Spanish Crown pursued a set of administrative and economic policies—known as the Bourbon Reforms—to revert declining trade and dwindling revenues in the Spanish American colonies, and to improve administrative efficiency and state authority in these areas. The underlying objective of these reforms was to enhance economic benefits and to realize greater political control over colonial territories. As a matter of fact, these liberalizing policies eventually set the stage for independence struggles and the breakdown of the entire colonial system (Brading 1987; Guerra 2000; Lynch 1986; Walker 1979).

In the center areas, where mercantilist states had been established, the Bourbon Reforms attacked local elite privileges, including the control of dominant conservative groups over the colonial state apparatus. For instance, Spanish monarchs attempted to stop the sale of offices and introduced a new layer of independent bureaucrats on temporary duty from Spain. In response, important conservative elite factions started to join liberal "Creole patriots" in questioning and opposing Spanish colonial rule. With independence and the removal of Spanish authority, these conservative elites were largely able to reestablish political dominance in the colonial centers, helping to fuel major divisions between conservative and liberal elite factions in these regions.

By contrast, in the peripheral areas, the Bourbon Reforms were often embraced by the incipient state apparatuses and local, mostly liberal, elites. These peripheral states emerged under a liberalizing Spanish colonial regime that gradually replaced the previous dominant mercantilist model. Moreover, unlike the mercantilist states, these new minimal states were not financially dependent on colonial monopolies and protections; rather, they were capable of functioning on their own in the immediate aftermath of colonialism. Hence, mercantilist states depended on the colonial relationship in a way that was not true of minimal states.

This brief discussion suggests some basic lessons about colonial states. Most obviously, the potentially evolving economic structures of the colonizing power are related to the kind of colonial states that are likely to emerge. Yet, it also suggests that colonial states are not simply reflections of the colonizing nation. Indeed, as a colonial settler population matures, it is almost inevitable that elite factions of this population will have conflicting interests with the colonizers. To the extent that elite segments of the settlers come to dominate local government and the local economy, colonial authorities may be unable to implement their policy agendas. In turn, however, the interests of elite settlers may not be the same across all colonial regions, and thus the extent to which colonial states are dependent on the colonial relationship may vary from one state to the other.[4]

Administrative Organization of the Empire

A bird's-eye view of the administrative structure of colonial Spanish America establishes a valuable entry point for explaining contrasting trajectories of state formation in the colonial centers and colonial peripheries. During the early and mid-colonial period, the central administrative division within the empire was between the Viceroyalty of New Spain and the Viceroyalty of Peru, the former eventually encompassing Mexico and Central America, as well as parts of Venezuela and the United States, and the latter including Panama and the Spanish possessions in South America except for parts of Venezuela. To establish more decentralized control within the Viceroyalties, the Crown founded *audiencias* in major colonial cities. These tribunals were originally intended to be judicial entities, but they also soon assumed legislative and executive functions, eventually becoming major governing bodies for the empire. From the *audiencias*, the Spanish Crown oversaw general administration, tax collection, public works, defense, and support for the Church.

With the rise of Bourbon reformers in the eighteenth century, the administrative organization of the empire was substantially revised. In 1739, the Viceroyalty of New Granada was permanently established, roughly comprising modern Colombia, Ecuador, and Venezuela. Then, in 1776, the Viceroyalty of Río de La Plata was created, which roughly encompassed modern Argentina, Bolivia, Paraguay, and Uruguay. Hence, the Viceroyalty of New Spain remained intact, whereas the Viceroyalty of Peru was reduced to modern Peru and most of Chile. Within the Viceroyalty of New Spain, the *audiencia* of Guatemala enjoyed the status of captaincy-general, making Guatemala City an important administrative district. In the South American viceroyalties, Lima remained the key administrative center, but Caracas and Buenos Aires now enjoyed substantial autonomy from this center, and Chile was also granted the status of captaincy-general. For our purposes, the critical implication of these administrative revisions is that state formation in the peripheries really began in the mid-eighteenth century, not the sixteenth century as it did in the colonial centers (Andrien 2001; Burkholder and Johnson 1994; Johnson and Socolow 2002; Lockart and Schwartz 1983).

Mercantilist States and Their Legacies

The Spanish imposition of mercantilist states occurred most dramatically in the two colonial centers of Mexico and Peru. These areas saw the first efforts by Spanish colonizers to create a set of administrative and coercive organizations in the aftermath of the military invasion, and they remained the bureaucratic cores of the empire throughout the colonial period. Less extensive but still important mercantilist state institutions could be found in territories within the productive orbit of Mexico or Peru, including what is now Guatemala, Bolivia, and Ecuador.

State Formation in the Colonial Centers

Spanish colonizers established state institutions in order to generate revenues for the Spanish Crown; the long-term socioeconomic effects of these state structures on the colonial territories were of secondary importance. In fact, the mercantilist goal of maximizing revenue extraction led to the creation of state institutions and orientations that would become burdens on long-run local development when incorporation into a global capitalist economy enhanced trade and market exchange in the eighteenth century.

As the colonial state gained strength in the sixteenth century, it was charged with wresting power away from the families of the original conquistadores and other emerging elites. The crown had to "conquer the conquerors" to control the financial resources of the Americas (Capdequí 1946, p. 45). For instance, officials of the Spanish Crown were eager to hold the reins over the *encomienda* (coercive labor allocation system) and to diminish the access of the original conqueror families to indigenous labor power, all with the aim to enhance royal revenues. In order to pursue these tasks, Spain created specialized bureaucracies with branches in both Spain and the Americas to staff and run the viceroyalties and *audiencias* (Andrien 2001; Lockart and Schwartz 1983).

Once colonial state institutions extended their reach, revenue extraction increased substantially during the early colonial period. Taxes imposed on indigenous communities and on mineral production were mostly spent locally and financed support for the Church, public works, defense, and the education of the colonial elite. Nonetheless, the internal organization of colonial states in sixteenth- and seventeenth-century New Spain and Peru was rather limited in its capacities to effectively intervene in society. Officeholders and bureaucratic structures lacked clear procedures, instructions, and executive power to implement decisions. Moreover, problems associated with infrequent and slow communication between Spain and the colonies made it difficult to supervise the royal bureaucratic apparatus in the New World (Andrien 1985).

Colonial state structures initially displayed relative autonomy from domestic elites. High-ranking officials were Spanish men who met educational and professional requirements and who were regarded as part of the elite in the colonial stratification system. In the colonial centers, a reasonably well-defined process of promotion known as *ascenso* established predictable career trajectories through a seniority system. However, the *ascenso* also made it difficult for Spaniards born in the New World— known as Creoles—to control political offices. The Crown "firmly believed that appointees who owed their careers solely to royal pleasure would perform more reliably than men of independent fortune already resident in the Indies" (Burkholder and Chandler 1977, p. 5). Thus, during the early colonial period, local Creole elites were systematically denied influence within the Spanish bureaucracies.

In the seventeenth century, however, this pattern of colonial state autonomy was gradually dismantled. Educated Creoles increasingly entered public positions in the *audiencias*, representing some 15 percent of all new appointments by mid-century. Then, in 1687, Charles II opened the doors to local elite influence by permitting the sale of New World *audiencia* appointments as a means to increase royal income. Those who purchased these offices did so with the full understanding that they would be able to use the office for private gains. The massive sale of offices therefore extended direct political control to local elites, and ultimately undermined much of the crown's independent authority (Andrien 1982).

Declining state autonomy enhanced rent seeking and severe disorganization within colonial state agencies. Local elites forged ties with state officials to block or alter Crown policies, ignore dictates from the colonial bureaucracy, and control forced labor quotas and tax collection. For example, a common strategy among new officeholders was to falsify census information in order to undercount the taxable indigenous population in reports to the Crown and keep the taxes collected from tributaries not officially listed. Moreover, the *ascenso* system went into remission, allowing wealth, personal connections, and kinship networks to drive career advancement rather than seniority. This patrimonial structure was further enhanced by Madrid's difficulty in exercising control over royal bureaucrats themselves (Andrien 1985, p. 79).

Patrimonialism was also built into the monopolistic guilds and trade restrictions of the colonial state. Local merchant guilds—known as *consulados*—were powerful local allies and were granted a monopoly over colonial trade. The *consulados* were protected by strict prohibitions on the movement of goods within the colonies and between the colonies and ports in Spain. Moreover, alliances between merchant guilds and local state officials contributed to the gradual legalization of the *repartimiento de comercio*. Under this arrangement, both merchants and state authorities made great profits by forcing indigenous communities to purchase often useless merchandise for exorbitant prices (Brading 1971; Guardino and Walker 1992).

These various ties between officials and domestic groups undermined royal control of the colonial state and diminished its capacity to implement autonomous judicial and political decisions. At the same time, local elites were partly dependent on the colonial state and the mercantilist economy that it supervised. Merchants in New Spain and Peru derived their wealth and political influence from colonial monopolies; likewise, local elites relied on the royal institutions in these territories to oversee the transfer of remittances from the colonial peripheries to the colonial centers. Without these protections, neither the dominant economic mode of production nor the reigning political organization of the colonial centers could have easily maintained themselves. Hence, local elites had an ambiguous relationship with colonial authorities. On the one hand, they often resented the appointed royal officials who ruled on behalf of Spain. On the other hand, however, they depended on colonial authorities to uphold the mercantilist state from which they ultimately benefited.

Successes and Failures of the Bourbon Reforms

During the eighteenth century, in response to dwindling revenues and political control, the Bourbon kings sought to reform a colonial trade system marked by contraband, burdensome regulation on dilapidated fleets, and trading monopolies confined to a few ports (Lynch 1958). Moreover, the Bourbon reformers envisioned a more coherent bureaucracy directed by a salaried administrative elite tied closely to Spain rather than being tightly interconnected with local elites. Such a more insulated bureaucratic apparatus would be more capable of collecting taxes, distributing resources for economic growth, and promoting defense through new troop lines.

In important respects, the Bourbons were successful at restructuring the colonial centers of Mexico, Peru, and Bolivia along these lines and to a lesser degree in other regions such as Guatemala and Ecuador. The Spanish Crown gradually lifted many monopolistic controls over trade, abolished the fleet system, and made provisions for the greater use of registered ships—all of which helped combat contraband, expand the flow of silver and other goods between the Americas and Spain, and thereby increase royal profits. Moreover, the Crown was successful at undermining local elite control over high-level colonial offices. Crucial in this regard was the termination of office sales and a renewed crown bias for *peninsulares* in the commanding positions of the colonial administration. When Creoles were appointed, they were now usually "outsiders" from peripheral regions of the Americas rather than the "native sons" who comprised the conservative elite. Furthermore, the *ascenso* was reinstated, and nearly all appointees were now university-educated men. With these reforms in place, promotions in government and the courts were increasingly based on individual merit—or at least seniority—rather than full-blown patrimonialism (Burkholder and Chandler 1977).

Despite these important successes, however, the Bourbon Reforms laid the foundation for postcolonial states that were more characteristic of the earlier patrimonial and elite-dominated mercantilist states. One major consequence of the reforms was the isolation of Creole elites, the very actors who had enjoyed such extensive control over state institutions before the mid-eighteenth century. As long as the local elite benefited from the colonial state, it displayed strong interests in maintaining the colonial relationship. Yet, with the Bourbon Reforms, especially conservative domestic elites became bitterly frustrated with this arrangement; they mobilized against the limited number of political appointments for native sons, and the decline of the substantial indirect influence Creole elites still marshaled over government decisions. For example, an established practice among viceroys and other executives was to consult local elites when making key decisions. Likewise, social ties cemented local elite influence, as top-ranking colonial officials often became the sons-in-law of the wealthy elite (Kicza 1983). In the late eighteenth and early nineteenth century, however, Spain undercut this informal influence by replacing local elite consultants with professional, salaried legal advisors. Furthermore, the Crown formulated new laws to restrict local marriages for governing elites and actively sought to enforce them. These reforms threatened to undermine the last safety net of local elite control over the state, and opposition toward them was an important impetus for the independence movements of the early nineteenth century.

The independence wars brought political chaos to the region, especially in the colonial centers where important battles were fought. Not until the 1820s or 1830s did political stability permit the first steps toward sovereign state formation. In this process, conservative factions of the local elite—especially wealthy landowners—reestablished substantial political authority in the colonial centers. However, they did so in a very different context than in the pre-1750 period. Political control over the new postindependence states was highly contested by competing domestic elites, who were divided into warring liberal and conservative factions. Further, these incipient sovereign states did not maintain a relationship of colonial dependence with Spain anymore, but rather served the interests of the particular elite faction that happened to exercise power. Thus, the incipient states of Mexico, Peru, and other important former colonies were deeply constrained by dominant class interests. And though no longer engaging in mercantilist policies or being dependent on Spain, these states nevertheless featured a corrupt bureaucratic corps, including military officers who now commanded great influence in the unstable politics of the early nineteenth century.

The Descent of the Colonial Centers

The period from 1750 to 1850 not only corresponds with the Bourbon Reforms and the emergence of independent states in Latin America, but it also overlaps with the economic decline of the most prosperous colonial territories. Although this decline had various causes (see Mahoney 2003), mercantilist state formation and its legacies were among the more important ones.

In the eighteenth century, Peru declined from the jewel of the Spanish Colonial Empire to a territory that could no longer compete with rising peripheries such as Argentina and Uruguay (Coatsworth 1998). Peru's silver production continued to grow, but the mining industry consisted mostly of small-scale operations that were dramatically undercapitalized and lacked modern drainage systems and adequate amounts of mercury and gunpowder. These problems existed in part because the colonial state was ineffective at initiating even the most basic reforms to enhance profitability and induce competition. Moreover, despite the fact that Peruvian ports enjoyed a privileged place within the empire, profits from Spanish imports did not stimulate modern urban development on a scale comparable to Argentina, Uruguay, and perhaps even Venezuela. Rather, the colonial state apparatus in Peru was unable or unwilling to extract resources from local elites, and profits quickly evaporated. Thus, despite increasing silver output for much of the eighteenth century, revenue collection did not increase from 1700 to 1760; when revenues did increase in the 1760s, they were still inadequate to allow Peru to remit any mineral profits back to Spain (Burkholder and Johnson 1994; Klein 1998).

In Ecuador and Guatemala, mercantilist state structures were in large parts responsible for the failure of these regions to take advantage of enhanced colonial trade after 1750. In Guatemala, the Bourbon Reforms never displaced the political power of traditional elites. Guatemalan merchants resisted the Bourbon Reforms through a quasi-state guild that oversaw the export of indigo produced in El Salvador (Woodward 1993). Although the failure of the Bourbon Reforms left the Guatemalan economy impoverished, the state monopolies, nevertheless, allowed a small class of merchants and landed elites to enjoy substantial prosperity. In Ecuador, the state was responsible for overseeing public monopolies that controlled the wool economy. Yet, with free trade reforms, the state was unable to adjust and compete with foreign textiles, which soon came to dominate the Andean market. Moreover, the state failed to reinvest resources from the wool industry into other potentially profitable sectors (Andrien 1995). At the time of independence, Ecuador was among the poorest countries in Latin America.

Bolivia's descent occurred much earlier as a result of the collapse of silver production in Potosí in the mid-seventeenth century. In fact, the period from 1750 to 1800 actually saw the expansion of this now depressed economy. In turn, this expansion was very likely related to the ability of liberal merchant groups from Buenos Aires to exercise influence over Bolivian state officials, even against the will of the local merchant elite. Indeed, as Bolivia was incorporated into the Viceroyalty Rio de la Plata, the regional state organizations became staffed by relatively well-paid and educated administrators who at least temporarily revived silver mining by lowering taxes, providing credit, and reorganizing the corrupt mercury trade networks (Klein 2003, pp. 67–71). All of this produced important growth, which only came to an abrupt halt with the general crisis for mining in the early nineteenth century, returning Bolivia to a state of severe economic depression.

Finally, Mexico was the last of the colonial centers to fall, and though it did not reach the bottom of the regional hierarchy, it nevertheless declined dramatically given its position as the wealthiest region of the colonial empire in the eighteenth century. Mexico was arguably wealthier than the United States in 1700, but it was poorer than Argentina and Uruguay, not to mention the United States by 1850 (Coatsworth 1993). Much of this descent took place in the three decades after independence (i.e., 1820–1850), when the collapse of the silver market produced a major depression. The inability of Mexico to redirect economic activity toward profitable sectors during early and mid-nineteenth century can be traced to many factors, but explanations centered on state structures and alliances stand out in some of the major works by economic historians. For example, Haber (1997) stresses the inability of the corrupt Mexican state to establish capital markets, whereas others point to the powerful political influence of landed elites and mineral interests as undercutting movement toward successful capitalist development (Hansen 1971). Thus, Mexico had great difficulty overcoming its mercantilist heritage in the aftermath of independence and descended rapidly into the periphery of the world economy.

Minimal States and Their Legacies

Colonial peripheries such as modern Argentina, Uruguay, and Costa Rica saw the formation of minimal states. Throughout most of the colonial period, these territories were of little importance to Spanish colonizers and were, therefore, marked by the relative absence of mercantilist state institutions. Only during the late colonial period did these areas witness the emergence of proto-states with semi-developed administrative and coercive apparatuses. Other colonial backwaters such as modern Chile, Colombia, and Venezuela featured minimal states, though mercantilist institutions could also be found in these territories.

Statelessness in the Colonial Periphery

During much of the colonial period, territories such as modern Argentina, Uruguay, and Costa Rica played a marginal role for economic production and political administration in the Spanish colonial system. Spanish settlements in Buenos Aires and Asunción were fortified mud-and-straw villages with minimal military and administrative facilities. High-ranking royal bureaucrats from Spain could not be found here; instead, state organizations in these backwaters were largely run by marginalized native-born administrators and soldiers, most of them Creoles or *mestizos*, the latter born from unions between Spaniards and indigenous people (Mörner 1967; Rock 1987).

Moreover, the colonial peripheries did not see the transfer of control over compulsory labor services from private hands to the royal domain. For instance, in parts of Chile, remote territories of Central America, and northwestern Argentina, forms of the *encomienda* persisted until the late eighteenth century. In Tucumán (Argentina), for instance, *encomenderos* forced indigenous people to work in textile factories. Royal administrators did not consider these areas important enough to extend the reach of state control and actively repress the private practices of exploiting indigenous labor (Burkholder and Johnson 1994; see also Newson 1986).

Another indication of statelessness in the colonial peripheries was the relative absence of alliances between powerful merchants and state officials. Merchants in these areas did not enjoy comparable protections to the *consulados* of Lima and Mexico City. Instead, they were exposed to more direct competition from legal rivals and from contraband. In Buenos Aires, the largest merchants achieved their position through short-term partnerships or price-fixing agreements rather than through a monopoly system created by the Spanish Crown. At the same time, some incipient regulation of the colonial economy took place in colonial backwater regions. For example, state-sponsored trading companies provided merchants with monopolistic protections in peripheral areas such as Venezuela. Nevertheless, for most of the colonial period, colonial peripheries were marked by the relative absence of administrative, legal, and coercive organizations and did not feature any significant forms of state intervention in economic relations (Halperín Donghi 1985).

The Bourbon Reforms and State Formation

With the onset of the Bourbon Reforms during the eighteenth century, the peripheral territories saw the gradual implementation and expansion of state institutions. The creation of new viceroyalties of New Grenada and Río de la Plata brought high-ranking bureaucrats to provincial cities such as Caracas, Bogotá, Buenos Aires, and Santiago, and the public sector became the single largest employer in these urban areas. The appointment of numerous new officials was accompanied not only by increased tax revenues, but also by the construction of new government buildings and investment in infrastructure such as roads or public sanitation. Likewise, new viceregal courts raised the legal authority of the state in these backwater regions. Spanish garrisons gained in size and were better trained and equipped because of growing investment in military expenditures (Kuethe 1978; Lynch 1958; McFarlane 1993; Socolow 1988).

Yet, while these emerging states provided an adequate institutional framework for commercialization and trade, the peripheral regions did not feature efficient and coherent bureaucracies necessary for the implementation of broad-based economic development projects. Royal bureaucrats in late colonial Buenos Aires or Caracas largely abstained from extending public investments in communication, transport, or education beyond their provincial capitals. Tax revenues were mostly spent on military expenditures and the maintenance of basic legal order (Burkholder and Johnson 1994). By virtue of their relative smallness, peripheral state agencies did not experience the blatant forms of rent seeking present in the colonial centers. Nonetheless, these minimal states lacked the strength to actively intervene in economic affairs and create the infrastructural basis for state-led development.

The most powerful domestic actors in the periphery were liberal elites, largely composed of export merchants endowed with substantial capital resources, and landowners engaged in the production and global sale of agricultural exports. Many of the merchants were immigrants from Spain who capitalized on ties to European ports and cities. They became wealthy through export goods that carried little traditional prestige and thus were not subject to extreme royal protections, such as coffee, sugar, and cattle. Moreover, cacao growers in Venezuela or cattle ranchers in Argentina were "new men" who did not belong to the traditional colonial elite. The incipient bourgeoisie that emerged around these exports naturally opposed colonial institutions that interfered with market mechanisms, and actively sought to abolish mercantilist practices of state protection and monopolies, advocating instead the expansion of market relations (Halperín Donghi 1988; Knight 2001). These liberal elites forged alliances with local state officials and exercised considerable control over political and administrative decisions. Thus, minimal states in peripheral areas were limited in their autonomy from domestic groupings that mobilized for export-oriented economic activities.

The Rise of the Colonial Peripheries

The expansion of state institutions in the colonial backwaters provided the basic legal and administrative infrastructure to sustain export economies. As tax revenues were gradually invested in the local economy, opportunities for commerce and trade expanded, and these export economies witnessed tremendous growth. In the last two decades of the eighteenth century, imports from Spain increased tenfold, while exports to the colonial territories increased fourfold (Fisher 1998). This increase in trade volume was mostly due to new economic activities in the colonial peripheries. For example, by the late eighteenth century, Caracas had become a major port city, and Venezuela landowners began to export cacao to Mexico and then to Spain, realizing huge profits in the process (McKinley 1985). Likewise, in rural areas of modern Argentina and Uruguay, new elites capitalized on expanding markets and invested in the production of wheat and livestock (Rock 1987). By the early nineteenth century, these sectors had become so profitable that Argentina and Uruguay were among the richest nations in the non-European world. Even landlocked Paraguay experienced substantial growth on the basis of enhanced yerba production (Whigham 1991).

Moreover, the reorganization of administrative structures—especially the creation of the two new viceroyalties—contributed to the formation of new trading networks. In Buenos Aires, merchants sent imported goods such as textiles, slaves, and iron to mining areas in Upper Peru and Chile in the exchange for bullion. In turn, the position of the city as a new center of regional commerce and as the entry point to the Atlantic economy attracted immigrants and capital (Socolow 1978, 1991). The administrative reforms also fostered more direct public investments in the former peripheral areas. The appointment of high-ranking royal bureaucrats resulted in the construction of government facilities and other measures such as new streets, clean water, and rudimentary healthcare to improve the infrastructure of provincial cities. The large numbers of new state officials tended to spend their salaries locally, thereby further stimulating markets for upper end goods and services.

Thus, during the late-colonial period, the economies and populations of the peripheries grew faster than the rest of the Spanish Empire in Latin America, resembling the rapid growth Peru and New Spain experienced during the mining boom in the sixteenth century. In Chile, for instance, the population increased from 184,000 in 1775 to 583,000 in 1810, and the mining production more than doubled within this time frame (Burkholder and Johnson 1994). Most of the major urban centers in the territories such as Buenos Aires, Bogotá, and Caracas saw dramatic demographic growth and changing consumption patterns.

With the wars of independence, the former colonial peripheries of Spanish America entered a period of political turmoil and economic stagnation. Different liberal elite factions competed for political influence and state control, and members of these groupings increasingly occupied the most important public offices. Elite-level conflicts often turned into military campaigns and sometimes even became larger civil wars between different political leaders and their allies. The authority and capacity of state structures in the colonial peripheries diminished; tax revenues and public investments dwindled during the 1820s and 1830s. By 1830, most regions in Spanish America were poorer than they were in 1800.

Yet, the former colonial backwaters suffered less and recovered faster when compared to the previous colonial center regions (see Coatsworth 1998). By 1850, new exports and new markets had overcome the costs of independence in most of the former peripheral areas, and public revenues again increased. Liberal elite movements with small ideological differences continued to fight for political control, and state power remained contested in unstable alliances. Official policies aimed to generate economic modernization and to promote private property and the destruction of communal land holdings. Nonetheless, there were important checks on the extent of this economic resurgence. Unpredictable caudillo politics tended to undermine the effectiveness of states to actually implement these policies. In Argentina, for instance, a split between white urban liberal elites and more conservative mestizo rural federalists dominated much of national politics, and worked against broad-based economic development projects (Rock 2002; Rock and López Alves 2000).

Overall, then, the peripheral colonial economies had never been dependent on royal protections and were therefore less affected by the breakdown of colonial state structures. Further, postindependence conservative elite factions interested in protectionist economic policies did not gain the same political influence in the periphery as in the former colonial centers. The incipient sovereign states in the marginal colonial territories did not suffer from extensive mercantilist legacies, and state intervention in the economy remained constrained, with beneficial implications for long-run economic development. It is important to note, however, that limited state capacities and liberal capture of these minimal states facilitated commercialization and trade but constrained industrial production and broad-based development. Rather, the economic model prevalent in these minimal states promoted growth on the basis of agricultural export products and industrial raw materials, thereby increasing their vulnerability to world market prices and dependent economic relationships.

Concluding Reflections on States and Development

A striking feature of Spanish America is the relative continuity of levels of development after the "great reversal" during the late-colonial and early-postindependence periods. Roughly between 1750 and 1850, marginal colonial backwaters tended to emerge as the wealthiest countries of the region. By contrast, the economically prosperous colonial centers often became the poorest areas in Spanish America. In the aftermath of this critical historical epoch, countries displayed significant stability with respect to their relative levels of economic development (Mahoney 2003).

In this chapter, we have explored how state formation helped establish this development hierarchy. In the economic and political centers of the Spanish Empire, largely resembling the modern countries of Peru, Mexico, and to a lesser extent Bolivia, Ecuador, and Guatemala, Spanish colonizers installed state institutions for the coordination of a mercantilist economy aimed at the extraction of precious metals and the exploitation of indigenous labor. These mercantilist states witnessed corruption, conservative elite control, and dependence on royal authorities in Spain. By contrast, no significant states were present in backwater regions such as modern Argentina, Uruguay, or Costa Rica for much of the colonial period. Only during the late-colonial period did minimal states emerge in these areas, marked by a laissez-faire internal organization, the absence of colonial dependence, and liberal elite control of the state apparatus. With the Bourbon Reforms and the gradual incorporation of Spanish America into the global capitalist economy, regions with minimal state structures were able to capitalize on the increased opportunities for free trade and market exchange. For their part, mercantilist state institutions proved to be a substantial burden for the former colonial centers and tended to hinder long-run development prospects.

Looking beyond this specific argument, we suggest that the historical experience of Spanish America offers some useful lessons for thinking about states and development more generally. These lessons grow out of the three underlying dimensions of our typology of colonial states: internal organization, domestic autonomy, and external dependence. First, with respect to the internal organization of states, we find support for Weber's argument that rational-bureaucratic states perform better than patrimonial states. Yet, in the historical context of Spanish America, where an efficient and modern bureaucracy could hardly be said to exist in any full-blown way, the *size* of the state had consequences that Weber did not fully recognize. In particular, minimal states were less patrimonial than mercantilist states in significant measure because they were protostates; that is, they were states with a rather limited organizational infrastructure, composed of few personnel, and therefore constrained in the capacity to become involved in economic development projects. Although in contemporary times the claim that "small" states are inherently better for economic development than "large" states is often driven more by ideology than by evidence, there is substantial reason for believing this claim to be true when the orientation of the top state leadership is mercantilist but the global economy is capitalist. Under these circumstances, less is indeed more, as revealed by the rapid economic growth of cases such as Argentina, Uruguay, and Venezuela in the late eighteenth and early nineteenth centuries.

Second, our analysis of historical state-society relations highlights the importance of theorizing "instrumental states," a category that has partially dropped out of discussion because of the focus on various kinds of state autonomy. We argued that both mercantilist and minimal states are largely controlled by domestic elites and therefore lack autonomy to pursue economic projects that clash with the fundamental interests of these social groupings. The key difference between these types of states is *what* specific domestic group captured the state. In minimal states, the social base of the controlling elite was composed of export merchants, urban elites, and intellectuals. By contrast, mercantilist states tended to be captured by conservative elites, especially protected guild merchants, higher clergy, and large landowners, all interested in maintaining major elements of the mercantilist status quo. Thus, just as scholars of contemporary states are very concerned with theorizing the implications of different *kinds of state autonomy* for development, scholars of historical states need to theorize carefully the implications of different *kinds of instrumental states* for long-run development.

Finally, we suggest that it is important to differentiate between "internal autonomy," or the nature of ties between state agents and domestic actors, and "external dependence," or the extent to which a state is financially and organizationally dependent on another state for its existence. As we have argued in this chapter, the orientation and policies of colonial states tend to be heavily skewed toward the interests of the colonizing power. A typology for explaining development prospects in postcolonial nations therefore needs to incorporate both internal autonomy and external dependence, but so too may a typology designed to explain development in the contemporary world. For instance, state action in developing countries tends to be strongly influenced by economic dependence on wealthy nations. Such a non-colonial form of economic domination represents a different form of international dependence, because these affluent external powers need to appeal—at least to a certain degree—to local political and economic interests. Thus, future research may extend our focus and move beyond the domain of colonial states, with the aim of better specifying distinct modes of international dependence and their implications for long-run development.

Notes

We would like to thank Matthew Lange and Dietrich Rueschemeyer for their helpful comments on an earlier draft of this chapter. James Mahoney's work on this chapter was supported by the National Science Foundation under Grant No. 0093754.

1. In our understanding, mercantilism as an economic model includes at least two highly interrelated dimensions. First, mercantilism envisions the promotion of "national interests" as the primary principle of political and economic organization. Institutions and policies shaped by mercantilism are oriented toward this aim. Second, mercantilism propels and justifies measures such as the implementation of trade restrictions, monopolies, and antimarket institutions in order to secure political and economic autarchy, the preferable way to ensure the protection of national interests (see Heckscher 1935). We suggest that mercantilism best describes the economic model prevalent in the centers of Spanish colonialism.
2. Evans (1995) also explores linkages to other organized groups in the conclusion of his book.
3. If predatory and developmental states are added to our typology, one might conceptualize a continuum of four states that range from worse to better for development as follows: predatory, mercantilist, minimal, developmental.
4. The three dimensions of our typology—internal organization, domestic autonomy, and external autonomy—do not exhaust the range of structural features that might be used to distinguish mercantilist and minimal states. Nor do we situate these states in relationship to all leading typologies of states. For example, one might also evaluate mercantilist and minimal states in light of Migdal's (1988) distinction between strong and weak states or along Centeno's (2002) dimensions of pacification and centralization. However, we believe that the three dimensions examined here are especially relevant for understanding patterns of economic development during the critical 1750–1850 period. By contrast, other distinctions such as those proposed by Migdal and

Centeno are more relevant for explaining long-run patterns of social control and political development in Latin America.

References

Acemoglu, Daron, Simon Johnson, and James A. Robinson. 2001. "The Colonial Origins of Comparative Development: An Empirical Investigation." *American Economic Review*, 91: 1369–1401.

———. 2002. "Reversal of Fortune: Geography and Institutions in the Making of the Modern World Income Distribution." *Quarterly Journal of Economics*, 117: 1231–1294.

Andrien, Kenneth J. 1982. "The Sale of Fiscal Offices and the Decline of Royal Authority in the Viceroyalty of Peru, 1633–1700." *Hispanic American Historical Review*, 62, 1: 49–71.

———. 1985. *Crisis and Decline: The Viceroyalty of Peru in the Seventeenth Century*. Albuquerque: University of New Mexico Press.

———. 1995. *The Kingdom of Quito, 1690–1830: The State and Regional Development*. Cambridge: Cambridge University Press.

———. 2001. *Andean Worlds: Indigenous History, Culture, and Consciousness under Spanish Rule, 1532–1825*. Albuquerque: University of New Mexico Press.

Brading, David A. 1971. *Miners and Merchants in Bourbon Mexico, 1763–1810*. Cambridge: Cambridge University Press.

———. 1987. "Bourbon Spain and Its American Empire." In *Colonial Spanish America*, edited by L. Bethell. Cambridge: Cambridge University Press, 112–162.

Burkholder, Mark A. and D. S. Chandler. 1977. *From Impotence to Authority: The Spanish Crown and the American Audiencias, 1687–1808*. Columbia: University of Missouri Press.

Burkholder, Mark A. and Lyman L. Johnson. 1994. *Colonial Latin America*. New York: Oxford University Press.

Capdequí, José Marí. 1946. *El Estado Español en las Indias*. 2nd edn. Mexico: Fondo de Cultura Económica.

Carnoy, Martin. 1984. *The State and Political Theory*. Princeton: Princeton University Press.

Centeno, Miguel Angel. 2002. *Blood and Debt: War and the Nation-State in Latin America*. University Park, PA: Pennsylvania State University Press.

Coatsworth, John H. 1993. "Notes on the Comparative Economic History of Latin America and the United States." In *Development and Underdevelopment in America: Contrasts of Economic Growth in North and Latin America in Historical Perspective*, edited by W. Bernecker and H. Werner Tobler. Berlin: Walter de Gruyter, 264–302.

Coatsworth, John H. 1998. "Economic and Institutional Trajectories in Nineteenth-Century Latin America." In *Latin American and the World Economy Since 1800*, edited by J. Coatsworth and A. Taylor. Cambridge, MA: David Rockefeller Center for Latin America Studies, Harvard University, 23–54.

Engerman, Stanley L. and Kenneth L. Sokoloff. 2002. "Factor Endowments, Inequality, and Paths of Development among New World Economies." *Economia*, 3: 41–88.

Evans, Peter. 1995. *Embedded Autonomy: States and Industrial Transformation*. Princeton: Princeton University Press.

Evans, Peter, Dietrich Rueschemeyer, and Theda Skocpol (eds.). 1985. *Bringing the State Back In*. Cambridge: Cambridge University Press.

Fisher, John. 1998. "Commerce and Imperial Decline: Spanish Trade with Spanish America, 1797–1820." *Journal of Latin American Studies*, 30: 459–479.

Gootenberg, Paul. 1996. "Paying for Caudillos: The Politics of Emergency Finance in Peru, 1820–1845." In *Liberals, Politics and Power: State Formation in Nineteenth-Century Latin America*, edited by V. Peloso and B. Tenenbaum. Athens: University of Georgia Press, 134–165.

Guardino, Peter and Charles Walker. 1992. "The State, Society, and Politics in Peru and Mexico in the Late Colonial and Early Republican Periods." *Latin American Perspectives*, 19: 10–43.

Guerra, Francisco-Xavier. 2000. "The Implosion of the Spanish Empire: Emerging Statehood and Collective Identities." In *The Collective and the Public in Latin America*, edited by L. Roniger and T. Herzog. Brighton: Sussex Academic Press, 71–94.

Haber, Stephen. 1997. "Financial Markets and Industrial Development: A Comparative Study of Government Regulation, Financial Innovation, and Industrial Structure in Brazil and Mexico, 1840–1930." In *How Latin America Fell Behind: Essays on the Economic Histories of Brazil and Mexico, 1800–1914*, edited by S. Haber. Stanford: Stanford University Press, 146–178.

Halperín Donghi, Tulio. 1985. *Reforma y disolución de los imperios ibéricos, 1750–1850*. Madrid: Alianza Editorial.

———. 1988. "Argentina: Liberalism in a Country Born Liberal." In *Guiding the Invisible Hand: Economic Liberalism and the State in Latin American History*, edited by J. Love and N. Jacobsen. New York: Praeger, 99–116.

Hansen, Roger D. 1971. *The Politics of Mexican Development*. Baltimore: Johns Hopkins University Press.

Heckscher, Eli F. 1935. *Mercantilism*. London: G. Allen & Unwin.

Johnson, Lyman L. and Susan M. Socolow. 2002. "Colonial Centers, Colonial Peripheries, and the Economic Agency of the Spanish State." In *Negotiated Empires: Centers and Peripheries in the Americas, 1500–1820*, edited by C. Daniels and M. Kennedy. New York: Routledge, 59–78.

Kicza, John E. 1983. *Colonial Entrepreneurs: Families and Business in Bourbon Mexico*. Albuquerque: University of New Mexico Press.

Klein, Herbert S. 1998. *The American Finances of the Spanish Empire: Royal Income and Expenditures in the Colonial Mexico, Peru, and Bolivia, 1680–1809*. Albuquerque: University of New Mexico Press.

———. 2003. *A Concise History of Bolivia*. Cambridge: Cambridge University Press.

Knight, Alan. 2001. "Democratic and Revolutionary Traditions in Latin America." *Bulletin of Latin American Research*, 20: 147–186.

Kuethe, Allan J. 1978. *Military Reform and Society in New Grenada, 1773–1808*. Gainesville: University Presses of Florida.

Lockhart, James and Stuart B. Schwartz. 1983. *Early Latin America: A History of Colonial Spanish America and Brazil*. Cambridge: Cambridge University Press.

Lynch, John. 1958. *Spanish Colonial Administration, 1782–1810: The Intendant System in the Viceroyalty of Rio de la Plata*. London: Athlone.

———. 1986. *The Spanish American Revolutions, 1808–1826*. 2nd edn. New York: W.W. Norton.

Mahoney, James. 2003. "Long-Run Development and the Legacy of Colonialism in Spanish America." *American Journal of Sociology*, 109: 50–106.

McFarlane, Anthony. 1993. *Colombia before Independence: Economy, Society, and Politics Under Bourbon Rule*. Cambridge: Cambridge University Press.

McKinley, P. Michael. 1985. *Pre-Revolutionary Caracas: Politics, Economy, and Society 1777–1811*. Cambridge, UK: Cambridge University Press.

Migdal, Joel S. 1988. *Strong Societies and Weak States: State-Society Relations and State Capabilities in the Third World*. Princeton, NJ: Princeton University Press.

Migdal, Joel S., Atul Kohli, and Vivienne Shue (eds.). 1994. *State Power and Social Forces: Domination and Transformation in the Third World*. New York: Cambridge University Press.

Mörner, Magnus. 1967. *Race Mixture in the History of Latin America*. Boston: Little, Brown.

Newson, Linda. 1986. *The Cost of Conquest: Indian Decline in Honduras under Spanish Rule*. Boulder: Westview.

Rock, David. 1987. *Argentina, 1516–1987: From Spanish Colonization to Alfonsín*. Revised ed. Berkeley: University of California Press.

———. 2002. *State Building and Political Movements in Argentina, 1860–1916*. Stanford: Stanford University Press.

Rock, David and Fernando López Alves. 2000. "State Building and Political Systems in Nineteenth Century Argentina and Uruguay." *Past and Present*, 167: 176–202.

Rueschemeyer, Dietrich and Peter Evans. 1985. "The State and Economic Transformation: Toward an Analysis of the Conditions Underlying Effective Intervention." In *Bringing the State Back In*, edited by P. Evans, D. Rueschemeyer, and T. Skocpol. New York: Cambridge University Press, 44–77.

Socolow, Susan M. 1978. *The Merchants of Buenos Aires, 1778–1810: Family and Commerce*. Cambridge: Cambridge University Press.

———. 1988. *The Bureaucrats of Buenos Aires, 1769–1810: Amor al Real Servicio* Durham, NC: Duke University Press.

———. 1991. "Buenos Aires: Atlantic Port and Hinterland in the Eighteenth Century." In *Atlantic Port Cities: Economy, Culture, and Society in the Atlantic World, 1650–1850*, edited by F. Knight and P. Liss. Knoxville: University of Tennessee Press, 240–261.

Walker, Geoffrey J. 1979. *Spanish Politics and Imperial Trade, 1700–1789*. Bloomington: Indiana University Press.

Weber Max. 1972. *Wirtschaft und Gesellschaft: Grundriß der verstehenden Soziologie* (5.Aufl.), Tübingen: J.C.B. Mohr (Paul Siebeck) Verlag.

Whigham, Thomas. 1991. *The Politics of River Trade: Tradition and Development in the Upper Plata, 1780–1870*. Albuquerque: University of New Mexico Press.

Woodward, Ralph Lee. 1993. *Rafael Carrera and the Emergence of the Republic of Guatemala, 1821–1871*. Athens: University of Georgia Press.

CHAPTER SIX

British Colonial State Legacies and Development Trajectories: A Statistical Analysis of Direct and Indirect Rule

MATTHEW LANGE

In his work on colonial legacies in sub-Saharan Africa, Crawford Young (1994) calls the colonial powers *Bula Matari*, a KiKongo phrase meaning "he who crushes rocks." The term not only refers to the extreme power of the European imperialists in Africa but also to the revolutionary changes that colonization began. Indeed, beginning with Ceuta, the Azores, and the Canary Islands during the mid-fifteenth century and continuing to this day with a few outposts, colonization of foreign lands has been a cataclysmic series of events that dramatically transformed the lives and lifestyles of peoples throughout the world. Whole populations were annihilated while others went to live in far-off places as part of the colonial machine, either as settlers, administrators, or laborers. As a consequence of this contact, local religions, markets, and states were either extensively transformed or completely destroyed and replaced by new ones.

Over the past half century, most scholars have analyzed the great colonial transformations from one of three primary perspectives. First, prior to the 1970s, most work supported modernization theory and emphasized positive changes. In particular, they described colonialism as a period of trusteeship, with Europeans bringing new technologies and better lives to their colonial subjects (see Bryce 1914; Hailey 1938; and, for a more recent and less one-sided work from this perspective, Ferguson 2002). Beginning some thirty years ago, the study of colonialism began to experience a powerful backlash against this view. Academics such as Frantz Fanon and Edward Said described the very negative and destructive aspects of colonialism, work that corrected many of the biases of the previous view and that has become institutionalized as a new academic discipline: colonial and postcolonial studies. Finally, over the past few years, more empirically driven social scientists within the field of development studies have tried to avoid questions about good and evil, which are inherent to the two previous perspectives. Instead, these scholars simply analyze the effects colonial rule had on broad-based development, recognizing that atrocities were committed but that colonialism might have had some positive effects on developmental processes as well (see Acemoglu, Johnson, and Robinson 2001, 2002; Brown 2000; Grier 1999; Kohli 1994; Lange 2003; Mahoney 2003; Sokoloff and Engerman 2000).

Situated in the third vein of colonial research, this chapter analyzes whether the form of colonial domination left legacies that have shaped developmental trajectories. It investigates whether the states that were constructed by the colonial powers to dominate foreign peoples have had long-term effects on developmental processes through state institutional reproduction and constant institutional effects. To do so, I create a variable that measures the extent to which British colonialism institutionalized indirect forms of rule and test its relationship with postcolonial levels of state governance and social development while controlling for various colonial and precolonial characteristics.

Variation in British Colonialism: Direct and Indirect Rule

Much of the recent qualitative work on colonialism investigates its impact on long-term developmental trajectories through institutional reproduction and institutional effects. Boone (1994), Mamdani (1996), Migdal (1988), and Reno (1995), for instance, describe how the legacy of indirect rule in Africa has impeded political development. These works focus on how indirect rule decentralized legal-administrative institutions, empowered local chiefs, and thereby institutionalized a system of decentralized despotism that has left the state both ineffective and near collapse. Alternatively, Amsden (1989), Huff (1994), Kohli (1994), Lange (2003), and Wade (1990) suggest that direct colonial rule left legacies that made possible effective states and thereby state-led development. They focus on bureaucratization and the state's ability to provide a variety of public goods (education, health care, sanitation, roads, law and order) and steer the national economy. Thus, qualitative scholars who analyze colonial state legacies emphasize both positive and negative effects on development and suggest that direct rule promoted the former while indirect rule promoted the latter.

Popular understandings of direct and indirect rule differentiate the two based on who holds what positions within the colonial state. Yet, colonial scholars and even Lord Lugard—the figure often given credit for inventing indirect rule—focus on structural differences rather than on the ethnic origin of the colonial administrators (Fisher 1991; Lugard 1922). According to the latter perspective, direct rule creates a complete system of colonial domination that lacks any relatively autonomous indigenous component even if staffed by indigenous actors, whereas indirect rule combines a central legal-administrative institution based on bureaucratic principles with peripheral legal-administrative institutions based on the colonial power's reconstruction of traditional authority (Mamdani 1996).

The state in directly ruled British colonies generally had levels of bureaucratic organization similar to those of their colonizers. Direct rule provided an administrative structure based on formal rules, as opposed to individual decisions, and had a centralized legal-administrative structure with a formal chain of command that linked the diverse state actors throughout the colony to the central colonial administration and thereby back to the British Government. This centralized and rule-based organization was possible because state actors were employees whose positions could not be owned, were based on merit (and usually race), and were the only means of income for the officeholders. Besides the organization of the colonial administration, the regulation of society was also guided by rules in directly ruled colonies. Large police forces and courts based on British law were constructed, and both collaborated with one another in order to create a broad and centralized legal framework regulating societal and state-society relations.

The legal-administrative institutions of indirectly ruled British colonies differed considerably from those of directly ruled colonies. Indirect rule was based on a tripartite chain of patron–client relations linking the colonial administration to the population via chiefs. While the members of the colonial administration were generally recruited and employed along bureaucratic lines, the position held by chiefs was based primarily on patrimonialism. In particular, chiefs were selected to rule according to their lineage and—most importantly—their willingness to collaborate with colonial officials. Moreover, although often receiving a salary, chiefs earned most of their livelihood through the control of land and direct extraction from their subjects. The chiefs were given executive, legislative, and judicial powers to regulate social relations in their chiefdoms, vast authority that was supposed to be grounded in preexisting tradition or custom, not bureaucratic rules. Thus, indirect rule often took the form of numerous patrimonial kingdoms linked together only weakly by a foreign administration.

Much of the recent qualitative work on colonial state legacies focuses on three aspects of indirect rule that, in combination, promoted local despotism at the expense of centralized control. First, the central legal-administrative institution was miniscule, concentrated almost exclusively in the colonial capital, and had very little interaction with the colonial population, characteristics that endowed it with very little infrastructural power (see Mann 1984). As a result, the colonial state in indirectly ruled colonies lacked the capabilities to implement policy outside of the capital city and often had no option other than coercion for pursuing policy. Next, indirect rule endowed chiefs with great institutional powers (Boone 1994; Chanock 1985; Mamdani 1996; Merry 1991; Migdal 1988; Roberts and Mann 1991). Chiefs were given control of "customary law" and, because it lacked formalization, were able to mold and wield it for personal benefit. Customary law also endowed chiefs with control over communal lands and chiefdom police, both of which could be coercively employed to dominate local inhabitants. Finally, the institutional powers of chiefs were augmented by their intermediary positions, which enabled them to control information and resource flows between the colonial administration and the local population and avoid colonial supervision (Clapham 1982; Lange 2004b; Reno 1995; Scott 1972). Consequently, chiefs were able to play administrators and local subjects off against one another in order to maintain considerable autonomy from each, allowing them to be rent-seekers extraordinaire whenever exchanges between the administration and local population occurred.

The Determinants of the Form of British Rule

Within the British Empire, numerous factors shaped the extent of direct or indirect rule. The importance of these factors, however, was not constant but instead varied from colony to colony. While an exhaustive discussion of the determinants of colonialism is beyond the scope of this chapter, it briefly outlines the primary factors that affected the form that British colonialism took, whether direct or indirect.

Settlement
The form of Brtish colonial rule was shaped by the presence or absence of large numbers of European settlers, with settlement colonies having direct

forms of rule and non-settlement colonies tending to have more indirect forms of rule. Settlement appears to have had a direct effect on the form of colonialism through institutional transfer: settlers reconstructed state institutions similar to those that they participated in prior to immigration.

Economics
The economic potential of a colony affected its form of rule in two ways. First, the extensiveness of the colonial administration depended on its ability to raise local resources. Second, settlers chose to migrate to lands with economic opportunities.

Disease
The extensiveness of colonial rule depended on the disease environment of the colonies (Acemoglu, Johnson, and Robinson 2001). Since much of Africa was a "white man's grave," for example, neither settlement nor the use of numerous European officials was feasible even if great economic potential existed. As a consequence, the continent was usually ruled indirectly.

Precolonial Populations
The presence of local populations shaped the form of rule in two primary ways. First, large local populations limited settlement by obstructing access to land and greatly increasing the costs and risks of large-scale settlement. Second, as the Indian Mutiny of 1857 showed, indigenous peoples were more likely to revolt against invasive forms of colonialism and were therefore most effectively ruled through more "customary" and indirect forms of rule (Porter 1996, pp. 29–48).

Time
The period of colonization was an extremely important determinant of its form. All territories conquered prior to the Indian Mutiny were ruled directly, while most conquered afterwards were ruled indirectly. This difference was due in part to the existence of a new model of rule after the 1857 rebellion, greater British sensitivity to indigenous opposition to colonial interference, and pressure from humanitarian and religious groups for the maintenance of precolonial institutions.

Geopolitics
Strategic geopolitical importance also affected the willingness of colonial powers to invest in direct forms of rule. When colonies were

vital to national interests, more extensive forms of rule—that is, direct rule—were established to protect them.

Statistical Analysis of British Colonial Legacies

Although the British have been credited with inventing indirect rule, Tilly (1992) recognizes that it has long been a form of rule over peripheral areas and describes how it was a difficult obstacle that had to be overcome for the construction of bureaucratic national states in early modern Europe (pp. 103–117). More recently, the French, Portuguese, and Belgians all used indirect forms of rule throughout their colonies in Africa and Asia (Bayart 1993; Boone 1992, 1994; Cruise O'Brien 1975; Mamdani 1996; Robinson 1972). In fact, excluding their colonization of the Philippines, the Spanish appear to have been the only modern colonial power that did not rule through non-European middlemen, although Spanish rule in the Americas was much more patrimonial than bureaucratic and might be viewed as a type of indirect rule through regional strongmen of European descent.

While recognizing that the British were neither the creators nor the sole colonizers employing indirect forms of rule, British colonialism was exceptional in at least one aspect—namely the size and diversity of the British Empire, which caused Great Britain to rely much more extensively on both direct and indirect modes of domination than any other colonial power. For example, colonial Uganda and Nigeria were extreme cases of indirect rule, Malaysia and Fiji had larger colonial legal-administrative orders yet were still heavily dependent on chiefs, and Singapore and Jamaica lacked chiefs completely. The British Empire therefore provides an opportunity to analyze the different institutional legacies of direct and indirect rule while controlling for the colonial power, the latter of which appears necessary given the numerous statistical analyses that find a positive and significant relationship between British colonialism and various development indicators (Bollen and Jackman 1985; Brown 2000; Grier 1999; LaPorta et al. 1999). The remainder of this chapter uses statistical methods to test whether the extent of direct and indirect colonialism within the British Empire is related to postcolonial indicators of state governance, economic development, and societal health.

Case Selection

The cases used for the statistical analysis are limited to 33 national states that are former British colonies (see table 6.1).[1] As such, the set includes

Table 6.1 Former British colonies used in analysis: dates and duration of colonialism

Country	Onset of colonialism	Conclusion of colonialism	Duration of colonialism
Bahamas	1783	1973	190
Bangladesh	1756/1857	1947/1971	190
Barbados	1627	1966	339
Belize	1798	1981	183
Botswana	1885	1966	81
Brunei	1888	1984	96
Cyprus	1878	1960	82
Fiji	1871	1970	99
Gambia	1888	1965	77
Ghana	1874	1957	83
Guyana	1814	1966	152
Hong Kong	1842	1999	157
India	1757/1857	1947	190
Jamaica	1655	1962	307
Kenya	1886	1963	77
Lesotho	1884	1966	82
Malawi	1891	1964	73
Malaysia	1824/1880	1957	77
Mauritius	1810	1968	158
Myanmar	1826/1885	1948	132
Nigeria	1861/1885	1960	75
Pakistan	1857	1947	90
Sierra Leone	1787/1896	1961	65
Singapore	1819	1957/1965	138
Solomon Islands	1893	1978	85
Sri Lanka	1798	1948	150
Sudan	1898	1956	58
Swaziland	1894	1968	74
Tanzania	1918	1961	43
Trinidad/Tobago	1797	1962	165
Uganda	1893	1962	69
Zambia	1890/1923	1964	74
Zimbabwe	1895/1923	1965/1980	70

colonies that were conquered between 1627 and 1918 and were colonies anywhere between 339 and 43 years. Despite this considerable variation, the cases are restricted to those colonies that lacked large numbers of European settlers, had over 100,000 inhabitants at independence, were ruled for more than 30 years, and did not merge with non-British colonies after independence. Although decreasing valuable degrees of freedom, such case restrictions are employed in an attempt to make the sample more homogeneous and thereby increase insight gained from cross-case comparison.[2]

The first restriction—which excludes Australia, Canada, New Zealand, South Africa, and the United States—is used in order to focus on non-settlement colonies and the variation of rule within this sub-set of colonialism. Because settlement colonies did not comprise subordinate populations (at least after disease, warfare, and exclusion marginalized the indigenous populations), they were closer to extensions of Great Britain than to colonies of foreign peoples. As a result, settlers were not prone to the same levels of exclusion and exploitation as other colonial peoples and therefore experienced distinct forms of colonial domination. Second, small island colonies such as St. Kitts and Nevis and Malta are excluded from this analysis because they are microstates that are analytically distinct from other national states in terms of size and population. Next, the set is limited to those colonies that were formal British colonies for more than 30 years, which excludes the British mandate territories in the Middle East. Finally, colonies such as Somaliland and British Cameroon are excluded because they merged with non-British territories at independence and therefore experienced hybrid colonial legacies.

Using these case restrictions, the set of former British colonies is also limited to those former colonies that gained their independences after World War II. This commonality is important for two reasons. First, beginning in the late 1930s and continuing into the 1960s, extensive reforms occurred throughout the British Empire. These reforms increased popular participation in local, district, and legislative councils; expanded the size of the colonial state; and boosted investment in education, health care, roads, and other public goods (Lee 1967). As a result, legacies of British colonialism were likely to be transformed to various extents during the postwar period. Second, the statistical analysis attempts to investigate the determinants of levels of development at the end of the colonial period as well as changes in development since independence. Data for level of development at the independence period and for change in development level since independence are unavailable for former colonies that received their independence before World War II.

Operationalizing the Form of British Colonialism

The primary explanatory variable used in the analysis measures the form of British colonial rule. In particular, the *extent of indirect colonial rule* is operationalized by dividing the number of colonially recognized customary court cases by the total number of court cases in 1955, the latter of which includes both customary cases heard by chiefs as well as magistrate court cases presided over by colonial officials. As such, it ranges between zero—a score shared by several former colonies—and 93—the score of colonial Nigeria—and measures the extent to which British colonial rule depended on customary legal institutions for the regulation of social relations. The variable also captures the size of the legal-administrative apparatus since indirectly ruled colonies had significantly fewer police officers per capita: the correlation between the customary court variable and per capita police officers in 1955 is −0.82. The customary law variable therefore provides a direct measurement of the level of colonial dependence on customary courts for local law and order and an indirect measurement of the lack of legal-administrative personnel under centralized administrative control. The data on British colonial legal systems were collected from the 1955 annual *Colonial Report, Annual Judicial Report*, and other colonial documents available at the Public Records Office in the United Kingdom (see Lange 2004a for more information on the data).

Compatible data for the extent of indirect rule are not available for Bangladesh, India, Myanmar, and Pakistan, all of which were ruled through the same colonial legal-administrative institutions until late colonialism.[3] During British colonialism, approximately two-fifths of these territories consisted of indirectly ruled princely states, suggesting an indirect rule score somewhere around 30 percent. Other factors suggest a higher score, however. As mentioned above, police officers per capita is one alternative means of generating a proxy for the extent of indirect rule. In 1938, the four former South Asian colonies had 0.4 police officers per 1,000 people, a ratio that is less than all other former British colonies except Nigeria (0.3 per 1,000) (Griffiths 1971, p. 422).[4] As such, the simple use of police officers per capita suggests a score of approximately 90 percent. Similarly, qualitative works describe how the minimal colonial state created local institutions—even in the more directly ruled regions—that were similar to those in indirectly ruled Africa and therefore provide additional evidence that a score measuring the extent of indirect rule in colonial India should be higher than that suggested by the percentage of land under indirect rule.[5] Noting these factors, this analysis splits the difference and gives the four South Asian colonies a score of 60 percent.

Dependent Variables

The four dependent variables used in this analysis are proxies for political, economic, and human development. First, five World Bank indicators are combined and used for an aggregate measurement of state governance. The indicators range from −2.5 to 2.5 and include variables for (1) state effectiveness, which measures the quality of the public service provision and the bureaucracy; (2) state stability, which measures perceptions of the likelihood that the government in power will be destabilized or overthrown; (3) lack of state corruption, which measures the extent to which state power is exercised to benefit the general public; (4) freedom from regulatory burden, which measures the absence of excessive regulation; and (5) rule of law, which measures the incidence of crime, the effectiveness and predictability of the judiciary, and the enforceability of contracts (see Kaufmann, Kraay, and Zoido-Lobaton 1999). Notably, because of availability, the state governance variables are limited to a single point in time: 1997–1998.

Average level of democratization is a second indicator of political development. The democracy variable combines the Freedom House indices of political rights and liberties, inverts the scores, and averages them over a 28-year period. As such, the democracy measurement is continuous and ranges from 1 (least democratic) to 13 (most democratic). The Freedom House data are available from 1972 to 2000 and are combined to create a variable measuring the average level of democratic rule over the period.

Per capita GDP in 1960 (constant 1995 U.S. dollars) is used to operationalize the level of economic production and therefore provides a crude indicator of the ability of individuals to pursue their material well-being during the late-colonial or early-independence period. Besides analyzing level of per capita GDP, models also analyze average annual growth in per capita GDP between 1961 and 2000.

Finally, because health is a necessary requirement for one to pursue her/his well-being, life expectancy is used to operationalize average societal health. Like the economic variable, models use both life expectancy in 1960 and absolute change in life expectancy between 1960 and 1990.[6]

Table 6.2 shows the bivariate relationships between the extent of indirect rule and level of development. The colonial variable has strong and negative relationships with all development indicators, ranging from a low of −0.63 with the average Freedom House democracy index between 1972 and 2000 and a high of −0.88 with life expectancy in 1990. In all cases, the p-values are equal to or below 0.0001. As such, a strong, negative, and general relationship exists between the extent of indirect rule and postcolonial state governance, postcolonial democratization, per capita GDP in 1960 and 1990, and life expectancy in 1960 and 1990.

Table 6.2 Bivariate correlation between the extent of indirect rule and various postcolonial development indicators

	Aggregate state governance, 1997–1998	Average Freedom House democracy index, 1972–2000
Correlation	−0.71	−0.63
Number of cases	32	32
	Per capita GDP, 1960 (log)	Per capita GDP, 2000 (log)
Correlation	−0.77	−0.83
Number of cases	32	32
	Life Expectancy, 1960	Life Expectancy, 1990
Correlation	−0.88	−0.88
Number of cases	33	33

Multivariate Analysis

In order to take into account other factors that might have shaped postcolonial development, five control variables are used for multivariate regression analysis. In particular, the variables control for *precolonial* and *colonial era conditions* that possibly shaped both the form of colonialism as well as developmental processes. First, because recent statistical analyses of economic and political development find a strong African regional effect (see Englebert 2000), and because Jeffrey Herbst (2000) suggests that regional characteristics hinder state building in sub-Saharan Africa, an African control variable is employed (1 = African, 0 = non-African). Next, the analysis controls for precolonial societal characteristics in an attempt to limit the possibility that relationships between the form of colonialism and postcolonial development are spurious and driven by precolonial development levels. Population density at the onset of formal colonization is used as a proxy of precolonial economic and human development. In particular, areas with more intensive agriculture are able to sustain larger populations who, in turn, participate in more diverse types of production, and Jared Diamond (1997) and Louis Putterman (2000) contend that population density is a long-term proxy for "broad human capital" level as well. The data for the variable were gathered from Kuczynski (1948, 1949, 1953) McEvedy and Jones (1978) or *Annual Colonial Reports* for the colonies.

Finally, three variables control for societal characteristics that were either wholly or partially shaped by colonization. First, the analysis includes a control for the extent of ethno-linguistic fractionalization since other analyses find a significant relationship between ethnic diversity and both economic performance and the quality of government (Easterly and Levine 1997; LaPorta et al. 1999). The variable is operationalized as the probability that two randomly selected co-nationals in 1960 spoke different languages, and the data came from LaPorta et al. (1999).

A binomial variable measuring whether or not plantation-based socioeconomic institutions were present during the colonial period is an additional control (1 = presence of plantation-based institutions, 0 = absence of plantation-based institutions). To be categorized as a plantation colony, plantations must have been major social institutions that affected the daily lives of most individuals and shaped the overall economic, political, and social institutions of the colony. As such, the Solomon Islands and Malaysia are not categorized as having plantation institutions because, although present, the plantations were economic enclaves and were not as dominant as they were in Jamaica, Barbados, or Mauritius. Data on the presence and extent of plantations are from Beckford (1983).

Finally, the analysis controls for European population as a percentage of total population at the end of the colonial period. Notably, this variable measures to some extent the form and intensity of colonialism and might simply be viewed as an alternative indicator of the form of colonialism (see Acemoglu, Johnson, and Robinson 2001). By measuring the European population, however, the analysis investigates the effects of direct colonialism on developmental processes that are *not* attributable to the presence of a large number of Europeans. In addition, since Europeans generally settled in areas without deadly diseases, the variable indirectly controls for disease environment. The data for the variable were gathered from Kuczynski (1948, 1949, 1953) McEvedy and Jones (1978) or *Annual Colonial Reports* for the colonies.

Diagnostic exams have been performed to check for outliers, nonlinear relationships, and collinearity. In most cases, the data are consistent with the assumptions of linear multivariate analysis. Per capita GDP and the percentage of total population of European descent, however, have curvilinear relationships with other variables, so their logarithms are used for the analysis. Next, the models testing change in GDP and life expectancy include controls for previous levels of development (per capita GDP in 1960 and life expectancy in 1960), both of which—as shown above—are very strongly related to the extent of indirect colonial rule. Collinearity might therefore be obscuring relationships in the models analyzing change in development level.

Multivariate Findings: Political Development

Table 6.3 gives the results of the multivariate analysis using the aggregate score of the World Bank governance indicators as the dependent variable.[7] In the table and all tables that follow, model 1 includes the extent of indirect rule but excludes the five control variables, model 2 includes all control variables but excludes the indirect rule variable, and model 3 includes all six independent and control variables. Model 1 of table 6.3 shows that by itself the extent of indirect rule accounts for half of the variation in the aggregate state governance indicator. Alternatively, the five control variables in model 2 have an adjusted R-squared value of only 0.2. When all six independent and control variables are included in model 3, the model again accounts for half of the variation in the dependent variable. The indirect rule variable therefore appears to underlie the power of the overall model.

Indeed, of the independent and control variables in model 3 of table 6.3, the extent of indirect rule is the only variable significantly related to the aggregate measurement of state governance, and its significance level is below 0.001. Its sign shows that the extent to which

Table 6.3 Multivariate analysis of state governance among former British colonies, 1997–1998

	Model 1	Model 2	Model 3
Variable coefficients			
Intercept	0.527***	0.288	0.410
	(0.130)	(0.306)	(0.243)
Extent of indirect rule, 1955	−0.015***		−0.018***
	(0.003)		(0.004)
Plantations		−0.250	−0.331
		(0.350)	(0.279)
European settlement, 1955 (log)		0.236*	0.120
		(0.099)	(0.083)
Precolonial population density		0.002	0.003
		(0.003)	(0.002)
Africa control		−0.490+	0.014
		(0.273)	(0.248)
Ethnic diversity, 1960		0.002	0.006
		(0.005)	(0.004)
Model			
F-Value	<0.001	0.048	<0.001
Adj. R-Squared	0.494	0.207	0.508
Number of cases	33	32	32

***p < 0.001; *p < 0.05; +p < 0.10.

colonies were ruled indirectly is negatively related to postcolonial state governance levels. And, the coefficients of the indirect rule variable are quite high, suggesting that an increase in the extent of indirect rule from 0 to 50 percent is associated with a one-point decrease in the governance score, an amount that separates Canada from Namibia and Hong Kong from Morocco. Thus, while controlling for other factors, the form of British colonialism remains very strongly related to present levels of state governance.

Table 6.4 gives the results of the models using the average Freedom House democracy score between 1972 and 2000 as the dependent variable. Unlike the analysis of aggregate state governance, model 1 accounts for less variance than model 2, and model 3 has only a slightly higher adjusted R-squared score than model 2, suggesting that the extent of indirect rule is not as strongly related to democratization as it is to state governance. Looking at the independent and control variables, although the extent of indirect rule is negatively related to average democratization and has a very significant relationship in model 1, it has only marginal

Table 6.4 Multivariate analysis of democracy among former British colonies

	Average FH Scores, 1972–2000		
	Model 1	Model 2	Model 3
Variable coefficients			
Intercept	9.625***	6.908***	7.201***
	(0.704)	(1.190)	(1.157)
Extent of indirect rule, 1955	−0.062***		−0.038+
	(0.014)		(0.021)
Plantation		3.827**	3.435*
		(1.363)	(1.329)
European settlement, 1955 (log)		0.342	0.202
		(0.416)	(0.408)
Precolonial population Density		0.013	0.021
		(0.016)	(0.016)
Africa control		−1.154	−0.193
		(1.034)	(1.135)
Ethnic diversity, 1960		−0.002	0.010
		(0.019)	(0.019)
Model			
F-Value	<0.001	0.001	<0.001
Adj. R-Squared	0.373	0.437	0.479
Number of cases	32	32	32

***p < 0.001; **p < 0.01; *p < 0.05; +p < 0.10.

significance once the control variables are added in model 3. This weaker relationship appears to be due to several directly ruled colonies in Asia that have had only low levels of democratization since independence—Malaysia, Singapore, and Brunei—and the wave of democratization in Africa during the 1990s.[8] Somewhat surprisingly, the plantation control variable has the most significance in model 3 and is positively related to postcolonial levels of democratization, a finding that might be due to lack of militaries at independence, relatively high levels of education, and strong societal demand for democratization as a result of past discrimination and exclusion.

Multivariate Findings: Economic Development and Societal Health
Having shown a negative relationship between various aspects of political development and the extent of indirect colonial rule, this chapter now investigates whether such institutional legacies also affected developmental processes. Tables 6.5a and 6.5b give the results of the multivariate regression analysis testing the determinants of level of economic production in 1960 (per capita GDP in constant 1995 U.S. dollars) and average annual rate of change in per capita GDP between 1961 and 2000. Similar to recent analyses of growth rates over extended periods, the logged value of per capita GDP in 1960 is also included as a control in all three of table 6.5b's models in order to take into account previous level of production. Looking at table 6.5a, the extent of indirect rule is significantly and negatively related to per capita GDP in 1960 in models 1 and 3. Indeed, it has the strongest relationship of all variables in model 3, suggesting that indirect rule affected level of economic production in 1960 somehow.

The analysis of GDP growth over time in table 6.5b has considerably lower adjusted R-squared scores than the models testing level of GDP at a set point in time. Of the models in the table, those including the extent of indirect rule account for the most variation in average annual GDP growth between 1961 and 2000, with model 1 accounting for nearly 20 percent of the variation, model 3 accounting for 11 percent, and model 2 accounting for nothing. Similar to table 6.5a, the indirect rule variable is negatively and significantly related to average annual per capita GDP growth between 1961 and 2000 in models 1 and 3, although its level of significance is lower than in table 6.5a. In model 3, the negative coefficient of the indirect rule variable suggests that a 50-point increase in the percentage of total court cases heard in customary courts in 1955 is associated with nearly 2.5 percent drop in average annual per capita GDP growth between 1961 and 2000. No other variable has even

Table 6.5

	Model 1	Model 2	Model 3
(a) Multivariate analysis of per capita GDP in 1960 (log)			
Variable coefficients			
Intercept	7.481***	7.281***	7.392***
	(0.207)	(0.418)	(0.372)
Extent of indirect rule, 1955	−0.028***		−0.018**
	(0.004)		(0.006)
Plantation		−0.094	−0.223
		(0.463)	(0.413)
European settlement, 1955 (log)		0.436**	0.344*
		(0.136)	(0.125)
Precolonial population density		−0.000	0.001
		(0.004)	(0.004)
Africa control		−0.950**	−0.431
		(0.361)	(0.368)
Ethnic diversity, 1960		−0.003	0.003
		(0.006)	(0.006)
Model			
F-Value	<0.001	<0.001	<0.001
Adj. R-Squared	0.583	0.534	0.634
Number of cases	33	33	33
(b) Multivariate analysis of average annual per capita GDP growth, 1961–2000			
Variable coefficients			
Intercept	7.465*	2.305	7.166
	(3.287)	(3.833)	(4.068)
Per capita GDP, 1960 (log)	−0.579	0.188	−0.440
	(0.434)	(0.505)	(0.534)
Extent of indirect rule, 1955	−0.044**		−0.047*
	(0.016)		(0.020)
Plantation		−0.707	−1.096
		(1.193)	(1.108)
European settlement, 1955 (log)		−0.080	−0.440
		(0.414)	(0.534)
Precolonial population density		−0.000	0.003
		(0.011)	(0.010)
Africa control		−0.488	0.246
		(1.047)	(1.009)
Ethnic diversity, 1960		−0.021	−0.810
		(0.016)	(1.603)
Model			
F-Value	0.017	0.145	0.205
Adj. R-Squared	0.192	−0.060	0.107
Number of cases	33	33	29

***p < 0.001; **p < 0.01; *p < 0.05; †p < 0.10.

moderate significance. As such, the extent of indirect rule is strongly and negatively related to both level of economic development in 1960 as well as change in economic development since then.

Tables 6.6a and 6.6b give the results of the models testing the determinants of life expectancy in 1960 and absolute change in life expectancy between 1960 and 1990. Notably, the models in table 6.6b include life expectancy in 1960 as an additional variable in order to control for previous level of societal health.

The models in table 6.6a account for much of the variation in life expectancy, with adjusted R-squared values of nearly 0.8 in both models 1 and 3 yet only 0.6 when the indirect rule variable is excluded in model 2. Considering the independent and control variables individually, the extent of indirect rule is negatively and very significantly related to life expectancy in models 1 and 3. According to the coefficients in model 3, an increase in the extent of indirect rule variable from 0 to 50 is associated with an 11-year decrease in life expectancy in 1960. The African control variable is also negatively and significantly related to life expectancy in models 2 and 3, although its significance level and coefficient value decrease considerably in model 3, suggesting that the form of colonialism accounts for much of the African effect.

Similar to the economic growth models, the overall predictive power of the models testing change in life expectancy between 1960 and 1990 is quite low. Indeed, the adjusted R-squared values range from a high of only 0.13 in model 3 to a low of 0.01 in model 2, suggesting that the historical factors included in the model are not among the most important determinants of recent changes in societal health. Of the independent and control variables, two are significantly related to the dependent variable. First, life expectancy in 1960 is negatively related to change in life expectancy, suggesting that former colonies with lower life expectancy in 1960 have generally had greater improvements. Next, the extent of indirect rule also has negative and significant relationships with change in life expectancy. In model 3, the indirect rule variable's large and negative coefficient shows that a 50 percent increase in the extent of indirect rule is associated with a four-and-one-half-year reduction in health improvements between 1960 and 1990, demonstrating that the legacies of indirect rule are negatively related to health care development since the 1960s. Thus, like the economic development models, the form of colonialism appears to have affected societal health both during and after colonialism, with indirect rule having deleterious consequences relative to direct rule.

Table 6.6

	Model 1	Model 2	Model 3
(a) Multivariate analysis of life expectancy, 1960			
Variable coefficients			
Intercept	61.318***	57.935***	59.989***
	(1.436)	(3.347)	(2.491)
Extent of indirect rule, 1955	−0.294***		−0.213***
	(0.029)		(0.043)
Plantation		3.064	1.320
		(3.829)	(2.832)
European settlement, 1955 (log)		2.301*	1.000
		(1.097)	(0.847)
Precolonial population density		−0.012	−0.003
		(0.033)	(0.025)
Africa control		−11.907***	−6.505*
		(2.922)	(2.409)
Ethnic diversity, 1960		−0.027	0.033
		(0.052)	(0.040)
Model			
F-Value	<0.001	<0.001	<0.001
Adj. R-Squared	0.759	0.614	0.792
Number of cases	33	33	33
(b) Multivariate analysis of change in life expectancy, 1960–1990			
Variable coefficients			
Intercept	27.837***	19.236**	21.380**
	(7.093)	(6.188)	(8.187)
Life expectancy, 1960	−0.277*	−0.114	−0.309*
	(0.115)	(0.102)	(0.134)
Extent of indirect rule, 1955	−0.084*		−0.086*
	(0.038)		(0.041)
Plantation		−2.069	−2.178
		(2.060)	(1.936)
European settlement, 1955 (log)		−0.079	−0.157
		(0.629)	(0.592)
Precolonial population density		0.002	0.004
		(0.018)	(0.017)
Africa control		−2.276	−2.411
		(1.974)	(1.856)
Ethnic diversity, 1960		−0.027	−0.008
		(0.028)	(0.028)
Model			
F-Value	0.069	0.411	0.164
Adj. R-Squared	0.107	0.011	0.127
Number of cases	33	33	33

***$p < 0.001$; **$p < 0.01$; *$p < 0.05$; †$p < 0.10$.

Conclusion

The above statistical findings provide evidence that British colonialism shaped political, economic, and human development during colonialism and afterwards. The extent of indirect colonial rule is strongly and negatively related to level of postcolonial state governance, levels of economic production and life expectancy in 1960, and change in per capita GDP and life expectancy after 1960. Notably, it has a weaker relationship with average level of democracy between 1972 and 2000, yet the relationship is still negative and marginally significant. Together, these findings suggest that (1) the form of colonialism began developmental trajectories and (2) different legal-administrative legacies have reinforced them through institutional reproduction and constant institutional effects during the postcolonial period. As such, the analysis provides evidence that qualitative works on the developmental impact of direct and indirect rule provide general insight into broad-based and long-term development among former British colonies.

Besides these specific findings, the analysis also raises additional questions concerning non-British colonies and state building and development in general. Considering the former, past research suggests that the findings are also applicable to non-British colonies (Bayart 1993; Boone 1992, 1994; Cruise O'Brien 1975; Mamdani 1996; Robinson 1972). Mamdani (1996) notes that all of Africa was ruled through indirect colonial rule and that these legacies hindered postcolonial political development regardless of colonial power. Moreover, Bayart (1993) finds that predatory and patrimonial states are present in postcolonial French Africa and are the legacies of colonial rule. Some disagree, however, suggesting that French colonialism was more direct than British colonialism in Africa since chiefs were more formally incorporated into the overall administration (Fisher 1991). This is correct, yet formalization still placed chiefs in an intermediary position and gave them extreme power over local affairs while leaving the central administration incapacitated. In fact, Firmin-Sellers (2000) analyzes two neighboring regions—one in Cote D'Ivoire, the other in Ghana—and finds that the chiefs in the former French colony had greater control over land and fewer checks on their powers than those in the former British colony despite similar precolonial political institutions. Thus, although French colonies appear more direct, French colonialism had similar, if not more pronounced, effects on state governance and development.

Second, the chapter raises issues dealing with states and development in general. It provides evidence that states have tendencies to reproduce themselves even after such important events as colonial independence and, through their constant effects on numerous social processes, shape long-term developmental trajectories. In addition, it sheds some light on the kinds of states that deter development and that promote it. The chapter shows that fissiparous states dominated by rural power brokers have detrimental effects on state building and development: the state cannot control rural areas, and the local brokers are able to use their powers to obstruct developmental demands made either by the central authorities or the local populations. Alternatively, centralized legal-administrative institutions that are present throughout a set territory are far more capable of implementing developmental policy.

Notes

A special thanks is given to Jim Mahoney, Louis Putterman, and Dietrich Rueschemeyer for their very helpful comments on earlier drafts of this paper.

1. Although Hong Kong is not a national state, it is included in the analysis.
2. The limited number of cases undoubtedly compounds difficulties associated with statistical methods. Yet, in social science analysis, a sample size near 30 is often considered sufficient for the assumptions of the central limit theorem to hold true (Hays 1994, p. 252).
3. Myanmar was given its own legal-administrative institutions in 1938, some ten years before its independence. Alternatively, Bangladesh, India, and Pakistan were ruled through the same central administration until the independence period.
4. The 1938 total includes the police forces of present day Bangladesh, India, Myanmar, and Pakistan. Alternative data for Myanmar in 1898 and Bangladesh in 1953 give slightly higher figures for per capita police officer (Doha 1957, p. 5; Griffiths 1971, p. 202).
5. In directly ruled areas of colonial India, officials employed village headmen for a number of activities: he was "a policeman while conveying reports of crimes, a judicial officer while disposing of petty cases, a revenue officer while assisting Government officers in making collections, and an administrative officer while discharging general administrative duties" (Gopal 1963, p. 144). The concentration of these duties, in turn, made possible unbridled power and the hyper-exploitation of the peasants (Gopal 1963; Kumar 1989). Since colonial revenue was largely dependent on land taxes, colonial rule also transformed social relations by giving some individuals greater control of local lands (Edwardes 1967, pp. 75–79; Kumar 1989). In many instances, tax farmers and revenue collectors known as zamindars were given rights to large tracts of land and were thereby "made masters of village communities" who were "mere parasites, who fattened on the products of the cultivators" (Kumar 1989, p. 35). Such local despotism appears to have had its legacies: areas in which land rights were given to landlords during the colonial period have had much lower agricultural production and investment in public goods during the postcolonial period (Banerjee and Iyer 2003). Thus, even when indirect rule was not formalized, the tiny administration in colonial India appears to have created alternative forms of decentralized despotism at the local level that have hindered development.
6. The years after 1990 are excluded from the analysis in order to omit the HIV/AIDS epidemic that hit many of Britain's former colonies in Africa. Due to the concentration of the disease on the African continent, statistical analysis testing change in life expectancy during the 1990s finds a strong and negative African regional effect.
7. The relationships between the extent of indirect rule variable and each of the five governance indicators are all strong and negative. The strongest relationships are with the rule of law indicator, and the weakest are with the state effectiveness indicator. See Lange 2004a for a more

detailed analysis of the relationship between the extent of indirect rule and postcolonial political development.
8. During the 1970s and 1980s, the bivariate correlation between the extent of indirect rule and the level of democratization among the 15 former British colonies in sub-Saharan Africa was −0.75. During the 1990s, the correlation fell to −0.52.

References

Acemoglu, Daron, Simon Johnson, and James Robinson. 2001. "Colonial Origins of Comparative Development: An Empirical Investigation." *American Economic Review*, 9, 15: 1369–1401.

———. 2002. "Reversal of Fortune: Geography and Institutions in the Making of the Modern World Income Distribution." *The Quarterly Journal of Economics*, 117, 4: 1231–1294.

Amsden, Alice. 1989. *Asia's Next Giant: South Korea and Asian Industrialization*. New York: Oxford University Press.

Banerjee, Abhijit and Lakshmi Iyer. 2003. "History, Institutions and Economic Performance: The Legacy of Colonial Land Tenure Systems in India." BREAD Working Paper No. 003.

Bayart, Jean-François. 1993. *The State in Africa: The Politics of the Belly*. New York: Longman.

Beckford, George. 1983. *Persistent Poverty: Underdevelopment in Plantation Economies of the Third World*. London: Zed Books.

Bollen, Kenneth and Robert Jackman. 1985. "Political Democracy and the Size Distribution of Income." *American Sociological Review*, 50, 4: 438–457.

Boone, Catherine. 1992. *Merchant Capital and the Roots of State Power in Senegal, 1930–1985*. New York: Cambridge University Press.

———. 1994. "States and Ruling Classes in Postcolonial Africa: The Enduring Contradictions of Power." In *State Power and Social Forces: Domination and Transformation in the Third World*, edited by J. Migdal, A. Kohli, and V. Shue. New York: Cambridge University Press, 108–140.

Brown, David. 2000. "Democracy, Colonization, and Human Capital in sub-Saharan Africa." *Studies in Comparative International Development*, 35, 1: 20–40.

Bryce, James. 1914. *The Ancient Roman Empire and the British Empire in India: The Diffusion of Roman and English Law Throughout the World: Two Historical Studies*. New York: Oxford University Press.

Chanock, Martin. 1985. *Law, Custom, and Social Order: The Colonial Experience in Malawi and Zambia*. New York: Cambridge University Press.

Clapham, Christopher. 1982. "The Politics of Failure: Clientelism, Political Instability and National Integration in Liberia and Sierra Leone." In *Private Patronage and Public Power*, edited by C. Clapham. New York: St. Martin's Press, 71–97.

Cruise O'Brien, Donal. 1975. *Saints and Politicians: Essays in the Organization of Senegalese Peasant Society*. New York: Cambridge University Press.

Diamond, Jared. 1997. *Guns, Germs, and Steel: The Fates of Human Societies*. New York: W.W. Norton.

Doha, A. H. M. S. 1957. *Report of the Police Administration of the Province of East Pakistan for the Year 1954*. Decca: East Pakistan Government Press.

Easterly, William and Ross Levine. 1997. "Africa's Growth Tragedy: Policies and Ethnic Divisions." *Quarterly Journal of Economics*, 112: 1203–1250.

Edwardes, Michael. 1967. *British India, 1772–1947: A Survey of the Nature and Effects of Alien Rule*. London: Sidgwick and Jackson.

Englebert, Pierre. 2000. "Solving the Mystery of the AFRICA Dummy." *World Development*, 28, 10: 1821–1835.

Ferguson, Niall. 2002. *Empire: The Rise and Demise of the British World Order and the Lessons for Global Power*. New York: Basic Books.

Firmin-Sellers, Kathryn. 2000. "Institutions, Context, and Outcomes: Explaining French and British Rule in West Africa." *Comparative Politics*, 32, 3: 253–272.
Fisher, Michael. 1991. *Indirect Rule in India: Residents and the Residency System, 1764–1858*. Delhi: Oxford University Press.
Gopal, Ram. 1963. *British Rule in India: An Assessment*. New York: Asia Publishing House.
Grier, Robin M. 1999. "Colonial Legacies and Economic Growth." *Public Choice*, 98: 317–335.
Griffiths, Percival. 1971. *The History of the Indian Police*. London: Ernest Benn Limited.
Hailey, William. 1938. *An African Survey*. New York: Oxford University Press.
Hays, William. 1994. *Statistics*. New York: Harcourt Brace College Publishers.
Herbst, Jeffrey. 2000. *States and Power in Africa*. Princeton: Princeton University Press.
Huff, W. G. 1994. *The Economic Growth of Singapore: Trade and Development in the Twentieth Century*. New York: Cambridge University Press.
Kaufmann, Daniel, Aart Kraay, and Pablo Zoido-Lobaton. 1999. *Governance Matters*. Policy Research Working Paper 2196. Washington, DC: World Bank.
Kohli, Atul. 1994. "Where Do High Growth Political Economies Come From? The Japanese Lineage of Korea's 'Developmental State.'" *World Development*, 22, 9: 1269–1293.
Kuczynski, Robert. 1948. *Demographic Survey of the British Colonial Empire, Volume I*. New York: Oxford University Press.
———. 1949. *Demographic Survey of the British Colonial Empire, Volume II*. New York: Oxford University Press.
———. 1953. *Demographic Survey of the British Colonial Empire, Volume III*. New York: Oxford University Press.
Kumar, Anand. 1989. *State and Society in India: A Study of the State's Agenda-Making, 1917–1977*. New Delhi: Radiant Publishers.
Lange, Matthew. 2003. "Embedding the Colonial State: A Comparative-Historical Analysis of State Building and Broad-Based Development in Mauritius." *Social Science History*, 27, 3: 397–423.
———. 2004a. "British Colonial Legacies and Political Development." *World Development*, 32, 6: 905–922.
———. 2004b. "Structural Holes and Structural Synergies: A Comparative-Historical Analysis of State-Society Relations and Development in Colonial Sierra Leone and Mauritius." *International Journal of Comparative Sociology*, 44, 4: 372–407.
LaPorta, Rafael, Florencio Lopez-de-Silanes, Andrei Shleifer, and Robert Vishny. 1999. "The Quality of Government." *Journal of Law, Economics, and Organization*, 1, 15: 222–282.
Lee, John Michael. 1967. *Colonial Development and Good Government: A study of the Ideas Expressed by the British Official Classes in Planning Decolonization, 1939–1964*. Oxford: Clarendon Press.
Lugard, Fredrick. 1922. *The Dual Mandate in British Tropical Africa*. London: W. Blackwood and Sons.
Mahoney, James. 2003. "Long-Run Development and the Legacy of Colonialism in Spanish America." *American Journal of Sociology*, 109, 1: 51–106.
Mamdani, Mahmood. 1996. *Citizen and Subject*. Princeton: Princeton University Press.
Mann, Michael. 1984. "The Autonomous Power of the State: Its Origins, Mechanisms, and Results." *European Journal of Sociology*, 25: 185–213.
McEvedy, Colin and Richard Jones. 1978. *Atlas of World Population History*. New York: Facts on File.
Merry, Sally Engle. 1991. "Law and Colonialism." *Law and Society Review*, 25, 4: 889–922.
Migdal, Joel. 1988. *Strong Societies and Weak States: State-Society Relations and State Capabilities in the Third World*. Princeton, NJ: Princeton University Press.
Porter, Bernard. 1996. *The Lion's Share: A Short History of British Imperialism, 1850–1995*. New York: Longman.
Putterman, Louis. 2000. "Can an Evolutionary Approach to Development Predict Post-War Economic Growth?" *Journal of Development Studies*, 36, 3: 1–30.

Reno, William. 1995. *Corruption and State Politics in Sierra Leone*. New York: Cambridge University Press.

Roberts, Richard and Kristin Mann. 1991. "Law in Colonial Africa." In *Law in Colonial Africa*, edited by K. Mann and R. Roberts. Portsmouth, NH: Heinemann.

Robinson, Ronald. 1972. "Non-European Foundations of European Imperialism: Sketch for a Theory of Collaboration." In *Studies in the Theory of Imperialism*, edited by R. Owen and B. Sutcliff. London: Longman, 117–140.

Scott, James. 1972. "The Erosion of Patron-Client Bonds and Social Change in Rural Southeast Asia." *Journal of Asian Studies*, 3, 1: 5–37.

Sokoloff, K. and Engerman, S. 2000. "Institutions, Factor Endowments, and Paths of Development in the New World." *Journal of Economic Perspectives*, 14, 3: 217–232.

Tilly, Charles. 1992. *Coercion, Capital, and European States, AD 990–1992*. Cambridge, MA: Blackwell.

Wade, Robert. 1990. *Governing the Market*. Princeton, NJ: Princeton University Press.

Young, Crawford. 1994. *The African Colonial State in Comparative Perspective*. New Haven, CT: Yale University Press.

PART III

Building States—Inherently a Long-Term Process?

CHAPTER SEVEN

Building States—Inherently a Long-Term Process? An Argument from Theory

DIETRICH RUESCHEMEYER

The historical record as well as current experience with development efforts suggests two broad empirical generalizations about state building: A well-functioning state is difficult to construct, and success often comes slowly where it does come. Given the indispensable role of effective states in social and economic development, it is important to examine whether state building is inherently a slow process. More specifically, it is important to determine those aspects of state building that are most and those that are least of a long-term character, to explore the underlying mechanisms, and to identify possible conditions under which fast developments are possible.

Tackling these questions is the task of the following chapters. The present chapter lays out a number of theoretical considerations. It is followed by reflections on early modern European state development, by an examination of state building after major revolutions, and by an assessment of state development in Korea in the second half of the past century against the background of Korean history. We think that this dialogue between theoretical argument and historical analysis offers the best chance to evaluate and delimit the claim that state building is inherently a long-term process.

An effective state, even a moderately effective state, requires an appropriate internal structure as well as relations with society that allow the growth of "infrastructural" in addition to coercive power.[1] I focus first on the structure of the state itself and begin that discussion with a few comments on the slow rise of the bureaucratic state in Europe. Next,

I discuss how relations with society influence state effectiveness, suggesting factors that make the emergence of such relations a matter of long-term change. Finally, I explore the conditions that make state building possible in shorter periods of time.

Rationalizing State Organization and Its Obstacles

It would not be unreasonable to claim that the rise of the European state was a development that took close to a millennium to play itself out. Such a time span suggests itself, if we use as benchmarks the foundation of the University of Bologna in the eleventh century and the near-complete bureaucratization of northwestern European states in the middle of the nineteenth century. Legal studies at Bologna revived and transformed the legacy of Roman law for the use of the church, a quasi-state that self-consciously rationalized its internal structure in the Gregorian reforms, while insisting on celibacy and the exclusion of lay-aristocrats from appointment procedures in order to reduce the dependence of its officials on the surrounding society.[2] The legal studies that were instrumental in this transformation of the church became the foundation of the Western legal tradition and influenced profoundly the building of secular states. The centuries since the Gregorian reforms have seen long periods of stagnation and partial reversals in the development of states. As to the opposite benchmark, we can take relatively close approximations to Max Weber's model of bureaucracy (Weber 1968) as a reasonable "end" point of the rise of the modern state in Europe. Bo Rothstein has recently shown that in Sweden this point was not reached until the decades between 1840 and 1870; and that seems to be a plausible dating also for other northwestern European countries (Rothstein 1997).

Rothstein argues against ahistorical projections of bureaucratic rule into earlier periods. However, while his effort to date more precisely the near-realization of Weber's full model in northwestern Europe is valuable indeed, it seems justified to look for earlier attempts to rationalize the organization of rule even if they involved only partial and incomplete efforts along certain lines of Weber's model. For this broader purpose, the Gregorian reforms of the church in the eleventh century and the attendant revival of Roman law identify an early and self-conscious move toward rationalization of rule in the church. The more common dating of the first moves toward proto-bureaucracy focuses on the beginnings of a transformation of patrimonial rule in secular states.

Weber contrasted bureaucracy to two other forms of organizing rule—the patrimonial household of traditional rulers and the inner group of followers of a charismatic leader. The features of bureaucratic administration can be reduced to a few broad components:

- A more or less steep hierarchy of offices with specialized tasks.
- Impersonal and rule-based operation of these offices.
- Appointment and promotion of officials on the basis of ability and performance.
- Supervision with incentives and sanctions at its disposal.
- Norms and structural features inducing loyalty (*esprit de corps*; full-time employment, job security).

Weber claimed that, in a broad historical perspective, approximations to this model are the most efficient means of large-scale administration and rule and that such rational, bureaucratic organization is indispensable in all modern societies. At the same time, he recognized that this gain in efficiency comes at a price for the rulers. Building a more efficient state is inevitably also a delegation of power and entails the risk of losing power. This gives particular salience to issues of loyalty. However, the most easily available forms of securing loyalty build on kinship and other personal ties. These are not only in limited supply but are also at odds with the impersonal meritocratic standards stipulated by the model. These contradictions and dilemmas inhibited a headlong rush toward building efficient administrative staffs. Here is the first major factor that explains the slow growth of European states.

A second set of circumstances accounting for the slow emergence of effective states comes into view when we consider how the early approximations to Weber's model were achieved. The emergence of proto-bureaucracies—combining some of the efficiency enhancing features with a loyalty of officials largely independent of kinship and other personal ties—represents a major breakthrough in the development of a modern social order.[3] For a whole complex of reasons, these processes overcoming the blockages just mentioned were uncertain and slow:

> They involved the emergence of an *esprit de corps* among the higher officials grounded in such foundations as similar origins, shared education, stable career prospects and a common privileged status in society. What was required on the part of the ruler were two dispositions at odds with each other: a willingness to delegate and a determination to impose one's will on the administrative apparatus. Success at both required, in turn, a tremendous amount of power based on economic, political, cultural and personal resources. Given these resources, the

ruler could provide generous rewards without becoming dependent on his subordinates; he could secure honour and status for them; he could influence and shape the emerging group ethos by invoking old ideals and fostering new ones, as well as by controlling education and training; he could destroy hostile alliances and forge or support agreeable new ones; and he could coerce or threaten to coerce when necessary. The joint impact of such interventions had to be steady over time, exceeding the generational turnover of rulers and officials before new orientations were developed and firmly institutionalized—a new cultural amalgam supported by habit and upbringing, group pride and individual commitment as well as by the material and non-material interests of the core personnel.[4]

Institutionalizing New Norms and Values

The time consuming character of such developments can be elucidated further by viewing them as instances of the generic problem of institutionalizing norms and values. In the ideal typical model the solution of this problem is simple and elegant. Full institutionalization means that reactions to one's behavior are structured in such a way that conforming behavior becomes rewarding and deviations are punishingly sanctioned. Furthermore, the model stipulates that the values and norms have been internalized by actors so that self-validation and guilt accompany conforming and deviating behavior. Full institutionalization in effect involves a restructuring of the actors' interests, aligning them with the complex of values and norms in question. If in its pure version this model is radically unrealistic, it points to a number of relevant features of the problem of institutionalization.

Internalization of values and norms—at least by core officials—is a critical aspect of state building, since it makes it possible to delegate power, trusting that it will not be abused. Continuous detailed monitoring is expensive for subordinates with routine tasks; it is counterproductive where substantial authority is delegated. Since internalization often builds on orientations developed early in life, a significant role of internalization makes generational turnover into a relevant metric of social change.

Yet internalization of values and norms may not be a sturdy guarantee of compliance if it stands alone. It gains greatly in effectiveness if it is embedded in groups with similar orientations and a similar status—officials of the same governmental body with an *esprit de corps*, and also graduates of high status schools or members of honored professions. The shared sense of honor in such status groups makes people not only monitor each other's overt behavior but also search for subtle indications of attitudes and subjective commitments. The sense of shame that is generated, if even small norm violations are noted by peers, and the sense of validation derived from their approval constitute critical linkages between external social control and internal self-monitoring. Again, the growth of such status groups with a distinctive and effective ethos takes time.

Norms are most effective if the prescribed behavior is unquestionably taken for granted. Several conditions seem particularly important for such a "naturalization" of normative standards. They must be well aligned with other effective norms and not stand in the way of persistent interests. And violations must be rare in people's experience, especially in those groups that "count" for them. In effect, naturalized injunctions call for what "one does" or "one does not do."[5] Clearly, the development of these complementarities and their extension across different groups are incremental processes that take time.

The underpinnings of bureaucratic functioning, then, are found in complex social norms and values that involve much more than the specific legal regulations of a bureaucracy. It is only through them that these legal regulations gain force. Bureaucracies require non-bureaucratic normative foundations in the same way as, according to Durkheim's famous theorem, contracts cannot be effective without non-contractual underpinnings.

Theoretical considerations of the development of norms and institutions, then, offer several ideas why the emergence of effective state institutions will take time. A complementary set of ideas derives from a consideration of opposition and conflict.

Opposition and Conflict

The norms we have considered derive from the interests of the political center. As such they are—at least initially—impositions from above. They have to constrain and control powerful interests. Being the official of a state with coercive control of its territory offers great opportunities for enrichment; officials therefore have a very strong interest to acquire and maintain proprietary and hereditary rights in their positions, an interest that has often blocked moves toward increasing bureaucratization for long periods of time. An incipient bureaucratic administration is likely to retain the character of imposition unless it approaches at least to some degree the model of complete institutionalization; unless, that is, the interests of officials have been fundamentally restructured and are now satisfied within the bureaucratic context.

As impositions, proto-bureaucratic norms will often provoke opposition, and this opposition may take on coordinated forms. The threat of punishing sanctions, if not fully effective, may actually reinforce the development of networks and groups of officials resisting what they consider as impositions. Such developments can take a variety of shapes, but all have the effect of slowing the pace of organizational rationalization. Some of these deserve brief comment.

If external and internal controls are less than fully effective, pockets of self-interested officials are likely to exploit their official positions for private gain. Where this behavior is supported by interests, loyalties, and cultural orientations shared with powerful groups outside the organization, it will tend to crystallize into persistent opposition, even if the center with its proto-bureaucratic intentions defines it as corruption and seeks to punish it as individual deviation and crime.

Other instances of opposition and conflict derive precisely from the fact that some coherent culture has grown around a given organizational structure. Increasing or changing the division of labor in such an organization typically runs into the vested interests of those whose status and authority are decreased by the restructuring. Similarly, established orientations of a body of officials, grounded in their *esprit de corps*, may be so much at odds with policies initiated by the political center that sharp conflicts and renewed attempts at imposition result. For the present discussion, both of these kinds of conflict have the same critical consequence: more or less successful institutionalizations of supportive subcultures among core officials may turn into obstacles to new policies as well as to further advances in bureaucratization. Breaking these obstacles and reconstituting organizational structures with modified normative cultures represent yet other projects that slow the process of state building.

A final internal conflict seems inherent in the very logic of bureaucracy as an instrument of rule. The political center of a system of rule is inevitably constituted on different principles than the bureaucratic organization and its fundamental features of specialization, meritocracy, universalism, and relative detachment from the surrounding social structure. This is the case whether the top positions are filled by kinship line, popular acclamation, dictatorial usurpation, or democratic procedure, because the political center sets goals, while the bureaucratic organization is defined by the instrumental logic of means for given goals. This dissimilarity may lead repeatedly to "invasions" of one side by the other. Core state officials may seek to "usurp" the power of the political center and to shape public policy (see, e.g., Rosenberg 1958), while members of the political elite may try to make allies—in political struggles or for more or less private gain—of useful members in the bureaucracy. The imbalances and conflicts arising from this inherent structural dissonance may require repeated restructurings of the organization of rule that—again—take time.

Theoretical arguments derived from norm theory as well as from conflict theory, then, make it plausible that building a machinery of rule that is an effective instrument in the hands of—individual or collective—rulers is likely to be a slow process. At the same time, these arguments begin to specify some of the mechanisms involved in slowing the process of state building. The same kinds of considerations are also illuminating if we now turn to state-society relations.

State-Society Relations and Their Impact on State Building

States cannot be effective simply because they acquire an efficient administration of rule. Effective state action calls for relations with society—as well as for social structures, interest constellations, and normative cultures within society—that are at least compatible with and at best conducive to successful state action. We will see that the considerations developed above about intra-organizational developments and blockages have counterparts that are also useful for understanding state-society relations and relevant developments in the wider society. Opposition and conflict as well as normative, institutional change play a critical role.

Opposition and Conflict

Conflicts play a much larger role in the state's relations with society than in intra-government developments. These conflicts similarly arise from impositions by rulers aiming for a stronger state, as well as from opposition and support mounted by vested interests; but they are much less amenable to central control than intra-organizational resistance and conflict. The major forces of opposition come from local and regional power holders likely to lose in the course of state development: from those who suffer from the state's attempts to increase revenue extraction without receiving substantial benefits, from the victims of warfare and different forms of conscription, and from those who resent the imposition of alien rule after conquest, be it alien in mores, language, or religion. Other groups may have strong interests in what the state has to offer. Historically, the most important of these are probably economic elites with an interest in having the state guarantee property rights and private contracts with its coercive power. Eisenstadt's (1963) analysis of premodern bureaucratic empires sees rationalizing states and these urban elites as sharing an interest in freeing human and material resources from ascriptive fixations and making them available for purposive projects.

Strong resistance from opposing interests and the frequently resulting stalemates are a major factor slowing state development. While resistance often flares up again, even after it was repressed, there seem to be turning points beyond which opposition dies down.[6] The conditions of these critical junctures deserve further careful exploration.

Beyond the dynamics of imposition and resistance, there is a related important factor. The rulers themselves are likely to have contradictory interests that make them hesitate and proceed with caution. While the interests associated with the rationalization of their apparatus of rule ally them with urban economic elites, the bases of their authority are in agrarian societies, very similar to those of other aristocratic power holders, who thus become, in this respect, natural allies. This dilemma accounts in Eisenstadt's view for prolonged "stagnation" in the process of state building as well as for the fact that "progress" toward more efficient states is no more an assured outcome than an eventual decay of the state organization, even in the long run.[7] We see here an interesting analogy to the intra-organizational problem of gambling on gains of efficiency in the face of the possibility of losing power through dividing authority, which is experienced by rulers who do not have fungible means of securing loyalty and trust.

Institutionalizing New Norms and Values

If interest constellations and conflicts between coalitions of interests play an even larger role in the external aspects of state building than in the internal problems of rationalizing rule, this is not true about normative, institutional developments. But these are nevertheless also of critical importance in state-society relations. In fact, in the long run normative and institutional transformations seem more important than turning resistance and opposition into acquiescence. At the same time, changing norms and institutions in society involves transformations on a much larger scale and of vastly greater complexity than changing the interests and the normative culture of the state's core staff.

What is it in the relations between society and the state that is required for effective state action? First, there is, the monopolization of violence by the state and an effective regularization of the use of that monopoly through the rule of law—creating a measure of internal peace rather than an imposed "pacification." Beyond that, much depends on compatible interests, compatible norms and values, and compatible understandings of how economy, polity, and society interrelate. What does this compatibility entail?

This is clearly a wide field of problems that transcends the confines of this chapter. Functionalist modernization theory had, at its most abstract level, a simple answer: the dominant institutions and attitudes have to become structurally similar to the bureaucratic organizations. They have to move from a status order and division of labor based on ascription and particularistic attachments toward meritocracy and an allocation of resources based on rational decisions. A social structure of unspecialized roles and collectives grounded in kinship relations and small local groups is to yield to an ever greater and far-flung division of tasks. And universalistic norms have to predominate in the culture and counterbalance the reduced sphere of particularistic loyalties.[8]

This theoretical perspective is not without value. It points to important global features; but it is flawed because it is too unspecific. It does not engage the analysis of actual historical trajectories, it tends to substitute claims about general cultural orientations for institutional and organizational developments as well as for changes in the attitudes of strategic subgroups, it neglects the role of power and conflict, and because of these neglects it fails to identify causal mechanisms and leverage points for transformational projects.[9]

I confine my argument here to just a few points. First, the development of state–society relations conducive to effective state action is not necessarily a matter of a global change in attitudes, value orientations, and understandings across the whole population. Changes that make for mutually productive exchanges between state and civil society are likely to be restricted for long times to certain enclaves where groups have interests that can be served by interaction with the state as well as orientations that are compatible with such interaction.

Second, what are at stake are not just aggregate attitudes and understandings, whether confined to circumscribed groups or spread across larger and more heterogeneous parts of society. Rather, the changes in attitudes and understandings must be grounded in institutional-organizational developments.

Third, as already noted, attitudinal and institutional changes that give state action greater traction and scope increase the infrastructural rather than the despotic power of states. "Infrastructural power is . . . collective power, 'power through' society, coordinating social life through state infrastructures" (Mann 1993, p. 59). Any development that creates institutions and spheres of activity in which the rational pursuit of goals—above all the pursuit of gain and status—is freed from traditional constraints and is regulated instead by impersonal norms, opens these spheres of activity to legal social control by the state, and at the same time mobilizes constituencies who seek to affect state action.[10] The prime instance of this interpenetration of state and society is the state's provision of the institutional infrastructure for economic production, market exchange, and investment in the slow joint rise of capitalism and the modern state in Europe. The expansion of market exchange and, subsequently, of dependent employment further had vast effects transforming societies and making broader groups receptive to and interested in state action, as it eventually materialized in the emergence of the modern service state.

A fourth point worth noting is that the transformations at stake do not and cannot come about once and for all. Particular state-civil society alliances of a limited character become obstacles to broader ambitions of the state and to the interests of newly empowered groups. The fundamental democratization of societies in the later course of capitalist transformation makes patterns of elite cooperation, which often were combined with traditional submission and acquiescence on the part of broad subordinate classes, unsustainable. A highly mobilized society requires—but does not necessarily have in easy reach—effective institutions and broad-based attitudes supporting active, demanding, and responsive citizenship within a political community that has at least a modicum of cohesion. In sum, "transitional" forms of compatible relations between state and society break down—or may have to be broken down—in order to arrive at new equilibria, which then require new institutional patterns. And these processes of change do not follow a single evolutionary path, even in rough outline, nor are they assured of success, even in the long run.

Closely related is a final point. The state's mode of operation will be effective only if it corresponds to the character of and the changes in society as well as to the problems tackled and the goals pursued. What in some societal contexts is effective intervention on behalf of certain interests, turns into "paternalistic" overreaching when these interests become more articulate and capable of mobilizing knowledge and activism on their behalf. While for some problems an organizational hierarchy with clear lines of command is of paramount importance, others require specialist expertise, and yet others the capacity to activate and integrate self-initiative on the part of different parts of the citizenry. Historical sequences of various equilibria and disturbances, then, result not only from changes in society but also from different modes of operation of the state, even where the state's organization has already closely approximated Weber's model of "bureaucracy."

The institutionalization of norms and value orientations appropriate for any of these equilibria is of the same fundamental character as we discussed for bureaucratic personnel; but it is inevitably more variegated, requires multifaceted adaptations among norm complexes, and is bound to be less successful when we speak of increasingly complex societies. Douglass North stressed in a recent essay that institutional development in society is a matter of incremental change and attributed that to "the economies of scope, complementarities, and network externalities of an institutional matrix" (North 1998, p. 496). At the same time, it is clear that the normative and institutional transformations in society and in state-society relations are ultimately far more important for effective action than overcoming opposition to the development of an effective state and the expansion of the scope of its actions.

Three Further Notes on the Slow Pace of State Building

We have considered many reasons why building an effective state is likely to be an incremental and slow process, a process that runs into opposition, and a process that is likely to encounter periods of stagnation and reversal (see table 7.1 for a compressed summary). Before we turn to the other side of the problem, the conditions of relatively fast developments, a few reflections on what has been said so far will round out the first side of the argument. We have to define a little more precisely what we mean by slow and fast developments in state formation; we will consider whether the phenomenon of "punctuated" change often encountered in history, of relatively fast developments separated by longer periods of stasis, has critical implications for a broader understanding of state formation; and we will ask whether the "developmental breakthrough" of bureaucratization in some parts of the world (Parsons 1966)—indeed a matter of slow and intermittent change—makes faster developments possible in "late comers," because precedents are now available in other countries.

Metrics of Time

I have so far bypassed an obvious question whose clarification is overdue: what is a slow development in state building, what a fast one? A first,

Table 7.1 Summary of factors slowing state development

	Normative, institutional change	Conflicts and stalemates
Within state organizations	• Tensions between loyalty based on personal ties and individual advantage and loyalty based on impersonal commitments and meritocracy prevent a fast pursuit of efficiency • Long-term institution building requires large economic, political, and cultural resources and may be disrupted and/or fail • Institutionalization of norms and especially their internalization takes time • Taken-for-granted norms, the most effective standards of behavior, are slow to develop • Cohesive status groups able to monitor and control behavior according to internalized norms take time to coalesce	• Officials seek to consolidate private gain by seeking proprietary and hereditary rights in their positions against the center's interest in control • Persistent opposition from pockets of officials especially if encouraged by outside interests, loyalties, and cultural orientations • Restructuring administrative organizations and reorienting public policy against resistance from a cohesive corps of officials may lead to repeated conflicts • Conflicts may arise out of the antinomy between the inherently non-bureaucratic issues of political direction and the instrumental logic of administration
In state-society relations	• Normative change may first come about only in certain institutions and in limited groups with a common status and/or shared interests • Change away from kin-based relations toward contractual and organization-based relations in the economic sphere tends to be slow and uneven • The spread of a normative conception of citizenship that is both demanding and responsive, possibly replacing earlier obedience-based acceptance, is likely to be slow and interrupted	• Rulers are likely to pursue efficiency goals with caution because of the contradictory nature of their alliance interests • Repeated and protracted conflicts with opponents who stand to lose power, economic resources, manpower, peaceful conditions, and/or cultural autonomy slow the imposition of state rule • Turning an eventual pacification into internal peace through the rule of law takes time and requires repeated adaptations

negative clarification is simple. If I started out with the revival of Roman law and the rationalization of rule in the church, I meant to convey some sense of the very long gestation of the rise of rationalized rule in Europe. I did not mean to introduce 900 or 500, or even 100 years as the relevant metric for any significant advance. Certain significant partial moves took a shorter time, measurable perhaps in decades though probably more often in generational turnover. Frequently, these were separated by longer periods of "stagnation," when further developments were blocked or when the decisive political actors considered things perhaps "good enough."

Politically, one might consider any development as long-term whose results lie beyond the time horizon of politicians and state managers. This is clearly, and admittedly, a variable yardstick. It is made shorter by pessimism, induced perhaps by a history of failure; it is made longer by optimism, induced sometimes by urgent necessity; it is made variable by the variable duration of expected political tenure; and it may be extended by the development of a culture of *raison d'etat* that defines the state's interest over a longer time span. Despite these variations, any development that approaches 25 to 30 years in duration may safely be called long-term if we take the time horizon of politicians as a point of reference. This also corresponds to the metric of generational turnover, itself a mechanism that opens the chance for deeper going social and cultural change.

Partial but critical advances toward the bureaucratic pole of state organization—say, the establishment of meritocratic careers in a core department or a decisive defeat for certain patrimonial patron-client relations—can be fast or short-term by this standard, but very often they are not. About apparently fast developments we may also ask to what extent they were prepared by previous developments as well as whether their actual implementation took longer than the legislative imposition.

For longer periods of observation and analysis there arises another question: did certain critical moves constitute nearly sufficient conditions for eventual later complementary and "completing" developments? If not, the overall trajectory becomes long-term indeed.

Continuous Development and Punctuated Change

The historical record of state formation, in Europe as well as in other parts of the world, is full of more or less long periods of "stasis,"[11] while at certain critical points, significant changes occurred. Such historical observations raise questions that seem critical for a better understanding of state formation. What are the conditions of slow incremental change and of accelerated if partial breakthroughs in state formation? Of the factors and mechanisms considered earlier, do some favor continuous incremental change, while others make breakthroughs or, for that matter, decline more likely? And, most ambitiously, can we identify conditions that make certain developments irreversible?

A rough generalization worth considering may be that normative change, especially normative change in the wider society, is more likely to be an incremental process than the outcomes of overt conflict. Where conflict results in decisive defeat of one side, rapid developments become possible once obstacles blocking them have been removed. Yet this generalization is surely not a hard-and-fast rule. The obstacles represented by—say—forces resisting certain forms of levies and taxation may be only part of the difficulties standing in the way of a more effective state action. Furthermore, even change in norms and values may—under as yet not very well understood conditions—come at a comparatively swift pace as has been documented for many societies in the twentieth century.

In a formal way, one can say that fast developments become possible once the major underlying factors of an old order have vanished or been severely weakened, while those supportive of new developments have come to predominate. Rapid change in fertility offers an example of this. It is an example that actually involves relatively fast normative change. I take the liberty of drastic simplification: the underlying factors favoring lower fertility—lower mortality of offspring, higher costs (including opportunity costs) of child raising, lower economic benefits from having children, and technical advances making fertility control more easily available—stand against established norms about fertility and sexual behavior. As the costs of norm-conforming behavior rise and even highly regarded people increasingly violate these norms, norm maintenance by established institutions may suddenly cease to be effective—as witnessed in the recent fertility declines in such countries as Ireland and Italy.

The critical question remains, of course, which factors we can identify—across different historical constellations—as the main underlying factors favoring the formation of effective states and synergistic state-society relations. We will have to return to this question when we review the dialogue of theoretical argument and historical analyses in the concluding chapter.

Where the underlying factors—also known as necessary and nearly sufficient conditions—are not yet ready for the emergence of effective states and synergistic state-society relations, mutual accommodation between opposing interests seems a major factor accounting for long periods of "stagnation." However, differences in the readiness to acquiesce in stagnation may account for major differences in the overall pace of state formation across different historical constellations.

It is only if we can gain a better—even if still rough—understanding of the necessary and sufficient conditions underlying the development of effective states and synergistic state-society relations (as well as the transformations resulting from their interaction) that we can begin to approach questions about reversible and irreversible developments. The same goes for the related issue of long-term tendencies toward a "completion" of state formation, once certain transformations have been achieved.

Precedents and the "Advantages of Backwardness"

My arguments, both with respect to the state's organization and its relation to society, have often referred to the first emergence of the modern state. This raises the question whether diffusion and imitation make these developments easier and potentially faster at later points in world history. There is little reason to expect that such "advantages of backwardness"[12] should play a significant role in industrialization but not in state formation. The opportunity to see and study the effective operation of other states as well as the competitive pressures that these other states are likely to exert, should not only make it easier to achieve reform but also provide the motivation to do so; ruling groups will not be as easily content with long periods of stagnation. The Japan of the Meiji Revolution provides as clear-cut an example of such learning across borders and cultural divides as one might wish.[13]

However, the "advantage of backwardness" may have severe limitations in state formation as well as in economic growth, as is suggested by the uneven and halting pace of economic development across the globe. The conditions of an initial institutional development found appealing by powerful elites may be different and more complex than the conditions of later successful adoption, but the conditions of later adoption may represent severe hurdles nevertheless. In fact, both sets of conditions may have a good deal in common with each other.

If major underlying conditions for effective state formation and synergistic state-society relations are given, we can expect latecomers to shorten the period of state formation significantly. We would then, especially, expect that they can avoid long periods of "stagnation." Without such conditions, the "advantages of backwardness" will be elusive and remain as oxymoronic as the formulation strikes us at first sight.

There is then reason to be skeptical about giving this mechanism too much weight. The success of neighbors and competitors may give cognitive clarity to what is required for effective administration and may even create the motivation to reach for those conditions; but cognitive clarity and political will on the part of some are only one part of the solution. The human resources required for building an effective state apparatus—their skills, their structural location in society, and their cultural orientations as well as prevailing patterns of state-society relations are conditions independent of the understanding and the will of elites aiming for an effective state. Engineering human social relations has to deal with much more recalcitrant "materials" than mechanical and chemical engineering. And the human "materials" in any given country—the pool of possible recruits for official positions, the constellations of opposing and supporting interests, and the historical shape of the many relevant different subcultures—are local in character.

Conditions of Faster State Building

It is now time to turn the question around and ask about the chances of relatively fast developments. Do the same considerations sketched above imply anything about this reverse problem? From the very inception of this project, we were aware of instances of apparently fast state building. This is the reason why two of the following chapters focus on state construction and reconstruction after revolutions and on the dramatic success of the developmental state in South Korea. Whether these analyses suggest limitations of the arguments developed so far is, however, an issue that will be taken up only in the conclusion.

Fast development in state structures seems to be a mark of modernity. Between 1960 and 1995, central government spending as a proportion of the GDP doubled in the OECD countries. Differences between countries reveal even more rapid developments: "Thus, from a point of rough equivalence in 1960, the Swedish state grew to nearly twice the size of that in the United States by 1995, in terms of both spending as a share of income and public employment as a share of population" (World Bank 1997, p. 22). True, one may consider these developments as mere expansions of state activity, which did not involve important institutional and organizational innovation. However, the development of the Scandinavian welfare state and also of Roosevelt's New Deal policies involved fairly radical new designs of public policy, and that entailed new institutions and organizations affecting and penetrating new spheres of social life. In some sense, these developments are analogous to the successful adoption of state institutions and state-society relations in countries that took others as a model: the new institutions and policies become effective because within modern societies the major underlying conditions are right.

If the welfare states of northwestern Europe must be ranked among the more successful rapid transformations of states and state-society relations on a very large scale, the social and economic transformation of post-communist East European countries has yielded so far much more uneven outcomes. Yet here, too, we see rapid and dramatic changes in state structure and functioning as well as in state-economy and state-society relations. The differences in the success of these transformations—say between Belarus, the Ukraine, and Russia on the one hand, the Czech Republic, Poland, Hungary, and the Baltic states on the other—seem be related to the previous history of industrialization and its attendant social and cultural changes. As in so many other respects, the sudden changes in eastern Europe present us with a natural laboratory for analyzing states and their transformations.

Why should "modernity" make a dramatic difference in the pace of state building and rebuilding? In terms of ideal typical modeling the answer is simple, and here it may come close enough to reality to offer a roughly adequate explanation. The more developed countries tend to exhibit widespread norms, values, and understandings conducive to effective collective action that is independent of close personal and kin ties. These are institutionally and organizationally grounded, both in state and in society, in education, in the economy, and so on. Compared to less developed countries (and certainly compared to premodern state-society relations), all take a large role of the state in social and economic life for granted, no matter whether certain policies or the level of taxation is more contested in some countries than in others.[14]

At the same time, there are important differences among developed countries, and all represent only complex approximations to the ideal typical model. The more successful countries seem to have the least trouble of converting the inevitably diverse interests into more or less common goals or at least courses of action that are broadly tolerable. This lower level of political division may be due to structural conditions (social inequality, ethno-racial heterogeneity), a less divisive history, or some portion of political luck, for instance in the timing of the attempted transformation in relation to economic growth spurts and recessions as well as of other conditions and trends.

In more developed countries, the purposive creation of formal organizations becomes a routine option, even though we know from organizational sociology that the interplay between formal and informal organization and of legal and nonlegal social control is critical for a smooth functioning of the new unit; and it is clear that working these interactions out may take some time. In a broad comparative perspective, however, the purposive creation of corporate actors for chosen purposes is a mark of modernity, as James Coleman emphasized in his magisterial *Foundations of Social Theory* (1990, pp. 531–664). It separates our world from others—earlier and contemporary—in which the creation of organizations and collectivities is much more closely (though in varying degrees) tied up with family and kinship ties.

Institutional and organizational developments in the most developed countries, then, build on what is there already. They represent a restructuring of state organization and state-society relations, extending well-established normative and cognitive principles to new uses, rather than the creation of more radically new foundational institutions. This "building on what is there already" represents a point that can be usefully generalized.

Even in situations quite far removed from the model type of a modern society, looking for normative and institutional patterns already existing may give us cues to understanding fairly rapid developments. For one, this may partially explain swift postrevolutionary state developments that perhaps can be understood as repairs and extensions of state structures disrupted by the revolution. But the point may also apply to existing conditions other than earlier but now fragmented state structures.

Favorable conditions for successful advances in state building may often be of a rather unexpected character. We should be inured to such unexpected links ever since Max Weber made a plausible if in detail still disputed connection between the Protestant ethic and the ethos of early capitalists. Some possible examples from state building come to mind. I have noted above that appeals to and transformations of earlier established values were important in building a cohesive, effective, and loyal corps of officials. One argument, close to Weber's hypothesis on the ethos of capitalists, holds that a state elite with Calvinist orientations played a critical role in the process of building the Prussian state.[15] Similarly, one might explore the appeal to the long latent and already transformed ethos of the *samurai* as factors in the pace of state building in Japan's Meiji Restoration. Surprising linkages of this kind may have been serendipitous to the actors themselves, but they could also simply be ingenious uses of the "materials" at hand.

Finally, we have to consider the impact of crisis situations. In extraordinary emergency situations states that have already attained a certain capacity for action can expand and create new organizations that would otherwise not be possible. Emergency situations concentrate the political power of those ready to act, enfeebling various kinds of opposition, and make it possible to deploy unusual amounts of economic resources as well as threats of coercion. The most extreme examples are perhaps wars. Charles Tilly has made the linkage between war-making and state building a central theme in his work (Tilly 1990). A qualifying comparative perspective is offered by Centeno (2002). Similar reasoning may explain the success of postrevolutionary developments at the end of a period of divided and uncertain sovereignty in reestablishing a system of domination that now included a larger and more powerful role for the state.

An example of the effect of slightly less extreme crises on state building are the transformation and extension of welfare state institutions in the United States in response to Depression and War. However, it would be a mistake to assume that all crises lead to transformations in state structure and operation, enhancing state capacity. Even if the financial crisis of East Asia was not as severe as the Depression of the 1930s in North America and parts of Europe, attempts to transform state-economy relations and to expand the incipient welfare state in South Korea had a far more ambiguous and weaker result. Crises have to be understood as triggering and facilitating factors for developments that require a host of other conditions to be right as well. Thus, it seems unlikely that Rwanda will soon, acquire an effective modern state, even if its Tutsi minority seems to have created relatively effective one-party rule in the aftermath of the genocide of the mid-1990s.

Conclusion

I have sought to lay out a preliminary case for the claim that state building is a long-term process, while remaining at the same time open for qualifications and exceptions. Combining power-resource and norm-theory perspectives, I have developed a number of hypotheses explaining why some aspects of state development are likely to be long-term in character. Considerations about norm development, institutions, and solidarity formation as well as analysis of imposition, resistance, and conflict lead to insights about when in particular to expect slow, incremental, and interrupted change as well as reversals.

At the same time, they allow us to begin exploring under which conditions we can expect more rapid development and the purposive and fast creation of organizations. Once effective states emerge on the scene, others may—given that major conditions are favorable—achieve similar institutional development in a shorter time. Crisis situations of different kinds—including revolutions, major wars, and economic crises—also can hasten the development of effective states as they transform the underlying power relations and give urgency to the search for effectiveness. Within modern societies, where the foundations for such institutional developments are more or less established throughout, relatively fast development of new state institutions as well as the transformation of old ones are not rare at all.

Notes

I wish to thank the participants of the conference at which early drafts of these papers were discussed for their manifold comments. The presentation and comments of Tom Ertman were particularly useful. Beyond that, I benefited from comments on later drafts by Matthew Lange, Peter Uvin, and especially, James Mahoney.

1. Michael Mann has made the important distinction between "infrastructural" power and "despotic" or coercive power central to his work; see Mann 1984 and 1993. Infrastructural power is the state's capacity to undergird and transform social structures and processes. Earlier distinctions between zero-sum and positive-sum conceptions of power, between power defined by the outcome of conflicts and power as the ability to achieve collective goals (e.g., Parsons 1967), and, more colloquially, between "hard" (coercive) power and "soft" influence aim at similar contrasts.
2. See Berman (1988). The importance of celibacy as a tool of severing important attachments and obligations of officials to the surrounding society is obvious on reflection. That "nepotism," the favoring of nephews, became the expression for corruption based on personal ties is indirect testimony to the effectiveness of celibacy in limiting the role of such ties.
3. Talcott Parsons included bureaucracy in his "evolutionary universals" (1964) and identified it as a "developmental breakthrough" (Parsons 1966).
4. Quoted, with apologies for the self-citation, from the chapter on "Division of Authority, Legitimation and Control" in my *Power and the Division of Labour* (Rueschemeyer 1986, p. 60).
5. Notably, the observation "Everyone does it" marks both fully naturalized norms and—in the opposite case—the complete breakdown of norms forbidding a certain behavior. Weber stressed habit as critical for stable norm compliance. While clearly an aspect of "naturalization," habit emphasizes its individual psychological side; but it distracts from the social mechanisms involved.
6. See the recent paper by Kiser and Linton (2002) on the Fronde and similar turning points elsewhere.
7. Viewed in a different perspective, the negotiated relations between political center and diverse provincial interests and elites that result from this dilemma appear as a major factor explaining the longevity of early modern empires. This emerged as a major theme at two workshops at New York University in 1999 and 2000 on "Shared Histories of Modernity: State Transformation in the Chinese and Ottoman Empires, Seventeenth through Nineteenth Centuries"; see the introduction by Islamoglu and Perdue (2001) to a special issue of the *Journal of Early Modern History*.
8. Talcott Parsons's "pattern variables" of now faded fame, to which this brief sketch alludes, were actually derived from his reading of Weber's ideal type of bureaucracy. They define four dimensions of social relations on which market exchange and bureaucratic organization show remarkable similarities. Explicitly or implicitly these contrasts, which specified the older dual concepts of contract and status societies (Sumner Maine), *Gesellschaft* and *Gemeinschaft* (Tönnies) or Durkheim's *solidarité organique* and *solidarité mécanique*, informed much of modernization theory; see for instance Levy (1966). Fundamentally, modernization theory emerged as a rushed reformulation of the heritage of classic social theory when the social sciences were at the end of World War II, confronted with decolonization and the development problems of poor countries.

9. I see this lack of specificity as modernization theory's main flaw, rather than the ethnocentrism or the conservative bias with which it has been charged. The latter tainted some arguments and formulations, and those were reinforced by the ideological confrontations of the Cold War, which turned poor new nations of the "South" into "Third World" countries; but these ideological features were not inherent in the perspective of modernization theory. What was inherent was a "functionalism" that asks what is required if certain outcomes are to take place, a question that is of interest to radicals, progressives, and conservatives alike when they are interested in certain outcomes. It is because similar questions are involved in our inquiry—the issues of slow change in building effective states lead to the question of what it takes to make state action effective—that the argument moved into the neighborhood of modernization theory.

10. See Rueschemeyer and Evans (1985, appendix), who apply insights of Dror (1959) on the conditions of effective legal social control to questions of developmental state action.

11. Depending on one's problem focus and theoretical inclination, such periods of "stasis" may be considered evidence of "stability" or—as for instance in the context of the timing of eventual bureaucratization—"stagnation." See note 7 and the papers introduced by Islamoglu and Perdue (2001).

12. Thorstein Veblen coined this formulation in his polemical discussion of German industrialization, where he argued that latecomers can gain from the advance of others (Veblen 1915). The idea was forcefully brought into development studies by Alexander Gerschenkron (1952).

13. Furthermore, as in the case of industrialization and development, the model and the impact of effective other states may make not only for faster state formation; it may also make state building different in process and outcome because the institutional "transplant" has to be articulated with a different social and cultural context. But this is a matter that goes beyond the confines of this chapter.

14. This is not to proclaim a normative blessing to the course worldwide modernization has taken and is taking. Max Weber saw these developments as inevitably yet profoundly objectionable. We can here leave both the normative questions and the claim of inevitability out of consideration.

15. Philip Gorski (1993) makes a stronger claim—that "a disciplinary revolution unleashed by ascetic Protestant movements" played a critical role in early modern European state building—and exemplifies this thesis with state formation in Holland and Brandenburg-Prussia. His broader argument is that this kind of cultural explanation must complement Marxist and institutionalist theories of state formation. See also Gorski 1999.

References

Berman, Harold J. 1988. *Law and Revolution: The Formation of the Western Legal Tradition*. Cambridge, MA: Harvard University Press.

Coleman, James S. 1990. *Foundations of Social Theory*. Cambridge, MA: Harvard University Press.

Centeno, Miguel A. 2002. *Blood and Debt: War and the Nation-State in Latin America*. University Park, PA: Pennsylvania State University Press.

Dror, Yeheskel. 1959. "Law and Social Change." *Tulane Law Review*, 33: 749–801.

Eisenstadt, S. N. 1963. *The Political System of Empires*. New York: Free Press.

Gerschenkron, Alexander. 1952. "Economic Backwardness in Historical Perspective." In *The Progress of Underdeveloped Areas*, edited by B. F. Hoselitz. Chicago, IL: University of Chicago Press.

Gorski, Philip S. 1993. "The Protestant Ethic Revisited: Disciplinary Revolution and State Formation in Holland and Prussia." *American Journal of Sociology*, 99, 2: 265–316.

Gorski, Philip S. 1999. "Calvinism and State Formation in Early Modern Europe." In *State/Culture: State Formation after the Cultural Turn*, edited by G. Steinmetz. Ithaca, NY: Cornell University Press, 147–181.

Islamoglu, Huri and Peter C. Perdue. 2001. "Introduction." Special issue on Shared Histories of Modernity in China and the Ottoman Empire, *Journal of Early Modern History*, V, 4.

Kiser, Edgar and April Linton. 2002. "The Hinges of History: State-Making and Revolt in Early Modern France." *American Sociological Review*, 67, 6: 889–910.

Levy, Marion J. 1966. *Modernization and the Structure of Societies*. Princeton, NJ: Princeton University Press.

Mann, Michael. 1984. "The Autonomous Power of the State." *Archives Européennes de Sociologie*, 25.

———. 1993. *The Sources of Social Power. Vol. II: The Rise of Social Classes and Nation-States, 1760–1914*. Cambridge and New York: Cambridge University Press.

North, Douglass. 1998. "Where Have We Been and Where Are We Going?" In *Economics, Values, and Organization*, edited by A. Ben-Ner and L. Putterman. New York and Cambridge: Cambridge University Press, 491–508.

Parsons, Talcott. 1964. "Evolutionary Principles in Society." *American Sociological Review*, 29: 339–357.

———. 1966. *Societies: Evolutionary and Comparative Perspectives*. Englewood Cliffs, NJ: Prentice-Hall.

———. 1967. "On the Concept of Political Power." In *Sociological Theory and Modern Society*, edited by T. Parsons. New York: Free Press, 297–354.

Rosenberg, Hans. 1958. *Bureaucracy, Aristocracy and Autocracy: The Prussian Experience 1660–1815*. Cambridge, MA: Harvard University Press.

Rothstein, Bo. 1997. "State Building and Capitalism: The Rise of the Swedish Bureaucracy." Paper presented at the Annual Meeting of the American Political Science Association, August 27–31, Washington, DC.

Rueschemeyer, Dietrich. 1986. *Power and the Division of Labour*. Cambridge: Polity Press, and Stanford, CA: Stanford University Press.

Rueschemeyer, Dietrich, and Peter B. Evans. 1985. "The State and Economic Transformation: Toward an Analysis of the Conditions Underlying Effective Intervention." In *Bringing the State Back In*, edited by P. Evans, D. Rueschemeyer, and T. Skocpol. New York: Cambridge University Press.

Tilly, Charles. 1990. *Coercion, Capital, and European States, A.D. 990–1990*. Oxford: Blackwell.

Veblen, Thorstein. 1915. *Imperial Germany and the Industrial Revolution*. London Macmillan.

Weber, Max. 1968. *Economy and Society*. New York: Bedminster Press.

World Bank. 1997. *Word Development Report 1997: The State in a Changing World*. Oxford and New York: Oxford University Press.

CHAPTER EIGHT

Building States—Inherently a Long-Term Process? An Argument from Comparative History

THOMAS ERTMAN

In his contribution to this volume, Dietrich Rueschemeyer has presented an "argument from theory" that explores the extent to which state building is an inherently long-term process. At first glance, the European experience would seem to imply that it most certainly is, since most of the continent's polities can point to developmental histories that span many centuries. Yet Rueschemeyer is not interested in just any kind of state building, but rather in the sort that leads to the emergence and consolidation of "effective" states, those constructed around the modern bureaucracies famously analyzed by Max Weber. Viewed from this perspective, the European case appears more ambiguous, for it was patrimonial rather than "modern" state building that predominated there throughout much of the medieval and early modern periods. Furthermore, when breakthroughs to a more effective form of state organization finally occurred beginning in the 1600s, they did so at varying speeds and under diverse circumstances, thereby rendering generalizations more difficult though, I hope to show, not impossible.

In this chapter, I seek to provide answers to three questions. First, why did state building in Europe between the twelfth and the late sixteenth century for the most part *not* move in the direction of the Weberian modern state but rather toward various forms of patrimonialism? Second, under what conditions did proto-bureaucracies, the first step toward a qualitatively new kind of state, begin to appear in some corners of the continent in the seventeenth and eighteenth centuries and become dominant thereafter? Finally, what broader conclusions about the speed and character of "effective" state building can we derive from the European case?

Non-Modern State Building in Medieval and Early Modern Europe

As Max Weber never tired of pointing out, the breakthrough to the modern, "effective" state was a unique and unexpected development. In most times and places, including ancient Egypt, Mesopotamia, the Islamic Near East, China, and the Roman Empire, the predominant kind of large-scale polity was *patrimonial* in character, by which he meant a form of rulership in which a monarch exercises patriarchal authority over a staff that extends out beyond his or her private household (Weber 1978, pp. 231–232, 1013). At the same time, as Weber also ceaselessly emphasized, medieval and early modern Europe possessed a number of features that set it apart from these other great civilizations, namely the separation of political and religious authority; self-governing cities; the prevalence of autonomous markets; and strong traditions of procedural as opposed to material justice. Yet, during the first period of European state building, from roughly the eleventh through the sixteenth centuries, these conditions were clearly *not* in themselves sufficient to permit the construction of infrastructures organized around proto-, much less modern, bureaucracies. Here too patrimonialism triumphed. To understand why this was so, we need to examine more closely the dynamics of political change during the Middle Ages in the continent's western regions.

After several false starts, post-Roman state building in Europe took off during the 1000s with the founding of many new kingdoms (Sweden, Norway, Denmark, Poland, Hungary) and the reconstitution of a number of others (France, England, Scotland, Castile, Aragon, Navarre, Portugal, Sicily) upon territories that had previously experienced a collapse of central authority or had been overrun by foreign invaders. These polities initially possessed only very rudimentary internal structures, consisting largely of a small, itinerant royal court and a limited number of all-purpose officials in the localities responsible for collecting royal revenues, dispensing justice, and organizing defense. These fragile new political entities soon faced challenges from a number of directions. First, in the wake of the revival of the European economy after the turn of the millennium and the Investiture Crisis of the late 1000s, rulers needed to assert and consolidate their authority vis-à-vis expanding, independent-minded cities, an autonomous Church, and a nobility strengthened by growing land revenues and local market taxes. In addition to these domestic threats, the rulers of England, France, and the Iberian and southern Italian states also had to face up to growing military pressures from their neighbors that soon involved them in ever longer and more costly wars, wars that were increasingly fought with paid professional troops rather than feudal levies (Ertman 1997, pp. 48–67).

Over the next four centuries, these rulers responded to such internal and external challenges by constructing large-scale state infrastructures to maintain order and dispense justice, to raise and provision armies, and to collect and disburse the revenues needed to pay for these activities. By the 1500s, they had hundreds and, in the case of France, thousands of officials in their employ. Yet these officials were not organized along bureaucratic, but rather along patrimonial lines: they often possessed strong proprietary claims over their offices, claims that greatly limited the right of rulers to hire, transfer, or fire officials as they sought fit. Moreover, the financial resources of these polities were not in the hands of royal officials at all, but of financiers who had taken control of these resources in return for cash advances and long-term loans. Hence after many centuries of state building, rulers in Europe's wealthiest, most advanced states had relinquished much of their influence over the state apparatus that they and their predecessors had called into being (Doyle 1996, pp. 3–4; Ertman 1997, pp. 77–83, 88–89). In Weber's terms, these rulers had lost out in a struggle over the means of administration characteristic of patrimonialism, and their victorious staffs would fight tenaciously to prevent modernizing reforms that would undermine this outcome and with it their material and social interests. Why did this outcome occur?

When monarchs in western and southern Europe began to expand their state apparatuses in the 1100s and 1200s, they first filled new administrative positions with clerics, who at this time enjoyed a quasi-monopoly of administrative skills. Beginning in the 1300s, however, as tensions with the Church heightened and the demand for officials exploded in the wake of massive conflicts such as the Hundred Years War between France and England, rulers sought to replace churchmen on their staffs with more politically reliable laymen (Ertman 1997, pp. 78, 80). Initially the position of these lay officials was far more precarious than that of their clerical predecessors. If the latter were dismissed by their political master, they could fall back financially on the income from ecclesiastical benefices that they held independent of the royal will, and alternative positions within the Church hierarchy would undoubtedly be forthcoming. For laymen, by contrast, dismissal could spell economic and social ruin for themselves and their families. A principal goal of this new breed of lay officials was hence to gain security of tenure in their positions and the right to name their own successors—most often a son or close relative—thereby safeguarding the future social position of their families.

After nearly two centuries of struggle, officials in France, Iberia, and southern Italy achieved this goal by the late 1400s. They exploited the tremendous pressures of war and their own strong market position as holders of still relatively rare administrative, financial, and military skills and resources to force their royal employers to apply the Church's canon law conception of office to their own positions. This conception not only granted officeholders lifetime tenure in their positions, but also permitted them to sell those positions to a successor (called *resignatio in favorem tertii*) as long as they did not die within 40 days of doing so (i.e., no deathbed resignations) (Olivier-Martin 1929; Schwarz 1983). In effect, government posts had become property, and rulers sought to profit as best they could from an unfavorable situation by taxing such sales, by extorting payments through periodic threats to revoke officeholders' rights, and by creating new positions for direct sale to a public anxious to enjoy the social status, privileges (such as tax exemption or even ennoblement), and profits that came with many offices. Both the appropriation of offices by their incumbents and the multiplication of new positions for sale naturally undetermined any semblance of an organizational hierarchy within the financial and administrative infrastructures of these states.

By the seventeenth century, the high costs of this kind of state apparatus in terms of loss of control, organizational incoherence, and inefficiency were clearly recognized by contemporary observers. However, the vast wealth of the Spanish Empire and France allowed both, at least for a time, to tolerate high levels of waste and still remain formidable geopolitical competitors. By the 1640s, though, Spain's resources were exhausted and after 1659 she fell from the ranks of the great powers. On three occasions during the eighteenth century, France's rulers sought to avoid the same fate by installing ministers (Terray and Maupeou, Turgot and Necker) who aimed to replace the country's bloated patrimonial infrastructure with one organized along proto-bureaucratic lines. Each time, coalitions of officeholders and aristocrats whose standing and income were threatened by such reforms succeeded in reversing them (Ertman 1997, pp. 141–151). The truth was that by this time the interests of patrimonial officeholders were so closely intertwined with those of the entire social order of ancien régime France that to attack such interests was to risk a collapse of the entire system. True reform, as we shall see, could only come through revolution.

To recapitulate: over a period of some four centuries, rulers in western and southern Europe built large state apparatuses in order to consolidate their authority in the face of both internal and external threats. However, these apparatuses were not "modern" and the states associated with them not "effective." This was so because monarchs in England, France, Iberia, and Italy lost the struggle with their staffs over control of the means of administration and, except in England (see later) were never able to reverse this loss prior to the French Revolution thanks to the resistance of vested interests.

Modern State Building in Early Modern Europe

An important step in the direction of modern state building occurred in the German territories around the turn of the sixteenth century. Principalities like Bavaria, Wuerttemberg, electoral Saxony, Brandenburg, and Hanover had only crystallized as autonomous polities during the course of the 1400s with the decline in the central authority of the Holy Roman Emperor. After 1450, institutionalized tripartite assemblies began to appear in the large and medium-sized territories to represent the local nobility, clergy, and towns in negotiations with their prince over his need for additional revenue. In order to strengthen their own hand vis-à-vis the elites of their lands, the rulers of these territories in turn sought to build up permanent administrative infrastructures covering their entire realm that would be answerable only to them. They took as their inspiration the organizational structure introduced by the Emperor Maximilian into his Austrian lands in the 1490s (itself derived from Burgundian models) and consisting of a central royal council (later privy council), a financial chamber, a war council, an ecclesiastic board, and a chancery to carry out the clerical work of central government. With minor variations, this set of institutions soon spread to nearly every state of any size within the Holy Roman Empire (Oestreich 1970, pp. 83–85; Jeserich et al. 1983, pp. 307–346; Schulze 1987, pp. 205, 211–214).

More significantly, these new administrations were staffed largely by laymen with university educations, many of them with legal training. Between 1348 and 1498, 16 universities had been founded in central Europe and by 1648, 18 more would open. Together they were producing a "glut of jurists" by the late 1500s (Wunder 1986, p. 37). It was from this large pool of available talent, further widened by the cultural unity of the German-speaking lands, that rulers drew their new corps of officials. As their infrastructures greatly expanded during the late 1500s and 1600s in the wake of the Reformation and the religious wars that followed it, the princes fought to maintain their right to hire and fire at will, aware as they were of the negative consequences of the proprietarization of office in France (Stolleis 1990, p. 218). In this they largely succeeded, for until the end of the eighteenth century most German rulers could remove officials as they sought fit and "the purchase of office remained . . . the exception rather than the rule," even if the phenomenon was not unknown (Dipper 1991, pp. 215, 219; Malettke 1980, pp. 179–180). Since the military and financial pressures on Germany's territorial princes were, given their limited resource base, as great if not greater than those on their French or English counterparts during the 1300s and 1400s, one can only surmise that their ability to prevent the appropriation of the means of administration by their staffs was due not only to a knowledge of the French situation, but also to the weak bargaining position of their staffs given the oversupply of qualified replacements on the labor market.

It was during this period that a noticeable professionalization of German officialdom first began. Serving in the state administration came to be viewed as a full-time, salaried occupation demanding adherence to special behavioral norms (loyalty, honesty, impartiality) where business was to be conducted in writing and records retained, and for which a certain level of educational attainment was a necessary prerequisite (Stolleis 1990, pp. 197–231; Dipper 1991, pp. 211–212; Rabe 1991, pp. 136–138). The most significant manifestation of this new trend toward professionalization was the introduction of qualifying examinations for entry into government service, first required for admission to the Prussian high court in 1693, to all Prussian courts in 1755, and finally to the nonjudicial higher administration in 1770. Other German states quickly followed the Prussian example over the course of the eighteenth century. The examination system was mutually beneficial for both the new breed of officials and for princely employers since it aimed to reduce the influence over the administrative system of clientelist networks linked to dynasties of officials or to powerful local aristocrats, though nobles were often able to win personal exemptions from the examination requirement. At the same time, however, examinations also limited the ability of rulers to place unqualified outsiders in important positions (Dipper 1991, pp. 212–213).

The German administrative model extended its influence far beyond the borders of the Holy Roman Empire. In 1538, the dynamic Swedish monarch Gustav Vasa recruited a veteran Habsburg official, Conrad von Pyhy, to introduce the new German system of royal council, chancery, chamber of finances, and war board into his kingdom, the central government of which had hitherto been "rudimentary" (Roberts 1968, pp. 113–114, 121–124). Clearly the poor, isolated country did not yet possess the resources to consolidate such a system, and it quickly fell into decline. Between 1618 and 1651, however, as the Swedish-Finnish kingdom plunged into the Thirty Years War and briefly rose to great power status, successive rulers reintroduced an updated version of the German system, this time accompanied by a personnel policy that required those seeking admission to the upper reaches of Swedish administration to possess a university education and to have clerked either on an appeals court or in local government (Gaunt 1975; Roberts 1958, pp. 260–283). This policy served the Swedish proto-bureaucracy well over the next 80 years, providing it with a steady stream of officials as it expanded by 80 percent, from 381 to 687 administrators (Gaunt 1975, p. 86). Peter the Great, in turn, imported the Swedish system wholesale into Russia between 1715 and 1722 with the aid of a German administrator who had previously served in Sweden and a group of Swedish prisoners-of-war (Peterson 1979). Further, it was the military defeat at the hands of Sweden in 1660 that precipitated a royal coup against the aristocratic government in Denmark-Norway and the rapid introduction there of the German administrative model. The Danish proto-bureaucracy was characterized, to even a greater degree than in Germany, by tight royal control over the hiring, promotion, and dismissal of its highly professionalized officials (Bjerre Jensen 1987; Knudsen 1995, pp. 115–123).

Yet, this was one key respect in which Danish administration deviated from a Weberian bureaucratic model that in many other respects it closely approximated (Bjerre Jensen 1987, pp. 305–306). Excessive and sometimes arbitrary intervention on the part of absolutist monarchs in the internal affairs of their proto-bureaucracies was common in the eighteenth-century German states as well as in Denmark. In addition, despite the spread of examinations, nobles were often able to gain special treatment and rapid promotion for themselves, while extended officeholding families were still capable of placing relatives in advantageous positions. Petty corruption was also a common feature of all of these administrations (Dipper 1991, p. 215; Wunder 1986, p. 18).

The impetus to reform these and other shortcomings and finally transform the German-Scandinavian proto-bureaucracies into true modern bureaucracies first came from the enlightened Bavarian minister Count Montgelas. Between 1799 and 1806 he carried out a complete overhaul of the Bavarian state with the aim of expanding its military capacities and thereby catapulting it into the rank of the great powers (Wunder 1978). His reforms were soon taken up by neighboring states and were fully implemented throughout Germany and in Sweden and Denmark as well by the 1860s. They involved, on the one hand, a structural rationalization that swept aside the remnants of aristocratic administration, that replaced government boards with monocratically organized hierarchies of offices, and that reconfigured ministries along functional rather than territorial lines. On the other hand, Montgelas's reforms sought to place the position of the government official on an entirely new footing. Henceforth the state was to protect its administrators against arbitrary dismissal and guarantee their material security for life and even beyond (introduction of widows' and orphans' pensions) while retaining ultimate control over hiring, promotions, transfers, and the timing of retirement. At the same time, the examination system was extended and made more rigorous, and administrators were now to be subjected to a strict code of conduct that governed not only their professional behavior but also their private lives and that was enforced in many German territories by special courts (Wunder 1978, pp. 123–233; Wunder 1986, pp. 18, 22–68). Taken together, these changes created the modern bureaucracy and the modern bureaucrat of which Max Weber wrote.

Those polities in western and southern Europe that had constructed large patrimonial infrastructures during the Middle Ages and into the sixteenth century took a different path to modern state building than that followed by the German and Scandinavian states. A pioneer in this respect was England, where reformers set a qualitative change in the state apparatus in motion in the second half of the 1600s. Outrage over the waste, corruption, and inefficiency of the early Stuart state was a precipitating factor in the outbreak of the Civil War in 1641, and a victorious Parliament moved quickly to remove many former government officials (and with them their property rights over their offices) and to replace them with professional administrators who could be dismissed at will (Aylmer 1973, pp. 82–83, 326–328, 341–343). However, the collapse of the Protectorate and the restoration of the monarchy under Charles II in 1660 brought with it a wholesale return to the old administrative system. Five years later, the shortcomings of this system were clearly exposed when England suffered military defeat at the hands of the Dutch. This humiliation provided an opening for reformers within central government, many of whom—like Sir George Downing—had previously served under Cromwell and all of whom were committed to rationalizing the country's administration and finances in the interest of greater military effectiveness.

Over the next two decades (1665–1685) and with strong backing from Parliament, these reformers created a new master department, the Treasury, to manage government revenue, expenditure, and appointments to office; removed the customs from the hands of tax farmers and built up a new service to collect excise taxes; and introduced standard bureaucratic procedures to the Navy Board and Ordnance Office. Most significantly of all, Downing found a cheaper, more efficient way for the government to borrow the large amounts of cash it needed to pay for soldiers, sailors, and military supplies. Rather than rely on small cliques of financiers, his Treasury Order system turned to the general public for cash, guaranteeing repayment from a designated tax fund by an act of Parliament. When in 1672 Charles II reneged on loans that he had contracted on his own account without parliamentary backing, all Treasury Order loans continued to be repaid on time (Roseveare 1973, pp. 18–45; Ertman 1997, pp. 193–204). This graphic demonstration of the importance of loan guarantees from Parliament ensured the success of Downing's system and the demise in England of borrowing methods that had given financiers and officeholders with financial resources the upper hand in their struggle with rulers over control of the means of administration.

Following the Glorious Revolution of 1688, the nascent fiscal-military state constructed since 1665 was forced to face up to the daunting challenge of holding its own against Europe's greatest power, Louis XIV's France, in two sustained conflicts (Nine Years War, 1689–1697; and the War of the Spanish Succession, 1702–1713). This task was rendered more difficult by the new king William III's decision to appoint inexperienced political allies to key positions in the Treasury, Excise, and Navy. The result was military setbacks and financial crises that provoked an outcry from a press newly freed from censorship. Literally hundreds of pamphlets flooded the public sphere criticizing, often with great technical expertise, the inner workings of the state and its financial practices and proposing a variety of alternatives. Parliament responded to this public disquiet in two ways. First, it appointed a Committee of Public Accounts to monitor the behavior of officials during wartime, a form of oversight that resulted in the removal of a number of leading politicians, including the Speaker of the House, on charges of malfeasance. Second, it agreed to underwrite a plan put forward by a Scots promoter, William Paterson, to found a quasi-public bank to assist the government in raising long-term funds and meeting financial emergencies—this was the Bank of England (Ertman 1997, pp. 208–217).

It was only after 1702 that the very experienced First Lord of the Treasury, Sidney Godolphin, was able to act on the lessons of the 1690s and once again place the English administrative and financial system on a sound footing. Godolphin reorganized the Excise department along strictly bureaucratic lines and altered the way the land tax was assessed and collected. He did this in order to guarantee that the tax funds from which the lending public would be repaid met their targets, thereby bolstering investor confidence. He also worked to ensure that the Ordnance and the Navy, Victualling and Transport Boards, all of which issued their own short-term credit notes, were free of rumors of mismanagement or corruption since such rumors would have an immediate effect on the discount rate of this paper. The success of Godolphin's efforts is shown by the government's ability to borrow the equivalent of its annual budget of 4 to 6 million pounds *in cash* from the general public every year between 1702 and 1710 (Sperling 1955, pp. 15, 21, 26). By the end of the War of the Spanish Succession, then, Britain was equipped with a fiscal-military system built around a few key departments in which parliamentary oversight, a relatively free press, and financial markets all worked together to maintain honesty and efficiency to the benefit of the country's creditworthiness and defensive capacities.

After 1714, however, the British state's proto-modern core came under threat from another source: its own politicians. The withering of opposition following the failed attempt to challenge the Hanoverian Succession in 1714–1715 ushered in a period of overwhelming Whig dominance that would last until at least the 1760s. Rather than extend the modernization of the state outward from the fiscal-military core to the royal household, seals offices and courts, Whig politicians sought to preserve useless positions as lucrative sinecures for themselves, their political clients, and for members of Parliament whose votes the government needed to pass legislation. Thus while one part of the state was already modern or very nearly so—John Brewer has characterized the Excise as "more closely approximated to Max Weber's idea of bureaucracy than any other agency in eighteenth-century Europe" (Brewer 1989, p. 68)—another part remained tainted by the kind of patrimonial practices more commonly associated with Britain's great rival, ancien régime France. The very heavy costs of the (victorious) Seven Years War (1757–1763) and the American conflict soon led to deafening calls from taxpayers for "economical reform" directed against corrupt practices. In 1780, Lord North's government responded by appointing Commissioners for Examining Public Accounts. In their subsequent reports, the commissioners laid down a set of strikingly Weberian principles to guide subsequent administrative reform: that offices should be separated from the person of the officeholder, that they should be arranged in a clear hierarchy and compensated by salaries rather than fees, that public and private income should be strictly separated, that officials should be directly accountable to the public and see it as their duty to convince the latter that tax money was being well spent (Harling 1996, pp. 60–61). This claim that the primary obligation of government officials was to serve the *public* sets British development apart from that in Germany where civil servants were to owe their primary loyalty to the *state* (Dipper 1991, pp. 215–216).

Despite the passage of an act in 1782 to abolish about 130 sinecures and the reorganization of the offices of the secretaries of state into nascent departments of home and foreign affairs (Chester 1981, pp. 124–127, 238; Harling 1996, pp. 37–38), the cause of reform was much delayed by the political backlash provoked by the French Revolution and by the tremendous financial and military pressures associated with the struggle against a resurgent France. Thus the final assault on the last vestiges of patrimonialism did not resume again on a large scale until 1808. Thereafter a whole series of acts stretching into the 1840s finally did away with all property rights in office, sinecures, and rights of reversion as well as introducing pensions for public employees and replacing fees where they were still present with salaries. At the same time, most departments carried out internal reorganizations to ensure clear lines of authority and promotion. The final step in the complete modernization of the British state did not come until 1870, however, with the introduction of open, competitive exams for entrance into the civil service (Chester 1981, pp. 123–140, 155–161).

It was also, of course, the popular pressure culminating in the Revolution that forced the replacement of patrimonial with modern state building in France. In a fit of revolutionary zeal during the night of August 4, 1789, the new National Assembly decided to abolish all aspects of proprietary officeholding, thereby putting an end in one stroke to a system of administration that had endured for over four centuries, often in the face of substantial resistance (Doyle 1996, pp. 1–2). Over the next two years, the assembly set about laying the groundwork for what would be, despite some continuities in personnel, a transformed French state. It promptly set up a new system of taxation and tax collection, a framework for regional administration built around 83 *departements* overseen by prefects and subprefects, set up a treasury department with control over revenue and expenditure, and reorganized the executive around six ministries. It was only after the onset of war in 1792 against Europe's other powers and the transformation of the government into a revolutionary dictatorship that the new structures were filled out, and over the next two decades they expanded rapidly. The officials manning this apparatus, which soon encompassed some 250,000 positions, possessed no proprietary claims to their offices, were remunerated by salary, received pensions, and were organized in functional hierarchies (Church 1981, pp. 72, 94–98, 181, 189). However, there were no formal requirements for entry into the civil service and no exam system, though Napoleon did create a kind of apprenticeship for higher officials when he instituted the system of "interns" *(auditeurs)* of the Council of State in 1803 (Bergeron 1972, p. 38).

The influence of revolutionary France, whether direct or indirect, was the single most important factor in the modernization of other western and southern states that had previously experienced patrimonial development. Thus administrative centralization and rationalization based on the French model came to the northern Netherlands when the former Dutch Republic became first a satellite of France and then was directly incorporated into Napoleon's empire (1810). Annexation and the imposition of French administration arrived in Belgium even earlier, in 1793, though that country had experienced a prior round of reform under the Habsburg ruler Joseph II who in 1787 had rationalized the justice system, redrawn the boundaries of territorial administration, and introduced a council of ministers as the chief executive organ (Blom and Lamberts 1993, pp. 303–318). In Tuscany as well, reform had been initiated before 1789 by the enlightened Habsburg rulers Francis Stephen and Leopold Peter inspired by modern state building in Germany. Thus between 1737 and 1790 these princes replaced the old patrimonial administration with a proto-modern bureaucracy characterized by the separation of officeholder from office, a clear hierarchy of authority and advancement, remuneration exclusively by salary, and pension benefits for retired officials (Litchfield 1986, pp. 270–312). In the rest of Italy, however, it was the arrival of the French that brought a swift end to the old administrative and financial as well as social system (Woolf 1979, pp. 194–215). An exception here was Piedmont, where the modernization of the bureaucracy was not carried out until 1853 under Cavour, but then quickly became the model for the administration of the new Italian state, also constructed by Cavour after 1859 (Romanelli 1995, pp. 187–200; Woolf 1979, pp. 440–443).

Theoretical Conclusions

In my reading, the following theoretical conclusions can be drawn from the European case outlined above:

First, medieval and early modern Europe possessed a number of special features that set it apart from other areas of the world at that time and that Max Weber has plausibly identified as necessary conditions for the construction of modern bureaucracies and hence for a breakthrough to the truly modern, effective state. The most important of these perhaps was the failure of caesaropapism in the wake of the Investiture Crisis, an outcome that was foreshadowed by the independent development of the Church in the tenth and eleventh centuries following the collapse of the Carolingian imperial project. The absence of caesaropapism meant that, despite the ideology of "divine right," Western rulers and their staffs were secularized, that is, that they were not viewed as principal carriers of religious authority as was true in China, India, and the Islamic states. As a result, attempts to reform officeholding did not have to overcome the often nearly insurmountable religious or spiritual barriers to change that, for example, helped preserve Mandarin rule for nearly fourteen centuries. In addition, the failure of caesaropapism opened the door to the predominance of a formal, procedural as opposed to a material conception of justice ("kadi justice") within the new European polities (and even within the Church itself!). That a full-fledged system of procedural justice—the Roman law—stood waiting to be "received" certainly helped, but under different ideological circumstances it is doubtful whether the Roman law would have enjoyed such a warm welcome. Furthermore, it is worth remembering that procedural justice triumphed in England as well, despite only limited help from Roman or Roman-influenced canon law. The predominance of procedural justice was in turn so significant, Weber implies, because it provided the conceptual model for the procedure- and rule-bound administrative framework of modern bureaucracy—hence the preponderance to this day of trained jurists among continental Europe's administrators.

A further unique feature of the medieval West cited by Weber was the relative weakness of the clan (or tribe) compared to other areas of the world, a consequence above all of Christianity's "fraternalism," that is, its claim that all people, not just clan members, are brothers/sisters. If left unchecked, clan allegiances both undermine the socially constructed authority structure of the bureaucracy and hinder the ability of officials to grant that organization their primary loyalty. Finally, Weber frequently pointed to the relative autonomy of markets as a unique and crucial characteristic of post–Roman Europe. In all other advanced civilizations, including ancient Rome, markets were subjected to heavy state regulation in the interest of order and stability. Indeed, in most other times and places the idea that a task as important as the provisioning of major cities should be left to the vagaries of the market would have been considered absurd. Once again, it was the collapse of central political authority in the

West in the fifth and then again in the ninth century that made possible the emergence of first international and local markets (eleventh century) and then regional markets (twelfth/thirteenth centuries) relatively free—at least in world-historical perspective if not by current standards—from political tutelage. The autonomy of markets was so significant for state development because it eventually permitted the eternal problem of the government's immediate cash needs and the irregular flow of tax revenues to be solved by public (i.e., market-based) borrowing. At the same time, the profit-making opportunities offered by a robust market economy provided an alternative path to enrichment and social advance for ambitious men and families compared to that represented by the rent-seeking capitalism of contractors, tax farmers, and patrimonial officeholders. Put another way, the "non-political" market is able to channel the greed of those who under other circumstances would become corrupt and rapacious officials in a more socially useful direction.

Second, while these four conditions may have been *necessary* for a breakthrough to modern state building, the triumph of patrimonialism in late medieval western and southern Europe clearly indicates that they were not *sufficient* to produce that outcome. Why was this so? One important factor, I have argued, was the relative paucity of trained laymen capable of staffing infrastructures that were expanding rapidly under the impact of internal and external conflict. This in turn strengthened greatly the bargaining position of the small group that did possess the necessary expertise, thereby permitting them over the long term to win the struggle for control over the means of administration with their royal masters and acquire proprietary rights over their positions. A second was the immaturity of the market economy that made it impossible for rulers to meet their short-term financial needs through broad-based borrowing and instead drove them to make repeated concessions to officeholders in order to generate the cash needed for military campaigns.

Third, when "effective" state building did finally appear in Europe, it seems to have followed two distinct patterns. The first of these might be called the mandarin-authoritarian path to the modern state and was characteristic of Germany and Scandinavia. In this pattern, rulers who first began to expand their infrastructures in the late 1500s and early 1600s in the wake of the Reformation and the warfare associated with it drew on a much expanded pool of laymen with legal training to construct proto-bureaucracies in which they retained rights of appointment and dismissal. Imitation played a key role here as the same organizational model spread first throughout Germany and then to Sweden-Finland and Denmark-Norway and from there to Russia. During the eighteenth century ever more states introduced examination systems to choose qualified candidates for office and by the first half of the nineteenth century the triumph of meritocratic principles for selection and promotion marked the transition of these infrastructures from proto- to fully Weberian bureaucracies. As befits their origins, these bureaucracies were—and to some extent remain—characterized by a strong ethos of service *to the state*.

The other path was that exemplified by the case of England, where a patrimonial administrative system built up since the twelfth century was displaced by a new proto-bureaucracy beginning in the 1660s thanks to pressure from Parliament. In addition, the government turned to very broad-based public credit markets to meet its financial needs. Despite these notable reforms, it was not until the nineteenth century that the last traces of patrimonial practices were eliminated from the British state, thanks again to the efforts of Parliament and of public opinion. Once that state had been fully bureaucratized after 1870, its officials were chosen from university-trained generalists rather than from students with law degrees as in Germany and Scandinavia. Also in contrast to Germany and Scandinavia, the dominant ethos here has been, at least in theory, that of service *to the public*.

Other cases of modern state building in western Europe—in France, the Netherlands, Belgium, and Italy—contain elements of both these patterns. In France, the National Assembly swept away in one frantic night the old patrimonial state apparatus, but the construction of a new bureaucratic infrastructure based on educational qualifications was in part the work of successive authoritarian—revolutionary and Napoleonic—regimes down to 1814. The further development and final consolidation of this new bureaucracy then occurred under various kinds of legislative scrutiny culminating in the Third Republic after 1870. Likewise modern bureaucratization began in the Netherlands and most Italian states under the aegis of the French occupying forces or their local allies, though later in the century all became subject to various kinds of constitutionalist regimes.

Fourth, and most important, it is clear that the task of modern, effective state building—that is, the construction of an administrative, financial, and judicial infrastructure organized around the principles enumerated by Weber in his discussion of bureaucracy—most often took far *less* time than the length of the European state building process as a whole might lead one to expect. Thus state building in France began in the eleventh century, yet reformers needed less than a century—between the 1790s and late 1800s—to equip that country with a modern infrastructure, and the basic features of that infrastructure were already in place within 20 years of the Revolution. The same is true of those countries where modernization was imposed by French arms. But are these examples of "revolutionary" state building not the exception rather than the rule? And did the changes imposed from outside really take root, especially in Italy? That country is today hardly a watchword for bureaucratic efficiency.

To address the first point, while the modernization of the state in post-1789 France and its satellites may indeed have been exceptionally rapid, it is not that far out of line with the experiences of other European states. As I have argued at length elsewhere, the leap in England from a largely patrimonial to a predominately modern state took place within less than 40 years (1666–ca. 1710) and was the prerequisite for that country's rise to world power status during the eighteenth century. The German and Scandinavian states were also able to erect, though not fully consolidate, proto-bureaucracies within a few decades during the seventeenth and early eighteenth centuries. Once again, perfecting these systems—transforming them from imperfect bureaucracies to the full-fledged Weberian article, often required another century or century and a half. But the crucial *qualitative* jump occurred much more quickly, and once that jump had been accomplished *none* of the European states fell back into patrimonialism.

This is not to say that this new organizational form was not under threat from a variety of directions. In the so-called mandarin-authoritarian states, both family networks and aristocratic privilege affected hiring and advancement and undermined the principle that authority emanated solely from position within the organizational hierarchy. Ever further extensions of the examination system sought to address these dangers, but they would only fully disappear with the democratization of social conditions in the course of the twentieth century. Another danger inherent in this variety of state building cited by Weber was the usurpation of political leadership by an overpowerful bureaucracy ill equipped to play this role, a problem in late-nineteenth-century Sweden and above all imperial Germany. In those states like Britain and later Italy where legislative oversight was of greater direct relevance for public administration, the threat came rather from the "colonization" of the administration by politicians and political parties. This was a phenomenon that afflicted the British state apparatus throughout the eighteenth century, though it was kept in check by the parliamentary gadflies and investigating journalists. The late eighteenth century saw the emergence of a broad popular movement for civil service reform that led, after the end of the

Napoleonic Wars, to a series of changes that pushed Britain toward the examination-based bureaucracy of the continent. In Italy, and later in Spain and Portugal, however, the thoroughly clientelistic nature of political parties and the weakness of the public sphere allowed newly modernized infrastructures to fall victim to machine politics, a problem that continues to plague Italy to this day.

If we accept that the changes that permitted a qualitative shift in the nature of European state building were introduced over a period of decades rather than centuries, how can the counterintuitive speed of this transformation be explained? I have argued above, with Weber, that this was so because Europe after about 1500 met a number of conditions both necessary and sufficient for the construction of modern bureaucracies: a desacralized state, a tradition of procedural justice, weak clan influence, an autonomous market economy, and an adequate supply of university-trained laymen. From the eighteenth century onward, these were joined by an ever-stronger public sphere and permanent organs of political control such as national legislatures. It would of course be possible to argue that Europe required many centuries (at least five) before the first five conditions were met and another four to five centuries before the final two were obtained and the process of bureaucratization could be completed, and hence that state building is necessarily a very long-term process. Yet in relation to the contemporary world such a conclusion would probably be a logical fallacy. This is so because rapid social and economic change has brought these conditions to many areas of the world—notably Asia and with some reservations Latin America and the Near East—in a far shorter time than five to ten centuries and thus permitted countries there to lay the groundwork for modern—though often flawed—states in a matter of decades. The fact that many countries in Africa and the Middle East that are beset by serious ethnic/tribal cleavages and suffer from weak market economies have experienced such difficulties building effective states merely underlines this point rather than calling it into question. Other lessons of the European past, those related to the construction of consociational political systems, are perhaps of greater relevance to these cases, but that is the subject for another paper (Steiner and Ertman 2002).

References

Aylmer, G. E. 1973. *The State's Servants: The Civil Service of the English Republic 1649–1660*. London: Routledge & Kegan Paul.

Bergeron, Louis. 1972. *L'Episode Napoleonien*. Paris: Seuil.

Bjerre Jensen, Birgit. 1987. *Udnaevnelsesretten i Enevaeldens Magtpolitiske System 1660–1730*. Copenhagen: G.E.C. Gads Forlag.
Blom, J. C. H. and E. Lamberts (eds). 1993. *Geschiedenis van de Nederlanden*. Amsterdam: Agon.
Brewer, John. 1989. *The Sinews of Power*. London: Hutchinson.
Chester, Sir Norman. 1981. *The English Administrative System 1780–1870*. Oxford: Clarendon.
Church, Clive. 1981. *Revolution and Red Tape: The French Ministerial Bureaucracy 1770–1850*. Oxford: Clarendon.
Dipper, Christof. 1991. *Deutsche Geschichte 1648–1789*. Frankfurt: Suhrkamp.
Doyle, William. 1996. *Venality: The Sale of Offices in Eighteenth-Century France*. Oxford: Clarendon.
Ertman, Thomas. 1997. *Birth of the Leviathan*. Cambridge: Cambridge University Press.
Gaunt, David. 1975. *Utbildning till Statens Tjaenst*. Uppsala: Almqvist & Wiksell.
Harling, Philip. 1996. *The Waning of "Old Corruption."* Oxford: Clarendon.
Jeserich, Kurt, Hans Pohl and Georg-Christoph Unruh (eds). 1983. *Deutsche Verwaltungsgeschichte. Volume I: Vom Spätmittelalter bis zum Ende des Reiches*. Stuttgart: Deutsche Verlags-Anstalt.
Knudsen, Tim. 1995. *Dansk Statsbygning*. Copenhagen: Jurist- og Okonomforbundets Forlag.
Litchfield, R. Burr. 1986. *Emergence of a Bureaucracy*. Princeton: Princeton University Press.
Malettke, Klaus. 1980. *Ämterkäuflichkeit: Aspekte Sozialer Mobilität im Europäischen Vergleich (17. und 18. Jahrhundert)*. Berlin: Colloquium.
Oestreich, Gerhard. 1970. *Verfassungsgeschichte vom Ende des Mittelalters bis zum Ende des alten Reiches*. Muenchen: Deutscher Taschenbuch Verlag.
Olivier-Martin, Francois. 1929. "La Nomination aux Office Royaux au XIVe Siecle et d'apres les Pratiques de la Chancellerie." In *Melanges Paul Fournier*. Paris: Sirey: 487–501.
Peterson, Claes. 1979. *Peter the Great's Administrative and Judicial Reforms: Swedish Antecedents and the Process of Reception*. Stockholm: Nordiska Bokhandeln.
Rabe, Horst. 1991. *Deutsche Geschichte 1500–1600*. Muenchen: Beck.
Roberts, Michael. 1968. *The Early Vasas: A History of Sweden 1523–1611*. Cambridge: Cambridge University Press.
Roberts, Michael. 1958. *Gustavus Adolphus: A History of Sweden 1611–1632*. London: Longmans.
Romanelli, Raffaele (ed). 1995. *Storia dello Stato Italiano dall'Unita a oggi*. Rome: Donzelli.
Roseveare, Henry. 1973. *The Treasury 1660–1870*. London: George Allen and Unwin.
Schulze, Winfried. 1987. *Deutsche Geschichte im 16. Jahrhundert*. Frankfurt: Suhrkamp.
Schwarz, Brigide. 1983. "Ämterkäuflichkeit, eine Institution des Absolutismus und ihre mitteralterlichen Wurzeln." In *Staat und Gesellschaft in Mittelalter und Früher Neuzeit: Gedenkschrift für Joachim Leuschner*. Goettingen: Vandenhoeck & Ruprecht, 176–196.
Sperling, John. 1955. "Godolphin and the Organization of Public Credit 1702 to 1710." Unpublished Dissertation. Cambridge: Cambridge University.
Steiner, Jüerg and Thomas Ertman (eds). 2002. *Still the Politics of Accommodation? The Fate of Consociational Democracy in Western Europe, 1968–2000*. Amsterdam: Acta Politica.
Stolleis, Michael. 1990. *Staat und Staatsraeson in der fruehen Neuzeit*. Frankfurt: Suhrkamp.
Weber, Max. 1978. *Economy and Society*. Berkeley: University of California Press.
Woolf, Stuart. 1979. *A History of Italy 1700–1860*. London: Methuen.
Wunder, Bernd. 1978. *Privilegierung und Disziplinierung: Die Entstehung des Berufsbeamtentums in Bayern und Wuerttemberg (1780–1825)*. Muenchen: Oldenbourg.
———. 1986. *Geschichte der Bürokratie in Deutschland*. Frankfurt: Suhrkamp.

CHAPTER NINE

How Fast Can You Build A State? State Building in Revolutions

JAIME BECKER AND JACK A. GOLDSTONE

Introduction

Revolutions offer an opportunity to study state building under pressure. Revolutionary leaders come to power after the old state has collapsed or been defeated, and are faced with the need to quickly reconstruct the machinery of administrative, political, and economic control. In this chapter, we look at the resources that revolutionary leaders have drawn on for state building, and the factors that lead to rapid state construction or, in some cases, to slow or ineffective efforts at state building.

Our key point is that under conditions of revolution, construction of an efficient bureaucratic state apparatus can take place fairly rapidly, in a matter of a few years. The combination of mass mobilization of the populace under the guidance of revolutionary cadres, and the weakening or destruction of the elites that formerly dominated the state, allow the replacement of the former traditional or patrimonial states with new and generally larger and more bureaucratic states. Such speed and success, however, depends on several conditions. Where the old elite is able to resist, or where the new elites are not able to come to agreement on the powers and structure of the new state, the persistence of internal conflict can slow state development for many years, even for decades. Moreover, the speed of state building and the effectiveness of the postrevolutionary state depend on several prerevolutionary factors and the new regime's ability to exploit them: the civil service and military, human and cultural capital, and external support.

Finally—and this is a major caveat—revolutions often give rise to party-states or populist dictatorships in which the executive authority is not checked by other institutions or groups in society. The result can be a personalistic or corrupt regime that, despite the revolutionary creation of an extensive bureaucratic apparatus and far-reaching ability to reorganize society, fails to live up to Max Weber's vision of modern state authority as rule-guided and impersonal. In such cases, revolutions help modernize the state's *structure*, but do not truly modernize the state's *behavior*. Development of a fully modern state structure, with impersonal rule of law *and* an efficient bureaucracy, may then be delayed for several decades until the authority of the ruling party or personalist ruler is dramatically reduced. Indeed, for many of the states that have experienced major revolutions (Russia, China, Cuba, Iran), such development of a fully modern state has still not arrived, even many decades after their revolutions.

State Building after Revolutions: A Scorecard

It is interesting to look at the empirical record of state building following revolutions, to see how long it has taken in specific cases and regions to create new stable state institutions.

Table 9.1 gives data on the time from the collapse or overthrow of the old regime to the consolidation of a stable new regime state for 47 cases of revolution. These cases come from all major regions of the world, and cover a time span in state-making from the Netherlands Revolt of 1572 to the Albanian and Baltic revolts of the 1990s. Our criteria for inclusion in this list were that a revolutionary regime came to power after the collapse or forcible removal of the old regime and was supported by popular collective actions.

It is often difficult to precisely date the fall or consolidation of a state. Old regimes can last a long time while guerilla movements chip away at their control of the countryside, and the consolidated states that eventually emerge are sometimes the result of successful counter-revolution rather than consolidation of the original revolutionary state (as in the British Puritan Revolution of 1648–1660).

To allow for this uncertainty, we have grouped revolutionary state building efforts in a series of broad categories of times to state completion. We have also specified the events that we have taken to mark the onset of old regime overthrow or collapse, and new state consolidation. We consider a postrevolutionary state to have become consolidated when it no longer faces internal elite or popular challenges that pose

Table 9.1 Time-spans from state collapse to revolutionary consolidation

	Regime collapse	Beginning event	New state	Ending event	# years
One year					
Zanzibar (Tanzania)	Jan. 1964	Okello's popular coup	April 1964	Forms Tanzania w/ Tanganyika	<1
France	1830	Charles X removed	1830	Louise-Philippe "King of the French"	<1
Philippines	Feb. 1986	Marcos flees	Feb. 1986	Election of Corazon Aquino	<1
Bangladesh	1971	independence	1971	independence	<1
Iran (Islamic)	1979	Shah leaves	1979	Khomeini forms Islamic Republic	<1
East German	Oct. 1989	Krenz replaces Honecker	July 1990	unification	<1
Hungary	Oct. 1956	Nagy renamed Prime Minister	Nov. 1956	Red Army crushes revolution	<1
Costa Rica	1948	Figueres's armed revolt	1949	new constitution	1
Baltic Republics (Latvia, Estonia, Lith.)	1990, 1991	Independence	1990, 1991	independence	1
Two to five years					
USSR	1989	democratic election of soviets	1991	dissolution of the USSR into republics	9
Poland	1989	Solidarity wins majority	end of 1990	Lech Walesa president	2
France	1848	crisis of confidence in government	1851	established 2nd empire	2
Yugoslavia	1941	German defeat of monarchy	1953	Stalin's death	3
Grenada	1979	NJM takes power from Gairy	1983	U.S. invasion	4
Haiti (independence)	1800	ex-slave army gains control	1804	independence, Dessalines takes power	4
Algeria	1958	GPRA provisional government	1962	independence	4
Czechoslovakia	1989	communist government resigned, Havel elected	1993	republic broke up	4
Russia (1917)	1917	Tsar abdicated	1921	Bolshevik victory in Civil Wars	4
Greece	1928	Russian defeat of Ottomans	1933	independence under King Otho	5
Iran (constitutional)	1906	formation of Majlis	1911	Russian threat closes down Majlis	5
Six to ten years					
Irish	1917	Sinn Fein majority in Clare-by	1923	treaty with England	6
Romania	1989	Ceausescu flees	1996	election replaces Iliescu	7

continued

185

Table 9.1 continued

	Regime collapse	Beginning event	New state	Ending event	# years
Albania	1991	elections	1998	election of Prime Minister Majko	7
Bulgaria	1989	dictator Todo Zhivkov abdicates	1997	decisive victory of UDF	8
South Africa	1985	government declares state of emergency	1994	1st democratic elections-Mandela president	9
Haiti (democratic)	1986	Baby Doc flees	1995	new elections, Preval president	9
Cuba	1952	Batista coup d'etat	1961	Castro regime repulses Bay of Pigs attack	9
Guatemala	1944	dictator Ubico y Castaneda toppled	1954	Castillo Armas replaces Arbenz	10
Eleven to twenty years					
Nicaragua	1979	FSLN triumph over Somoza	1990	Violeta Chomorro (UNO) elected president	11
France	1789	convocation of the Estates-General	1801	Concordat of 1801	12
Puritan	1648	king executed, republic established	1660	monarchy restored	12
United States	1776	Declaration of Independence	1789	Government under the new Constitution	13
Ethiopia	1974	Haile Selassie overthrown	1991	Mengistu deposed, EPRDF in power	17
Dutch Batavian	1795	Orangists driven out	1813	French driven out	18
Mozambique	1975	independence	1994	multiparty elections	19
Twenty to thirty years					
Eritrea	1974	Haile Selassie overthrown	1997	constitution ratified	23
Cambodia	1975	CPK defeats Lon Nol regime	1998	Hun Sen Prime Minister	23
Indonesia	1942	Japanese occupation	1966	Gen. Suharto's coup	24
Angola	1975	MPLA proclaims independence	2000	decisive power shift to MPLA	25
Mexico	1911	Diaz overthrown	1940	Cardenas oil nationalization stands	29

More than thirty years

Bolivia	1934	end of civilian oligarchy	1964	MNR loses control	30
Afghanistan	1973	Daud Kahn topples King Zaher	2003	new government of President Karzai	30
Vietnam	1945	Japanese overthrow French	1976	Socialist Republic of Vietnam	31
India	1935	electoral reform	1971	formation of Bangladesh	36
Benin	1960	independence	1996	President Kerekou elected	36
Netherlands Revolt	1572	military command offered to Orange	1609	independence	37
China	1911	Republican revolution	1949	PRC established	38
Ghana	1951	CPP wins majority in Legislature	1993	4th Republic under Rawlings	42

BY REGIONS

Africa

Algeria	1958	GPRA provisional government	1962	independence	4
Angola	1975	MPLA proclaims independence	2000	decisive power shift to MPLA	25
Benin	1960	independence	1996	President Kerekou elected	36
Eritrea	1974	Haile Selassie overthrown	1997	constitution ratified	23
Ethiopia	1974	Haile Selassie overthrown	1991	Mengistu deposed, EPRDF in power	17
Ghana	1951	CPP wins majority in Legislature	1993	4th Republic under Rawlings	42
Mozambique	1975	independence	1994	multiparty elections	19
South Africa	1985	government declares state of emergency	1994	1st democratic elections-Mandela president	9
Zanzibar (Tanzania)	Jan. 1964	Okello's popular coup	Apr. 64	form Tanzania w/ Tanganyika	<1

Eastern Europe

Albania	1991	elections	1998	election of Prime Minister Majko	7
Baltic Republics	1990, 1991	independence	1990, 1991	independence	1
Bulgaria	1989	dictator Todo Zhivkov abdicates	1997	decisive victory of UDF	8
Czechoslovakia	1989	communist government resigned, Havel elected	1993	republic split (Czech and Slovak Republics)	4
East Germany	Oct. 1989	Krenz replaces Honecker	July 1990	unification	<1
Greece	1928	Russian defeat of Ottomans	1933	independence under King Otho	5

continued

Table 9.1 continued

	Regime collapse	Beginning event	New state	Ending event	# years
Hungary	Oct. 1956	Nagy renamed Prime Minister	Nov. 1956	Red Army crushed revolution	<1
Poland	1989	Solidarity wins majority	end of 1990	Lech Walesa president	2
Romania	1989	Ceausescu flees	1996	election replaces Iliescu	7
Russia (1917)	1917	tsar abdicates	1921	Bolshevik victory	4
USSR	1989	democratic election of soviets	1991	dissolution of the USSR into republics	2
Yugoslavia	1941	German defeat of monarchy	1953	Stalin's death	4
Western Europe					
Dutch Batavian	1795	Orangists driven out	1813	French driven out	18
France	1789	convocation of the Estates-General	1801	Concordat of 1801	12
France	1830	Charles X removed	1830	Louise-Philippe "King of the French"	<1
France	1848	crisis of confindence in government	1851	2nd empire established	3
Irish	1917	Sinn Fein majority in Clare-by	1923	treaty with England	6
Netherlands Revolt	1572	military command offered to Orange	1609	independence	37
Puritan	1648	king executed, republic established	1660	monarchy restored	12
Latin America					
Bolivia	1934	end of civilian oligarchy	1953? 1964?	64-MNR loses control	30
Costa Rica	1948	Figueres's armed revolt	1949	new constitution	1
Cuba	1952	Batista coup d'etat	1961	Castro regime repulses Bay of Pig attack	9
Guatemala	1944	dictator Ubico y Castaneda toppled	1954	Castillo Armas replaced Arbenz	10

Mexico	1911	Diaz overthrown	1940	Cardenas oil nationalization stands	29
Nicaragua	1979	FSLN triumph over Somoza	1990	Violeta Chomorro (UNO) elected president	11

East Asia

Cambodia	1975	CPK defeats Lon Nol regime	1998	Hun Sen Prime Minister	23
China	1911	Republican revolution	1949	PRC established	38
Vietnam	1945	Japanese overthrow French	1976	Socialist Republic of Vietnam	31

South Asia

Afghanistan	1973	Daud Kahn topples King Zaher	2003	new government of President Karzai	30
Bangladesh	1971	independence	1971	independence	<1
India	1935	electoral reform	1971	formation of Bangladesh	36
Indonesia	1942	Japanese occupation	1966	Gen. Suharto's coup	24
Iran (constitutional)	1906	formation of Majlis	1911	Russian threat closes down Majlis	5
Iran (Islamic)	1979	Shah leaves	1979	Khomeini forms Islamic Republic	<1
Philippines	Feb. 1986	Marcos flees	Feb. 1986	election of Corazon Aquino	<1

Carribean

Grenada	1979	NJM takes power from Gairy	1983	US invasion	4
Haiti (democratic)	1986	Baby Doc flees	1995	new elections, Preval president	9
Haiti (independence)	1800	ex-slave army gains control	1804	independence, Dessalines takes power	4

a significant threat to its existence and reaches a point where the basic structure of state-society relations have been settled. We recognize that acceptance of such states may remain contingent, but we accept the lack of major *overt* internal challenges as sufficient. Those who differ with our choices can then modify this table as they see fit, and see if that affects our results.

What we find is that the median time span to consolidate a postrevolutionary state is not excessive—only eight years. This suggests that new states can be built fairly rapidly. However, the *mean* average time span to a consolidated postrevolutionary state is somewhat higher: 12 years and 8 months, to be exact. This is because there has been an enormous range of time spans to consolidation, from less than one year to more than forty, with more than a dozen cases involving several decades before a newly stable state was created.

There is, perhaps unexpectedly, no clear pattern in time to consolidation by region or time-period. Short- and long-time cases are found in Africa, Asia, Europe, and Latin America, and from the early nineteenth to the late twentieth centuries. What most people consider to be the "major" social revolutions had widely varied time spans before postrevolutionary states were fully consolidated (or terminated); these are laid out in table 9.2, ranging from the briefest (Iran 1979) to nearly the very longest (China 1911). The mean time span (18.3 years) is somewhat longer for these major social revolutions than for all cases, however, suggesting that a larger degree of upheaval also requires a longer time span to reconsolidate state power.

One might think that authoritarian regimes consolidate more rapidly, but we find that is not the case. The communist and dictatorial

Table 9.2 Major social revolutions' time-span to consolidation

Country and year revolution began	*Years to postrevolutionary consolidated state (state faces no further violent challenges to its authority)*
France 1789	12
Mexico 1910	29
China 1911	38
Russia 1917	4
Cuba 1952	9
Bolivia 1954	30
Nicaragua 1979	11
Iran 1979	<1
Vietnam 1945	31

consolidations took from short periods (1 year in Iran and 4 years in Russia) to very long spans (31 years in Vietnam and 38 years in China). Similarly, some democratic state consolidations took place rapidly (Philippines 1986, Hungary and the Baltic republics in the 1980s); others took much longer—Haiti (1986) and Nicaragua (1979) taking more than a decade to establish democratic regimes following the overthrow of their dictators (indeed with the recent ouster of President Aristide in Haiti, one could argue that the Haitian revolution against the Duvaliers has yet to be consolidated).

The biggest obstacle to postrevolutionary state consolidation is clearly civil war. Where civil wars are absent or relatively brief, new regimes are consolidated very quickly. This was the situation in almost all of the regimes that consolidated in five years or less. Where regimes consolidated in six to ten years, we find sustained factional fighting, but not quite at the level of major civil wars. However, for regimes that took longer than ten years to consolidate, all of their revolutions were marked by lengthy and wide-ranging civil wars—from the Puritan and Netherlands Revolts to the Afghan and Chinese Revolutions. In a number of these cases, external wars combined with civil wars, or external support sustained civil war combatants. Often foreign intervention fueled or sustained these conflicts, as in the Netherlands, Afghanistan, China, Vietnam, and many other cases.

In some sense, this is a tautological finding—states experiencing lengthy and wide-ranging civil wars are by definition not "consolidated." Yet the contrast with foreign wars is striking. Revolutionary states are often quite good at meeting external threats, and wars that are mainly foreign-inspired (even if based on émigrés and exiles), rather than drawing on deep internal opposition, often strengthen new revolutionary states, and do so in short order. One can think of Iran's war against Iraq, Cuba's repulsion of the Bay of Pigs invasion, and even the White opposition to the Bolshevik's Red Army as civil wars that had greater foreign than domestic support. Only where indigenous opponents of the new regime are fairly numerous and well-entrenched does foreign support seem to be able to sustain postrevolutionary civil conflicts. These data make it clear that while Charles Tilly has argued that "wars make states," it is not that simple. In the case of postrevolutionary state-consolidation, ongoing or recurrent *civil* wars can delay the consolidation of states for many years, even decades.

Once this has occurred, however, the postrevolutionary elite can begin the task of constructing a new system of rule. This chapter now examines the factors involved in this process.

Requisites for a New State

Max Weber pointed out long ago that state authority, can be built on at least three different foundations: charismatic authority, patrimonial authority (personal authority buttressed by patron/client relationships and personal rewards that is based on some form of traditional legitimacy), or rational-bureaucratic authority. In a revolution, leaders usually draw initially on charismatic authority, but they realize that for the revolution to last, they must institutionalize that authority by building new state structures on patrimonial or rational-bureaucratic lines.

These are of course Weberian "ideal types." In reality, postrevolutionary regimes may mix or shift among these types. For example, in Cuba, even 46 years after the revolution of 1959, Castro's revolutionary charisma continues to be a pillar of the regime's authority, despite its rational-bureaucratic institutionalization in a national communist party apparatus. In Iraq, although the socialist Ba'athist party quickly established a rational-bureaucratic regime to replace the overthrown Hashemite monarchy, Saddam Hussein captured the regime and turned it into a more patrimonial system of rule dependent on his personal wishes and treating Iraqis from his home-region of Tikrit as a favored elite.

Rather than focusing only on the type of authority undergirding a state, it is useful to note that a state must also meet certain functional prerequisites and to recognize that charismatic, patrimonial, and rational-bureaucratic authority need to be deployed in a manner to meet these requisites. First, state leaders must assure the loyalty and cooperation of key elites. Otherwise, the state will be ineffective and undermined by competing power centers in the society. Second, they must assure the financial resources to maintain its civil service, military, police, and other employees; pay its debts; and carry out its expected responsibilities. Third, state leaders must be able to command or compel the obedience of the population in regard to following the law, paying taxes, and, in extremis, defending the new state. These three conditions are the requisites of a stable government. Until a revolutionary regime has secured these requisites, one cannot say that a stable new state has been created. But even these requisites tell us little of the precise *structure* and *behavior* of the state.

In regard to structure, what distinguishes the modern state—one that can be most effective in stimulating development by resource allocation and/or enforcement of market norms throughout society—is a high level of what Michael Mann (1986, 2004) has called "infrastructural" power. Infrastructural power is the ability of a state to obtain and direct material resources and mobilize populations for specific ends; it is the ability to act throughout society and redistribute and redirect resources and actions. As a rough measure of infrastructural power, we can observe that in premodern states with low infrastructural power the central government almost never obtained revenues of more than 10 percent of GDP. By contrast, in modern states with high infrastructural power government revenues tend to be at least 20 percent of GDP, and commonly rise to 50 percent (and in socialist states even higher).

Modern states control a vast apparatus of millions of officials and state employees. Such states therefore can deploy numerous bodies of officials who are capable of intervening in the behavior of people, and the distribution of resources in society, down to the level of ordinary individuals, a power lacking in premodern states. However, it requires extensive mobilization and coordination of cadres of officials, and sufficient resources to pay a vast officialdom.

In regard to behavior, a second distinguishing characteristic of the fully modern state is a low level of what Mann (1986, 2004) has called "despotic power." Despotic power is the ability of state leaders to act arbitrarily to reward or punish individuals and groups throughout society; it is the opposite of the impersonal rule of law.

High despotic power exists in the absence of such checks on arbitrary state actions as a legal code that effectively limits the scope of executive actions and guarantees the security of individuals and groups against state action (e.g., an effectively enforced bill of rights); an effective and independent judiciary that can overturn executive actions; an effective and independent legislature that can stymie or alter executive actions by withholding cooperation and funds, and autonomous federal or nongovernmental organizations that can mobilize people and resources through institutionalized and protected actions to effectively influence political decisions and outcomes in opposition to the central regime. Traditional and dictatorial regimes generally have a great deal of despotic power; indeed, lacking the infrastructural power to reshape society and extract extensive resources, such regimes often rely on exhibitions of despotic power to overawe potential opponents and to create elite and popular allegiance.

Of course, such despotic power is often inconsistent with enforcement of impersonal market norms. Some despotic states have chosen to enforce laws impersonally and thus to sustain large and vital markets (e.g., the Roman Empire under the Antonines, or China under the Kangxi emperor). In addition, states with despotic power can sometimes "force-feed" certain kinds of economic growth through forced allocation of investment. However, most often states with high levels of despotic power engage in favoritism toward cronies or dependents and harshly discipline ideological or political opponents. Such states are generally not favorable to long-term growth as their arbitrary and unchecked power is potentially hostile to the long-term investment and security of property needed for sustained long-term growth (North 1990). Instead, corruption and/or patrimonialism tend to dominate states in which despotic power is high.

In assessing the success of revolutionary state building, we thus wish to address three questions: (1) How rapidly are revolutionary regimes able to secure the requisites to establish a stable state? (2) What degree of infrastructural power is generally wielded by revolutionary states, and how rapidly is it acquired? and (3) To what degree is despotic power checked or produced in revolutionary regimes, and how long does it take to substantially reduce the despotic power of state rulers?

Revolutionary leaders, of course, cannot merely wave a magic wand labeled "authority" and create stable state institutions. These must be crafted from the resources at hand, and with attention to the domestic and international conditions and pressures facing their society. Fortunately, revolutionary leaders never start from a *tabula rasa*; rather, they in almost all cases are able to draw on resources inherited from the old regime.

Resources for State Building 1: The Civil Service and the Military

The first resource for revolutionary state building is the civil service of the old regime. The more developed, centralized, and professional the civil service of the old regime, the more readily the new regime can utilize it for rebuilding the state. On the other hand, the more patrimonial and personally tied to the leadership of the old regime is the civil service, the more likely it is that the new regime will find the loyalty of the old civil service questionable, and the more likely its members are to flee from the revolutionary state.

To be sure, even a fairly professional bureaucratic officialdom inherited from the old regime may be committed to certain policies, and may seek to steer the new regime toward supporting them. Yet while such efforts may affect the ability of the new regime to carry out certain policies, they generally do not threaten the authority or stability of the new state. It is mainly where the old officialdom was recruited and promoted on the basis of principles that were overturned by the revolution, or was chosen mainly for their personal loyalty to the old regime leadership, that major problems in continuity of the bureaucracy arise.

Thus, for example in France in 1789, those government officials who had been chosen and promoted for merit (many of whom were sympathetic to the revolutionaries) were available to work with the new regime, while those officials who had been chosen for noble rank and/or through personal patronage from the court joined the émigrés and fled. In the French revolutions of 1830 and 1848, however, the government officialdom was sufficiently developed in its professional service that almost all officials could be retained except for the immediate followers of Charles X and Louis Philippe (Woloch 1995).

By contrast, in Iran in 1979, the officialdom was so strongly associated with the regime of the Shah that almost all officials fled. In this case, the new regime drew upon an alternative hierarchical body of trained professionals, the clergy of the Shi'a Islamic faith. Although not a unified body in the sense of a civil service hierarchy (there were a number of Ayatollahs, each with their own circle of followers), the Shi'ite clergy nonetheless constituted a sufficient body of trained professionals that they could be called upon to staff key government positions. To be sure, the Iranian clergy had no expertise in economic policy and other such technical matters; the results of their domination of the government were thus predictably dismal for Iran's economy. Indeed, the dilemma for revolutionary governments in state reconstruction is how to weigh ideological conformity and loyalty to revolutionary ideals versus technical competence in recruitment of state officers and employees. Where too much weight is placed on the former (as in Maoist China as well as the Islamic Republic of Iran), the performance of the government suffers.

In some cases, as in Russia in 1917, the new regime needed to rely on the technical expertise of the old regime staff, but the patrimonial aspects of the old regime were such that they could not count on the professional loyalty of the old regime officials. The new regime then instituted a "dual government," with ideologically loyal commissars appointed to oversee the expert officials held over from the old regime in their work, and to report back to the revolutionary leadership on the latter's actions. This expedient, however, became a fixed pattern and resulted in the wasteful inefficiency of having a parallel hierarchy of party officials overseeing nonparty managers and technocrats throughout the life of the Soviet Union.

In other cases with a long, drawn-out guerrilla struggle in which the revolutionary forces have established a substantial base of operations in one region of the country, the guerrillas may have developed their own cadres of trained officials and simply replace most of the old regime officials with their own. Maoist China is an excellent example. However, even in this case the extent of China was so vast that many officials of the old Kuomintang regime remained and were employed by the Chinese Communist State. Only when the latter felt it had enough cadres to dispense with the old officials were the latter "outed," publicly shamed, and often dismissed and sentenced to reeducation facilities.

A second major resource for state building is, perhaps oddly, the military forces of the old regime. In most cases, the military—especially the enlisted personnel, noncommissioned officers, and lower-ranking officers—is the most professional body in the old regime, and can be readily reorganized and melded with the armed forces (if any) of the revolutionaries. Indeed, the lower officer and enlisted ranks are often sympathetic to revolutionary movements. Thus the bulk of the old-regime army is rarely dismissed or destroyed in a revolution; instead it is reorganized, and led by officers newly promoted from the middle officer ranks who have joined the revolutionary movement. Or where the revolutionary forces have themselves previously been organized for a guerrilla or civil war, the victorious revolutionary forces will place members of their own forces as officers and key subordinates in a reorganized military that includes members of the old regime.

Indeed, it is often professional military officers who have led popular revolutions, from Gamel Abdul Nasser in Egypt and Mustapha Kemal in Turkey to Simon Bolivar and George Washington in the Latin American and United States Independence Revolutions. In such cases, a faction of the military forces becomes a primary instrument of the revolution itself, and can provide security for the revolutionary leaders and the new state until civilian institutions are established. In many such cases (notably in Egypt after Nasser) former military men continue to dominate the highest positions in the government long after the revolution.

To be sure, in some cases the military (or factions thereof) are sufficiently politicized and tainted by patrimonial ties to the old regime that they cannot function effectively under the command of the revolutionary regime. Thus in the Philippines under Corazon Aquino, after the revolution that toppled the Marcos regime, renegade members of the armed forces repeatedly attempted military coups. U.S. forces intervened to protect the new regime while Aquino purged the officer corps. In some cases, as in the Bolivian Revolution of 1952, even efforts to purge and reconstruct a professional army failed to create a force subordinate to the regime; instead, conservative military officers eventually succeeded in gaining control over a weak revolutionary regime. Thus, as with the civil service, the degree of prior centralization and professionalization of the military determines the speed and effectiveness with which it can be used by a new, revolutionary regime in building a new state.

Resources for State Building 2: Human and Cultural Capital

As Jonathan Kelley and Herbert Klein (2003) have pointed out, one thing that a revolution does not destroy is the general level of human capital accumulated in the population. Although skilled individuals may perish in the revolutionary struggle, the broad base of the population, their literacy, their experience in agriculture and technical pursuits, and for many even their attitude toward the state, are not lost when governments change.

However, in almost all revolutions, the degree of human capital in the population at large has been quite low. In agrarian bureaucracies and most military dictatorships, a small elite of educated clerical, business, military, and professional elites has rested upon a mass of illiterate peasants, and a smaller group of urban or factory workers. Nonetheless, this does not seem to have been an impediment to state building. Whether in Soviet Russia, Communist Cuba, and Maoist China, or in Napoleonic France, Mexico under the Party of Institutionalized Revolution (PRI), or Nicaragua under the Sandinistas, relatively small cadres of skilled military or party elites were able to mold revolutionary states by drawing on the revolutionary zeal of their followers and the coercive force of their military.

Conversely, high human capital did not prevent adverse consequences of revolution. In all probability, the two most human-capital rich societies to experience revolutions were Germany in 1918 and the Soviet Union in 1991. (Hungary, Czechoslovakia, Germany, and Poland were also human-capital rich in 1989–1991, but their revolutions were highly dependent on changes in the Soviet Union.) Yet in Germany, this advantage did not prevent the conflict after the overthrow of Kaiser's government in 1918 between two highly educated and professional groups—the professional military and heavy industrialists on the one hand, and social democratic politicians on the other. Divisions within the German government helped lead to the policy failures of hyperinflation in the 1920s, depression in the 1930s, and the rise of Nazi dictatorship. In the Soviet Union, although the revolution to unseat communist rule succeeded and indeed was prominently led by distinguished scientists, professionals, and managers, these great human-capital resources did not prevent a precipitous decline in the economy and life spans in Russia from 1989 to 1999, fierce ethnic wars in Chechnya and Armenia, and a whittling away of freedom of the press and opposition.

The ability to build from revolutionary zeal points us to a factor more important than human capital, namely the cultural capital available to the revolutionary leadership. By this we do not mean personal cultural capital, in Bourdieu's sense of individual cultural accomplishments that indicate a high level of personal status (1990). Rather, we mean the ability of the new revolutionary state to draw upon widely recognized and resonant symbols of opposition and renewal to inspire and win the confidence of revolutionary masses (Foran 1997).

One of the chief difficulties in state building is to build enthusiastic support for the government among its critical supporters—the elites in the military and civil service who enforce its authority and implement its policies. A second problem is to win the loyalty of popular groups, so as not to require coercion to obtain obedience. The use of symbolic and cultural capital as a source of charismatic revolutionary authority can stand in for personal charisma and act to more broadly bind the revolutionary leadership and population. In England's Puritan Revolution, for example, religious imagery was used to justify the discipline and goals of Cromwell's army. In France, revolutionaries initially relied on symbols borrowed from Republican Rome to inspire the classically educated and urbanized elites; they then turned to populist images of liberty (Hunt 1992). Elsewhere, modern revolutionary movements have drawn on prior revolutionary traditions. The Nicaraguan "Sandinistas" took their name from the popular hero of Nicaraguan rebellion against the United States 60 years earlier; similarly the "Zapatistas" of Chiapas, Mexico, took their name from a major leader of the Mexican Revolution of 1910.

By contrast, the Bolsheviks lacked any such symbolic tie to the Russian populace, with the exception of industrial workers who identified with the Marxist ideology of building a workers' "utopia." To extract resources from the peasantry in the 1930s for industrialization, the revolutionary regime was forced to rely on brutal coercion until victory in World War II gave the Communist Party a new lease of life as the defender of the Fatherland in "The Great Patriotic War." This allowed the party to identify with Russian patriotism for at least a generation. In China, Mao's communist party similarly lacked any symbolic ties to the Chinese past, and had to generate their own symbolic capital through holidays, Mao's little Red Book, and repeated efforts to renew revolutionary enthusiasms through rituals of revolutionary activity (from reenactments of the Long March to the Cultural Revolution).

Perhaps the most potent cultural capital lies in nationalist symbols of group identity and their repression by colonial or authoritarian regimes. Thus the traditions of Shi'a Islam were a potent symbolic as well as organizational resource for Ayatollah Khomeini's Islamic revolution, as were claims of throwing off the "Norman Yoke" for English opponents of the Crown. In a variety of anti-imperial and anticolonial revolutions in Africa, Latin America, and Asia, it was the leaders who could best embody nationalist aspirations who were able to build revolutionary coalitions and sustain them into state building.

Resources for State Building 3: Visionary and Pragmatic Leadership

It has been fashionable since Theda Skocpol's (1979) great work on states and social revolutions to focus on structural causes for revolutions to the detriment of the role of leadership. Yet more recently an appreciation has reemerged for the critical role of leadership in revolutions (Aminzade et al. 2001; Selbin 1993). The importance of leadership is perhaps even more evident in state-building. Often, the old regime has perished due to military or fiscal problems of its own, rather than as a result of brilliant revolutionary leadership. Nonetheless, once the old states fall, a new state must be rebuilt, and there lies a severe test of the breadth and competence of revolutionary leaders.

Failures of revolutionary leadership in state building are all too common, even among leaders successful in starting revolutions. Francisco Madero, who successfully challenged Porfirio Díaz in Mexico, was quickly overthrown by a military coup, and it took the ability of generals Carranza and Obregon to forge a stable state. The failure of Kerensky in Russia after the fall of the Romanovs is a byword for revolutionary futility, although the New Jewel movement under Maurice Bishop did little better. Sun-Yat Sen was able to inspire a revolution against the Imperial government of China, but not to consolidate it.

By contrast, the ability of leaders such as Lenin and Trotsky in Russia, Castro in Cuba, and Ho Chi Minh in Vietnam to triumph over enormous odds was stunning. Not only did they overthrow their old regimes, they succeeded in building states capable of waging war and surviving against numerous challenges—both internal and external—for generations. Although all of these leaders were autocrats who ruled through one-party states, successful revolutionary consolidation can also take democratic form. In the United States, the Philippines, and South Africa, the leadership of George Washington, Corazon Aquino, and Nelson Mandela respectively were essential to overcoming factional conflicts and consolidating democratic outcomes. Indeed, it is hard to imagine democracy having survived in those new regimes without the moral leadership and dedication to democracy provided by those individuals.

Leadership in revolutions—as is true of leadership more generally—has two major components. First, creating a revolutionary coalition and fanning the enthusiasm of numerous supporters requires visionary and inspirational leadership, usually based in effective writing, oratory, or self-sacrifice, which can persuade people to risk leaving their normal routines to support revolution. Second, creating an effective and successful revolutionary movement and revolutionary state requires pragmatic organizational leadership, which can ensure that troops are supplied and properly deployed, that civilian officials are properly chosen and organized, and that funds are properly raised and spent.

In most great revolutions, such capabilities have been shared by partners in revolutionary leadership: in Russia, Lenin was the visionary and Trotsky the architect of the Red Army and its victories; in the American Revolution, Adams, Jefferson, and Franklin were the visionary writers and theorists and Washington and Hamilton the practical men of military and financial affairs; in France, Robespierre and Sieyes were the writers and orators with Napoleon the organizational and military genius; in Cuba, Fidel Castro was the inspirational leader and his brother Raúl Castro the cool organizer; in China, Mao played the visionary and Li Peng, Zhou Enlai, and Deng Xiaoping the pragmatic organizers; and in Mexico, Zapata and Villa served as the popular leaders, but Obregon and Carranza the pragmatic builders of the Constitutionalist armies and the Mexican revolutionary state. In some cases, both qualities are found in a single individual—Lenin was also a ruthless pragmatic organizer, and in Iran, Ayatollah Khomeini was both a masterful organizer and a brilliant propagandist of the Islamic revolution.

As is obvious from this recounting, it is the pragmatic leaders who eventually succeeded in consolidating power. Even in China, where Mao struggled desperately to keep his visionary and idealistic image of revolution alive, and repeatedly purged his practical partners for being excessively pragmatic and nonideological, it was Deng Xiaoping who finally came to shape the Chinese present. In the Czech republic, it was not Vaclav Havel's inspirational vision of a humanistic society, but Vaclav Klaus's vision of a compact national state that triumphed.

Where revolutions have had only visionary leadership, but lacked strong pragmatic leadership as well, those revolutions have foundered or swung toward uncontrolled extremism and burned out. For example, in Haiti, while Jean-Bertrand Aristide helped lead the opposition to the dictatorial Duvalier family and became Haiti's first president, he was never able to build an effective state and his own regime was overthrown; not once but twice. In Cambodia, the Khmer Rouge leaders led an extremist revolution that, following visionary belief rather than practical sense, came into fatal conflict with Vietnam and was thus short-lived. In Afghanistan, the idealistic but poorly executed effort of the Marxist regime to impose Communism on a tribal and deeply religious society produced an overwhelming Islamic counterrevolution. In Grenada, Maurice Bishop's idealistic plans for his "New Jewel Revolution" were overturned by his power-hungry Deputy Prime Minister, Bernard Coard, whose clumsy efforts to create a brutal Stalinist regime paved the way for a U.S. invasion to end the revolution.

In sum, having the right kind, and balance, of leadership skills within the revolutionary leadership is essential for effective state building in the new regime.

Resources for State Building 4: External Support

External intervention can be a valuable tool in state building. Whether it was the Soviet Union's essential military support for Mao's Chinese Revolution, or U.S. support for the Constitutionalists at a crucial juncture in the Mexican Revolution, external support can provide not only material resources, but also frameworks for new states. The family resemblances among North Korea, Vietnam, and Laos reveal a common heritage of Soviet guidance in state construction.

It might be thought that external pressure would also easily undo the early state building that follows revolutions. Yet that is not the case; instead external pressure seems to intensify nationalist support for a new revolutionary regime, and temper it in the fires of national crisis. The French Revolutionary regime became more centralized and powerful in the course of fighting the Vendée rebellion and external wars in Europe. The Iranian regime grew stronger, not weaker, in fighting a ten-year war against Iraq. U.S. pressure and sanctions were unable to overturn the Cuban revolution, to reverse the course of the Vietnamese Revolution, or to quickly undo the Sandinista regime in Nicaragua. The Soviet Union was unable to overcome the Islamic revolution in Afghanistan. Revolutionary states, even recent ones, can thus be quite resilient.

Nonetheless, overwhelming military victory *can* undo or reverse revolutionary state building. The defeat of Napoleon in France, of Hungarian uprisings in 1848 and 1956, of Czechoslovakia in 1968, and of Communards in Paris in 1871, testify to the ability of complete military victory and occupation to quench incipient revolutions. Yet such cases are the exception, not the rule. In most cases, external powers that have tried to act against new revolutionary regimes have paid the greater price (Halliday 1999). The combination of mass mobilization, tapping of nationalist symbols and ideology to inspire and unify support, and the emergence of highly pragmatic as well as visionary leadership, all of which generally attend successful revolutions, makes those new revolutionary regimes very difficult to overcome from outside.

Obstacles to Revolutionary State Building

Alexis de Tocqueville (1978) was right—the more the old regime has centralized its power and reduced that of local and autonomous authorities, the easier it is to build a powerful revolutionary state on the rubble of the old regime.

The greatest obstacle to revolutionary state building is the presence of powerful and autonomous elites remaining from the old regime who oppose the goals, financing, and organization of the new revolutionary regime. In France, conservative clerics and their followers in Brittany and other areas of western France created massive counterrevolutionary movements; so too did Federalist rebellions by municipal authorities in southern and western France seeking to maintain or increase their autonomy from Paris. In Russia, the "White" generals, loyal to the Tsar, who took their troops into opposition to the Bolshevik regime, threatened the life of the new government. In China, after the Republican revolution of 1911, local warlords remained sufficiently powerful to prevent reestablishment of a centralized government until the communist party triumph in 1949. In most cases, such local notables are eventually brought to heel and either replaced or subordinated to new revolutionary institutions. However, in some cases, as in Turkey after the Kemalist revolution of 1921, powerful local landlords not only retained autonomy but also were later able to capture control of the revolutionary institutions and limit further change (Trimberger 1978).

A second major obstacle to a stable revolutionary regime arises where prior religious, ethnic, or regional cleavages make it difficult to assemble various groups and regions into a single state under the authority of the revolutionary regime. To some degree, this factor may reflect the presence of prior elites left over from the old regime. But in other cases, such cleavages form the bases for new elites to emerge seeking to develop a newly autonomous power base.

Particularly when revolutions occur in multiethnic empires that have united diverse peoples, new nationalist leaders may emerge seeking to carve out independent nation-based regimes in resistance to the revolutionary state. In the anticommunist revolutions of 1989, not only did the

Soviet Empire fissure along nationalist lines, but even within the new Russian state, ethnic rebellion by Chechnya continued to challenge state authority. Czechoslovakia, shortly after its anticommunist revolution, split into the two states of Slovakia and the Czech Republic. Most tragic were the events in Yugoslavia, in which the initial efforts to replace Tito's communist regime, and secession by Croatia, Macedonia, and Slovenia, were soon followed by nationalist revolutions against Serbian/Yugoslav central authority in Bosnia and Kosovo. In all such cases, revolutionary action against the imperial regime led not merely to a revolutionary government taking over the empire, but to substantial territorial reshaping as parts of the old empire were lost. Even the Bolsheviks were unable to hold on to all the territories of the Tsarist empire, and their losses in the West resulted in new independent nations in eastern Europe and the Baltic region, which were not recovered until World War II. New revolutionary states thus may need to reduce their territories—often substantially—in order to consolidate their authority.

Revolution and New State Designs

The removal of old elites from power allows postrevolutionary leaders to implement reforms affecting the overall design of the state. Two major new designs for modern states—constitutional democracies and one-party states—were relatively late developments, appearing only in the eighteenth and twentieth centuries. Revolutions were crucial in the implementation and diffusion of both of these novel designs.

In chapter seven of this volume, Rueschemeyer points out that the roots of the modern state were planted in the eleventh century, when Roman law was adopted early in the Gregorian reforms of the Catholic Church as the basis for canon law. It was several more centuries before secular monarchs started selecting clerics with legal and administrative skills to staff their state administrations, and using university-trained administrators to develop their own legally shaped bureaucracies. Even then, as Ertman shows (chapter eight), in the major western and southern European states patrimonial nobilities retained their critical positions in local administration, the military, and consultative assemblies such as Britain's Parliament and the French Estates-General and provincial estates. Even in Germany and Russia, by the eighteenth century hereditary nobles had succeeded in softening the efforts of the Hohenzollern and Romanov rulers to mold totally bureaucratic civil and military machines by gaining sole authority on their estates and securing aristocratic dominance of the military officer corps.

The dominant role of these autonomous hereditary elites blocked the full implementation of modern impersonal bureaucracies. It was not until the French Revolution and the consequent Prussian Reform movement in the late eighteenth and early nineteenth centuries that the patrimonial features of national governments in Europe and America were swept away. In Russia, it would take the revolution of 1917 to overcome these obstacles. In Britain, despite an efficient and bureaucratic excise service developing in the seventeenth century, hereditary lords continued to play a dominant role in the government and military, shaping Parliament and policy, until the nineteenth-century reforms of Parliament and voting rights. Thus many centuries passed from the Gregorian model of Roman-law-based hierarchical bureaucracy as a template for governance to its full adoption by secular states. However, once the revolutionary movements of the eighteenth and nineteenth centuries swept away the autonomous power of the aristocratic elites, a fairly quick implementation of modern bureaucratic state structures could occur.

What Rueschemeyer and Ertman both overlook, however, is the further development of designs for the modern state, which was not merely a matter of increasing the degree of impersonal bureaucracy in the collection of revenue and the operations of administration. The patrimonial character of Europe's monarchies and empires—and those in the Middle East, China, and Latin America—was shaken by ideals of republican government or utopian party-based revolution. It was these revolutionary aims, based on new designs for state authority, and not merely efforts to rationalize and extend bureaucracy, that were key to overcoming entrenched patrimonial elites. Yet even these new, revolutionary designs took many decades to diffuse and to be implemented in various states.

Democratic institutions had been in severe decline in Europe since the sixteenth century. Indeed, the counterpart of an increasing role for church-trained administrators and their hierarchical bureaucratic vision of state structure in secular states was a decline in the role of democratic or republican institutions that had developed from medieval city councils, provincial self-governance, and rulers' counselors. From the suppression of the *Comuneros* in Spain, to the lassitude of the French provincial Estates and Estates-General, to the Prussian suppression of Estates in western Germany, to the efforts of Charles I and James II to rule without Parliament or subordinate it to royal will, the sixteenth and seventeenth centuries saw the spread of models of "enlightened absolutism" as the ideal for efficient and rational governance.

It was only in the late eighteenth century, after the death of William III and the increasingly powerful role of Parliament in British governance, and then far more importantly with the American and French Revolutions, that classical republican forms of government were recalled for the design of new national democratic institutions. The U.S. Constitution and the French Declaration of the Rights of Man and Citizen and subsequent constitutions, set off a wave of constitutional reform and revolution around the world.

Still, while efforts to rebuild states along constitutional lines spread throughout the nineteenth and twentieth centuries (the Revolutions of 1830 and 1848 in Europe, the Latin American independence movements of the 1820s, the constitutional/republican revolutions in Iran, Mexico, and China in 1905–1911, and the British reform movements of the 1820s and 1840s), such efforts faced entrenched opposition from both landed and military elites. In most regions, military leadership repeatedly interrupted the growth of democratic state designs. In large part, this was because the democracies faced severe obstacles to state building—many lacked pragmatic leadership, relying mainly on a vision of harmonious democracy; many faced conservative and entrenched autonomous landed elites who opposed democratization.

Thus by the 1950s, although the number of states operating as hereditary monarchies had dwindled to a handful, relatively few states had built effective republican/democratic states. Instead, the majority of the world's states were constructed as military or civilian dictatorships, or according to a new, twentieth-century design—the one-party state, in which a modern efficient hierarchical bureaucracy implemented the plans of an exclusive political elite organized as a "party" or corporate body.

This latter design—the one party-state—was developed with remarkable celerity by Lenin and the Bolsheviks in response to frustration with the slow development of worker power through gradual democratization in western Europe. Once the design was developed and publicized, it took some years to implement in Russia (total party dominance was relaxed—for pragmatic reasons—until Stalin's rule, and Trotsky's efforts to build the Red Army in tandem with cadres of party officials during the Russian civil wars were essential). Yet, once one-party rule was established in Russia, the model spread rapidly throughout Asia and Latin America and Africa, spawning revolutionary movements on all continents.

Not all one-party states were communist: populist and fascist party-states, based on a combination of patronage of supporters and harsh repression of opponents, also developed in early twentieth century in Europe, Latin America, and Asia, and in the later twentieth century in Africa, the

Middle East, and southeast Asia. Again it often took years or even decades to implement one-party states over the opposition of local elites. In some states, such as Afghanistan, the effort to implement a modern communist regime failed miserably; in others, such as Cambodia and Ethiopia, the revolutionary states overreached in their efforts to suddenly transform society and burned out in harsh internal conflicts.

To sum up, the design of modern states involved a small number of dramatic revisions that were quickly undertaken. Yet the implementation of these designs took centuries, and the time spans intervening between the development of new designs took a similar period. The Gregorian revolution developed the model of hierarchical meritocratic bureaucracy in a few decades in the eleventh century, drawing on Roman legal traditions to develop canon law. However, this model remained confounded with continued patrimonial/aristocratic authority throughout Europe until the late eighteenth century or early nineteenth century. It was only then that patrimonial and aristocratic dominance of the state apparatus was substantially reduced in the major European states, and a primarily meritocratic, bureaucratic state became the norm.

A key to this process was the development in the eighteenth century, by the Founding Fathers of the United States, of a constitutional form of government, drawing on classical republican forms of governance and ideals of citizenship, but modifying them to fit the needs of a large and diverse national state. Although the constitutional design was widely admired and imitated, most efforts at constitutional governance led to unstable states. It was only in the late twentieth century that many major states established stable governments on constitutional principles.

The one-party state was designed even more quickly by Lenin and the Bolsheviks, over a few years at the beginning of the twentieth century. This design was also widely imitated, and arguably spread more quickly and completely than any other state design. Yet, here too implementation was slow and sometimes unsuccessful.

In other words, the evolution of state designs, and their diffusion and implementation, has been a very slow process, more like the "punctuated equilibrium" of biological evolution than a steady process of rationalization. The primary modern state designs—constitutional and one-party states—arose only quite recently. Moreover, the implementation of those designs is still an ongoing process. Most nations of Africa, South Asia, and the Middle East, and many in Latin America, retain patrimonial government to this day, and many democracies and one-party states have been short-lived.

Revolutions, of course, played a crucial role in implementing these new state designs. But even though revolutions might rapidly change the principles of government, they have had mixed success in terms of building fully modern states.

The Structure and Behavior of Revolutionary States

The above analysis discusses how rapidly revolutionary states have been able to establish infrastructure making stable governance possible. In addition, the last section suggests that revolutions have affected the overall designs of states and thereby their very nature and behavior. Here we find a striking paradox. On the one hand, revolutions—especially major social revolutions—have been enormously successful in increasing the infrastructural power of the state. As Theda Skocpol (1979, 1994) has stressed, revolutions can draw on popular mobilization to increase state capacity substantially over that of their predecessor states. Both in extracting resources from society and in building military and bureaucratic organizations, revolutionary states tend to far outstrip the former regime. In this sense, revolutions have given a huge leap forward to states in regard to this element of building a modern state.

On the other hand, those same revolutions have produced one-party states or personalist dictatorships that often had even greater despotic power than the old regimes that they replaced. This amplification of despotic power created a tendency to renewed patrimonialism and corruption, and to sudden and arbitrary shifts in government actions. The result was that while revolutionary states gained the resources and vast officialdom to reshape society and promote rapid industrial growth, their despotic and arbitrary leadership often unraveled or wasted economic growth. While they exhibited a modern state *structure* in the degree of resources appropriated from society, and the deployment of a vast army of officials to regulate social life according to rules and regulations, revolutionary states rarely exhibited modern state behavior, insofar as they often found it difficult to regulate executive authority, or indeed to create any institutions capable of doing so.

The major revolutions that resulted in one-party states (Mexico, Russia, Cuba, China, Vietnam, and Iran) all fell victim in short order to patrimonialism and corruption (Mexico, Iran) or to the irrational whims of personalist dictators (Russia, Cuba, and China). In this respect, these states have still not become fully modern states in their behavior. Those revolutions that resulted in constitutional, multiparty states (the United States, France after 1870, the Philippines, the Baltics and eastern Europe in 1989–1991) have done much better in regard to checking executive authority. Yet in these cases, where economic development levels were low (the United

States and France in the eighteenth and nineteenth centuries, the Philippines in the twentieth) the development of high levels of state infrastructural power took many decades. It was only, as Reuschemeyer suggested in his chapter, where revolutions created constitutional regimes in countries with already relatively high levels of industrial development, that we see both the high infrastructural power *and* the low despotic power of the fully modern state in the wake of revolutionary change.

It is striking that for *all* of the major social revolutions listed in table 9.2, *none* except for France (1789) have yet produced a fully modern state with both high levels of infrastructural power and low levels of despotic power—and it took France well over a hundred years (until the late nineteenth century) to do so. Clearly, revolution may be a rapid way to implement new designs for states (including both modern constitutional and one-party state designs), and usually provides a rapid jump in state resources and infrastructural power. Yet we cannot, on the basis of the evidence, say that revolutions are a particularly rapid path to fully modern state creation. The tendency of revolutionary states to leave unchecked despotic power in the hands of state leaders works against the creation of the fully modern state, in which the impersonal authority of the laws takes precedence over the preferences of powerful individuals.

Conclusion

In the study of postrevolutionary state building, we can see the process of state building repeated in a diverse range of times and places. Rapid state building is possible in favorable circumstances. In particular, when a state can use a cadre of trained professional civil servants and military officers from the prior regime, when there is no sustained opposition to the new state from powerful autonomous elites, and where the state can secure financial resources to pay its officials and soldiers, new states can be erected in a few years, in some cases in a matter of months. Yet this is only where favorable conditions prevail.

Where a state must start from scratch to build an administrative and security apparatus; where a state lacks ready access to revenues, and in particular where autonomous elites oppose the new regime, consolidation can take decades. The most difficult circumstances for a new regime are when opposing internal forces are able to sustain a civil war against the new state, particularly if their opposition is sustained by external support. Aspiring states do not automatically prevail, or even dominate, in such conditions; at best their state-making efforts are set back for lengthy periods.

Revolutions do offer one major advantage for state building. Since the biggest obstacle to building new regimes (or making substantial changes in old ones) is opposition from entrenched autonomous elites, revolutions can utilize popular mobilization to either eliminate those elites, or their autonomy. Where successful, this can allow the relatively rapid construction of new political regimes. The downside risk, however, is that old elites will not be quickly overcome, but will raise domestic and international support to sustain a struggle against the new revolutionary states. In these cases, not only is state building delayed, but the costs in human lives can be extreme.

Most striking, however, is the way in which revolutions both accelerate and delay progress toward a modern, bureaucratic but rule-governed state. Revolutions, especially major social revolutions, have led to the rapid adoption of new designs for the organization and scope of state authority, and to vast increases in the bureaucratic and material resources that states can deploy to reshape society. Yet these revolutions also generally increased the despotic power of the new regimes, and thus led to arbitrary and personalist governance, rather than the impersonal rationality of a fully modern state. Perhaps surprisingly, this increased despotic power has often lasted many decades. Even where it is a party, and no longer a heroic revolutionary semi-deity that wields power, such parties tend to degenerate into patrimonial cliques, rather than become the basis for impersonal and rule-governed regimes.

Rueschemeyer argued that the state building process is lengthy in part because the operation of the modern impersonal state requires not merely the accumulation of resources for governance, but also the acquisition by elites and society of social habits regarding the relationships between state and society, and between state leaders and other officials, that involve the acceptance of *limited* and *rule-governed* behavior by state leaders and their officials. Revolutions may hasten the state's accumulation of resources for governance, but the dynamics of revolution—in which a small elite suddenly gains extensive power—often work against the acceptance of limited and rule-governed behavior by state leaders and officials.

Our investigation of revolutionary state building thus appears to support Rueschemeyer's view: even with revolutions, the creation of a fully modern state is a lengthy process, requiring a fundamental reshaping of attitudes and behaviors regarding governance, rather than merely an amplification of the material resources and institutions of state rule. With the exception of constitutional revolutions in the already-industrialized states, revolutions have often delayed the development of truly impersonal and rule-governed states. Revolutions may do part of the task of creating modern states, by implementing new state designs and eliminating the power of old elites. But they do only part—the process of limiting state authority takes rather longer, and appears to be the more difficult part of creating the modern, powerful, but rule-bound, state.

References

Aminzade, Ronald et al. 2001. *Silence and Voice in the Study of Contentious Politics*. New York: Cambridge University Press.

Bourdieu, Pierre. 1990. *In Other Words: Essays Towards a Reflexive Sociology*. Trans. M. Adamson. Stanford, CA: Stanford University Press.

Foran, John (ed.). 1997. *Theorizing Revolutions*. London: Routledge.

Halliday, Fred. 1999. *Revolution and World Politics: The Rise and Fall of the Sixth Great Power*. Durham, NC: Duke University Press.

Hunt, Lynn A. 1992. *The Family Romance of the French Revolution*. Berkeley: University of California Press.

Kelley, Jonathan and Herbert S. Klein. 2003. "Revolution and the Rebirth of Inequality: Stratification in Postrevolutionary Society." In *Revolutions: Theoretical, Comparative, and Historical Studies*, edited by J. Goldstone. Fort Worth, TX: Harcourt Brace Jovanovich.

Mann, Michael. 1986. *The Structure of Social Power, Vol. 1*. New York: Cambridge University Press.

———. 2004. *The Dark Side of Democracy: Explaining Ethnic Cleansing*. Cambridge: Cambridge University Press.

North, Douglas. 1990. *Institutions, Institutional Change and Economic Performance*. New York: Cambridge University Press.

Rady, Martyn. 1995. "1989." *The Slavonic and East European Review*, 73, 1: 111–116.

Selbin, Eric. 1993. *Modern Latin American Revolutions*. Boulder, CO: Westview Press.

Skocpol, Theda. 1979. *States and Social Revolutions*. Cambridge, UK: Cambridge University Press.

———. 1994. *Social Revolutions in the Modern World*. Cambridge, UK: Cambridge University Press.

Tocqueville, Alexis de. 1978. *The Old Regime and the French Revolution*. Trans. S. Gilbert. Gloucester, MA: Peter Smith.

Trimberger, Ellen Kay. 1978. *Revolution from Above: Military Bureaucrats and Development in Japan, Turkey, Egypt, and Peru*. New Brunswick, NJ: Transaction Books.

Woloch, Isser. 1995. *The New Regime: Transformations of the French Civic Order, 1789–1920s*. New York: W.W. Norton.

CHAPTER TEN

State Building in Korea: Continuity and Crisis

BRUCE CUMINGS

In the early twenty-first century, the hierarchy of advanced industrial nations remains quite similar to what it was at the end of the nineteenth century: the leading economy today, the United States, was the most productive industrial power then; the leading economy then, the United Kingdom, remains a powerful industrial economy today, its size roughly comparable to France and Italy; Germany is still the economic powerhouse of Central Europe, as it was then. A century ago, Japan's industrial prowess was just beginning to gain notice, however, and it would not become a major industrial power until the 1930s. A century ago, Korea had just begun to industrialize, something hardly anyone noticed, but today it is a major, fully industrialized country with state-of-the-art technology in many fields. Japan and Korea are striking examples of industrial development precisely because the new entrants to advanced industrial status are so few—or so familiar in their long-run continuity In 1900, a sage might have predicted this outcome for Japan, but no one but a clairvoyant would have picked Korea. South Korea's growth thus strikes observers as rapid, unusual, even miraculous. So how did it happen?

Generally speaking, there are two answers in the social science literature: for mainstream developmental economists, Korean growth began ca. 1960, when they "got their prices right" and market forces took over; leading from various comparative advantages in the world market, they began exporting textiles and light industrial products and quickly worked their way up the product cycle ladder to steel, autos, computers, and finally to state-of-the-art high-definition televisions. The second answer was nicely put by Alice Amsden: rapid growth began when Koreans "got prices wrong"(Amsden 1989) and in particular when the state began intervening in the market and directing industrial development—often against the advice of mainstream economists (who, for example, opposed Korea's move into heavy industries in the early 1970s). This second answer, however, remained grounded in recent history: Korea's "developmental state" is also a post-1960 phenomenon. Some studies push this history back to the 1930s, when Japan pioneered a forced-pace "late" industrialization that encompassed its colonies in Korea, Taiwan, and Manchuria, yielding a model that was particularly influential in South Korea (Woo 1991). But Korea is one of the oldest countries in the world, with a continuous presence on the same peninsula well back into antiquity. It therefore becomes an interesting case for the concerns of this volume, emphasizing that state building is inherently a long-term process.

Dietrich Rueschemeyer finds three reasons for this phenomenon: the growth of states involves both the development of institutions and of norms; it involves complex alignments of interests and the coordination of many different actors and units; and it embodies conflict, antagonism, winners, and losers, and long-term stalemates. The emergence of the European state took as much as a millennium, with many detours and little continuity; "proto-bureaucracies" began to emerge, but only very slowly did they take on the modern characteristics of Weberian bureaucracy. Central institutions often found themselves hamstrung by regional and local centers of power. Building the modern state is therefore a long and often incremental process, punctuated by unexpected and unpredicted crises.

The history of state building in Korea offers much testimony to support these insights, and some experience that does not. In this brief space and in broad sweeps, I want to isolate the following categories that long predate the presumed watershed year of 1960: (1) centuries of civil service and recruitment by merit; (2) the profound influence of education for socio-academic upward mobility; (3) tensions between the historically centralized state and local power; (4) a colonial experience that was unusually bureaucratic—"administrative colonialism"; (5) the continuity of the central state in South Korea after World War II; and (6) the crisis of war, revolution, and land reform in the same period. The state is not merely a domestic product, however, and Korean development during the colonial period and after 1945 cannot be understood apart from the political economy and security arrangements of the Northeast Asian region. Furthermore the roots of the basic conceptualization of the state in Japan and Korea go back to mid-nineteenth-century German thinking about state science (as opposed to political science) and national economy (as opposed to market economy) conceived in the context of the world economy (Cumings 1999). The modern state structures of the Northeast Asian region and the conceptions behind them have always been biased toward European continental theories and configurations of state behavior and political economy because of the "late" emergence in world time of this region's industrialization. Meanwhile, during this same long period of time, the Anglo-American configuration of states and markets or political economy, functioning under the name "liberal" (or now, neo-liberal) has had little influence in Northeast Asia. In other words, a strong and in times of crisis determining external regime has had far less impact than one would expect on the internal or domestic behavior of those countries inside the system. Finally, we briefly examine the Korean state in the past decade, as it was whipped by waves of democratization, crisis, and reform.

The Ancien Régime

A thumbnail sketch of the history of state building in Korea can at least impress upon us the fact of its extraordinary longevity. Centralized government emerged during the Silla Dynasty in the last half of the fifth century AD, as the capital at Kyongju became both an administrative and a marketing center. In the early sixth century, its leaders introduced plowing by oxen and built extensive irrigation facilities. Increased agricultural output was the result, enabling further political and cultural development including an administrative code in 520, a hereditary "bone-rank" system for designating elite status, and the adoption of Buddhism as the state religion around 535. In AD 682 Silla set up a national Confucian academy to train high officials, and later instituted a civil service exam system somewhat like that of the T'ang Dynasty, but with typically Korean hereditary restrictions on who could sit for the exams. Those hereditary requirements persisted down to the late nineteenth century, creating an aristocracy that was highly literate and merited, but less open to talent from below than was the Chinese bureaucratic system.

The civil service examinations constituted the core of Korean civilization, upon the outcome of which "hung preferment to office, a place in the sun and a name never to be forgotten."(Gale 1972, p. 181) For children, whose families could spare them from the fields, a regimen of study began when a child first acquired speech and did not end until he had reached the highest station his talents could afford him. Education meant socialization into Confucian norms and virtues that began in early childhood with the reading of the Confucian classics, something true for king and commoner alike, and cultivation of the skills of statecraft. The peak aspiration was to pass the highest level of exams and become a scholar-official, a person of unquestioned dignity and respect. Civil service was the most respected and sought after profession, making of the civil servant a stock character in Korean society long before the equivalent emerged in Europe—or more especially, Germany. In the modern period, the top universities funnel their best graduates into careers in government (or the *chaebol*, which are both business conglomerates and enormous bureaucratic organizations), much like Japan or France.

In spite of hereditary obstacles, long ago a remarkably strong cultural norm developed, focused on the education of the young as a means of family and communal upward mobility. This is testified to in numerous accounts by foreigners going back 400 years and more. In 1888, Percival Lowell (discoverer of the "canals" on Mars) remarked of Korean education, as compared to that of the West, "if the peaks of intellect rise less eminent, the plateau of general elevation stands higher" (Lowell 1888, p. 7). He was wrong about the "peaks," but right about the egalitarian belief, ultimately deriving from Confucian philosophy, in the inherent perfectibility of all humans. In the modern era, this norm focused on educating the entire population up to a high general level—a compulsory school system through the elementary level in the 1930s–1960s, and later including middle and high school levels—such that the broad Korean work force was better suited to industrial tasks than the population of many other countries, yielding a huge comparative advantage in human capital (Cumings 1997).

The long tradition of bureaucratic governance by scholar-officials, reaching pre-industrial peaks as high as anywhere else, was another essential background for building a modern state. As Etienne Balazs has argued, civil servants were also technocrats: their speciality was statecraft above all, and also agriculture, irrigation, hydraulic control of everything from rivers to lakes to reservoirs, military technology (armaments), even rockets (where, e.g., the Chinese excelled). The state was the embodiment of knowledge. Why should the state not play a major role in the economy? But the ancien régime's idea of what the state should do in the economy was hardly developmental: instead it sought to monopolize key commodities and to squelch enterprise that resisted state controls. Old Korea thus had an agrarian bureaucracy: it was bureaucratic because it possessed an elaborate procedure for entry to the civil service, a highly organized civil service itself, and a practice of administering the country from the center and from the top down. Unlike a feudal system Korea had strong central administration and many officials who ruled through a civilian bureaucracy, not through provincial lords who fused civil and military functions. But the system rested entirely upon an agrarian base, with weakly developed commerce, making it different from modern bureaucratic systems; breaking the hold of that base was essential to the emergence of a modern state in the twentieth century.

Conflict between bureaucrats seeking revenues for government coffers and landowners hoping to control tenants and harvests was a constant source of tension during the Chosôn Dynasty (1392–1910), and in this conflict over resources the landowners often won out. Theoretically owned by the state, private landed power was stronger and more persistent in Korea than in China. Korea had centralized administration, to be sure, but the ostensibly strong center was more often a facade concealing the reality of aristocratic power: "In fact," James Palais writes, "the social elite controlled the bureaucratic structure, kept it relatively weak, and used it to check royal authority." The rural aristocracy succeeded in blocking cadastral or land surveys for decades at a time—thus blocking the taxing powers of the state—with just a handful over several centuries (the state did major surveys in 1663–1669, 1718–1720, and 1820, the latter being very incomplete). The result was "the fusion of aristocratic status with private landownership, an amalgam that was almost as resistant to the fiscal encroachments of the central government as a bona fide feudal nobility" (Palais 1975, p. 58). The administrative setup was strong from the center down to the county level, as in China, with local magistrates appointed by the center and subject to frequent rotation lest they get too involved with the localities. Below the counties, however, local influentials (meaning strong clans and elders) controlled everything.

Thus Korea's agrarian bureaucracy was superficially strong but actually rather weak at the center. The state ostensibly dominated the society, but in practice landed aristocratic families could keep the state at bay and perpetuate local power for centuries. Precisely because of the tension between central power and landed wealth, however, Korea's leaders could achieve stability over time by playing one force off against the other, since both ends of this connection needed the other. This was a supple and adaptable system for governing Korea; otherwise how could it have lasted for 500 years? But it was not a system that could be mobilized to keep the imperial powers at bay in the late nineteenth century; instead it fell before them: "the balance of power between monarchy and aristocracy was an asset for the maintenance of stability," Palais writes, "but it was a liability when Korea was faced with the need to expand central power to mobilize resources for defense and development." This pattern persisted until the late 1940s, when landed dominance was obliterated in a northern revolution and deeply undermined in southern land reform; since that time the balance has shifted toward strong central power and top-down administration of the whole country in both North and South Korea.

Administrative Colonialism

When the Japanese took over in 1910, they rooted the landed aristocracy to the ground while quickly reforming and deepening the reach of the state, and putting the land system on a contractual or legal-rational basis. After the annexation they pensioned off some 3,645 civil service officials; the higher officials were replaced by Japanese, but lower ones were kept and Korean landlords were allowed to retain their holdings and encouraged to continue disciplining peasants (the vast majority of whom were tenants). These policies rooted Korean landlords more firmly to the localities by snipping their web of connections to political office in Seoul and using their traditional power and legitimacy to extract rice from peasants for the export market, more stably and effectively than if the Japanese had done it themselves. The state had been centralized in Seoul for 500 years, but the colonizers vastly increased the capacity and scope of the state. Japan did not send to Korea swashbuckling colonial conquerors, like Cecil Rhodes, but chose the civil service bureaucrat as the model overlord: the archetype was a man like Gōtō Shimpei, a colonial administrator in Taiwan and later active in Korea and Manchukuo, a man in a black Western suit with developmental plans in his briefcase.

The Japanese unquestionably strengthened central bureaucratic power in Korea, demolishing the old balance and tension with the landed aristocracy; operating from the top down, they effectively penetrated below the county level and into the villages for the first time. Added to the old county-level pivot of central magistrate, local clerks, and landed families, was a centrally controlled, highly mobile national police force, responsive to the center and possessing its own communications and transportation facilities. For decades black-coated policemen kept order and helped bring in the harvest, manning the ramparts of the rice production circuit from paddy field to middleman to storehouse to export platform, and thence to Japan. Here is how Patti Tsurumi described this new, multifunctional police system innovated in Taiwan by Gōtō Shimpei, a model later transferred to Korea:

> Under Gōtō the police became the backbone of regional administration. In addition to regular policing duties, the police supervised the

collection of taxes, the enforcement of sanitary measures, and works connected with the salt, camphor and opium monopolies. . . . They superintended road and irrigation improvements, introduced new plant specimens to the farmers, and encouraged education and the development of local industries. (Tsurumi 1967, pp. 117–118)

A horde of bureaucrats also descended on Korea. By the last decade of the colonial period some 246,000 Japanese civil servants and professionals ruled about 21 million Koreans, with about 46 percent of the colonizer population active in government service. In 1937, by way of comparison, the French ruled a Vietnamese population of 17 million with 2,920 administrative personnel and about 11,000 regular French troops, and the British had even smaller administrative and military forces in most of their colonies (proportionate to the populations) (Cumings 1981, p. 12). A majority of Japanese officials worked at one of the many government ministries in Seoul, a capital city that combined administrative, financial, commercial, and transportation centrality. Also visible as early as the 1920s was the developmental model of state-sponsored loans at preferential interest rates as a means to shape industrial development and take advantage of "product cycle" advantages, yielding firms whose paid-in capital was often much less than their outstanding debt. Businessmen did not offer shares on a stock market, but went to state banks for their capital. Strategic investment decisions were in the hands of state bureaucrats, state banks, and state corporations (like the Oriental Development Company), in ways that deeply influenced South Korea in the 1960s and 1970s.

We see the kernel of this logic in the colonial Government-General's Industrial Commission of 1921, which for the first time called for supports to Korea's fledgling textile industry and for it to produce not just for the domestic market, but especially for exports to the Asian continent, where Korean goods would have a price advantage. This was by no means a purely "top-down" exercise, either, for Koreans were part of the commission and quickly called for state subsidies and hothouse "protection" for Korean companies. That Japan had much larger ideas in mind, however, is obvious in the proposal for "General Industrial Policy" put before the 1921 conference:

> Since Korea is a part of the imperial domain, industrial plans for Korea should be in conformity with imperial industrial policy. Such a policy must provide for economic conditions in adjacent areas,

based on [Korea's] geographical position amid Japan, China, and the Russian Far East.

One of the Japanese delegates explained that Korean industry would be integral to overall planning going on in Tokyo, and would require some protection if it were to accept its proper place in "a single, coexistent, co-prosperous Japanese-Korean unit" (Eckert 1991, pp. 115, 128).

Colonial state subsidies to the first Korean conglomerate, Kim Sŏng-su's Kyŏngbang Textile Company began in 1924, amounting to 4 percent of its capital, and continued every year thereafter until 1935 (except for the depression year of 1932–1933), by which time they accounted for one-quarter of the firm's capital. Kim Sŏng-su got loans from the Industrial Bank of ¥80,000 in 1920 and triple that size in 1929, allowing a major expansion of his textile business. For the next decade Kyŏngbang got several million *yen* worth of loans from this bank, so that by 1945 its ¥22 million outstanding debt was more than twice the company's worth. By the 1940s, it had become Korea's first multinational firm, with a new textile factory in Manchuria. Its interests included three ginning factories, a huge factory for spinning and weaving in Yŏngdûngp'o, a bleaching and dyeing factory, silk thread and cloth factories; also industries such as ball bearings, brewing, gold mining, real estate, metal, oil refining, and even aircraft (Eckert 1991, pp. 58, 85–86).

By the mid-1930s, state financing of industry at highly preferential interest rates had became a standard practice; the key institution at the nexus of this model was the Korean Industrial Bank (*Chösen Shokusan Ginkö*), the main source of capital for big Korean firms (by the 1940s about half of its employees were Korean). Japan's closed door policy in the 1930s had clear Keynesian pump-priming goals—farm village relief, a military buildup and a "big push" in heavy industries, thus to pull Japan and its colonies out of the depression. Ugaki Kazushige was Governor-General of Korea from 1931 to 1936; he was "an ultra-nationalist, [who] deeply believed in the need for a Japanese imperium of economic autarky and industrial self-sufficiency." Korea was industrialized out of the depression, with growth rates in manufacturing averaging more than 10 percent annually; unlike Japan, Korea was a "capitalist paradise," with minimal business taxes and little regulation of working conditions and business practices. By 1936, heavy industry accounted for 28 percent of total industrial production, and more than half a million Koreans were employed in industry, a figure that had tripled by 1945. By 1943, the production ratio between Korea's heavy and light industry had become equal. Nor is it really the case that northern Korea had all the heavies and the South only light industry; the South surpassed the North in machine building, electric machinery, heavy vehicles, mining tools, and the like (Woo 1991, pp. 31, 34–36, 41). Thus Korea's industrial revolution began in earnest during the last 15 years of Japanese rule.

One observant scholar was much impressed by the rapid development of Korea in the late 1930s. Here was an "obvious, indeed astonishing success," even if the development was "oriented toward the needs of the empire." This, combined with a succession of excellent harvests in 1936–1938, yielded the idea of a "Korean boom": with "the rapid development of all of Korea's economic capacity . . . a certain amount of prosperity is beginning to enter even the farmer's huts." The northeast corner of Korea, long backward, was "experiencing an upswing unlike any other part of Korea," mainly because of its incorporation into Manchurian trading networks (Lautensach 1945, pp. 204–207, 383, 386–387).

The Developmental State and its Continental Background

Clearly by the 1930s the Japanese state and its imperial bureaucracies in Korea, Taiwan, and Manchuria were performing a developmental function. Chalmers Johnson is widely credited with coining the term "developmental state" and establishing it as a third category alongside liberal and Stalinist conceptions. He eschewed various explanations of Japanese success occupying the public mind in the 1980s, namely that the market drives it, or that collectivism drives it, or that national character is the explanation, or a diffuse notion of "culture" and "Asian values" identified with leaders like Singapore's Lee Kwan Yew. Johnson thought that much Japanese "difference" could be explained situationally, in terms of "late development, lack of resources, the need to trade . . . and so forth."

This was a key breakthrough in the American literature on Northeast Asia, but it is important to note that Johnson traces the lineages of this state form back to the late 1920s and 1930s. His argument took truly original and controversial form in the postulation of a genealogy of bureaucratic departments and careers (an "economic general staff") spanning the presumed 1945 watershed, preeminently the interwar forerunners of Ministry of International Trade and Industry (MITI) who industrialized Manchukuo and the dark knight of that industrial policy, Kishi Nobosuke (later the Japanese Prime Minister). Manchukuo is thus resituated not as a failed puppet state run by a restive Kwantung Army, but as the birthplace of the Japanese "miracle" (Johnson 1982, pp. 108, 122–124).

Mostly missed in this account, however, except for the implications of Japan's "situational" placement, is the shaping and constraining influence of international forces, such as American hegemony in the postwar period, or the collapse of the world system in the interwar period. Like nearly everyone else, Johnson takes "Japan" as his unit of analysis. He rightly traces a German lineage in Japan's success, but only to *Handlespolitik* or neo-mercantilism in the first instance, and with more emphasis on Japanese learning from Germany in the 1930s than the 1880s. In fact the German state was an object of extensive study in Japan from the 1870s onward, with "state science" and law being a far more important discipline than political science or sociology—then and, also, today.

When the Meiji leader Itò Hirobumi came back from Germany and quipped, "I understand the secret of the state, now I can die a happy man,"[1] it was first of all because he had met Lorenz von Stein, author of the classic text *The History of the Social Movement in France, 1789–1850*. As Immanuel Wallerstein argues, von Stein understood "society" to be a concept of state science (*Staatswissenschaft*) because it has meaning primarily "in the antimony, society/state."[2] For von Stein, society and state were not just linked inextricably in meaning, but were fused in a number of senses: for example, states decide who constitutes the citizenry ("civil society"); more powerfully, if for Hegel the monarch embodied the state and vice versa (a different fusion), the novelty of the French Revolution was that after it came along, the state embodied the popular will (or should). The question then becomes, who embodies (or creates, or knows) the popular will?

Fortunately, this last question is not one we have to solve. The point instead is that in German "state science," the conception of the fused state was born, or rather, first noticed in the aftermath of the French Revolution, as a point of definitional anxiety and political reality. It is then a short step to observe the disorders of that same revolution, to relate them to novel ideas about "popular will," and to conclude, well, who needs that? To put the point baldly, of what value is civil society in a race for industrialization? The Germans invented the field of state science not to solve the problems of liberty, equality, and fraternity at the dawn of the industrial epoch, but to solve the mid-nineteenth-century problems of the second industrial revolution and, more importantly, catching up with England. Here, in short, was a political theory of late development that put off to a distant future the magnificent obsession of the early industrializers with questions of popular will, democratic representation, public versus private, or state versus civil society.

Friedrich List always had a strong following in Japan, being by far the most influential foreign economist in the nineteenth century. His conception of national economy (*Nationalökonomie*) was an explicit antithesis to Adam Smith's market economy and provided a theory of "late" industrial development that, together with nineteenth-century German industrial practice, became a model for Japan (and later Korea). The late-developing state should regulate trade and foreign competition by opening and closing within the grand terrain of the world market, along the lines of Karl Polanyi's theory of the state, which in the milieu of the world economy becomes a guarantor of Polanyi's "principle of social protection" against the backwash and the ravages of world market competition (Polanyi 1957).

Japan, Korea, and China were drawn inexorably toward state science and national economy, whether of the von Stein or the Leninist variety. Sooner or later, all the Northeast Asian nations fashioned states worthy to the battle of late industrialization, and all of them did so in conditions ranging from the complete absence to the overwhelming presence of hegemonic American ideology (1930s Japan vs. 1960s Japan, North Korea vs. South Korea, post-1949 China vs. post-1949 Taiwan). The meaning of "state building" in Northeast Asia's fused state/societies is that recourse to the state comes first, followed by conscious or unconscious attempts to create industry and then and only then "civil society," that is, the groups requisite for and appropriate to contemporary imaginings of "modernity."

Chalmers Johnson's work postulated a trichotomy of states that are "plan rational" (Japan), "plan ideological" (Stalinist states) and "regulatory" (the New Deal American state). The virtue of this analysis is to suggest that planning can be as "rational" as market allocation, or more so. The vice is the aura of reification and righteousness surrounding the term "rational." But that is not surprising, since the real German lineage that Johnson asserts is from Max Weber to MITI. Modern bureaucracy for Weber is "the most rational and impersonal form of state administration," Johnson wrote, and he found no problem locating the angel of rationality: it is a technocratic elite of bureaucrats, signified above all by the Ministry of Trade and Industry, but embodied in the servants of the Japanese state more generally: the "way of the bureaucrat" is Japan's modern substitution for the "way of the warrior" (Johnson 1982, pp. 22–23, 36–37, 39–42). As many critics have pointed out, Johnson is at a loss to show how and why the angel of rationality got things right in Japan, and of course for the past decade "the way of the bureaucrat" has been to get things wrong in an economy stuck in the low-growth doldrums. Johnson uncovered a truth about Japanese state practice that had eluded a generation of analysts, and thereby revalued the entire field of modern Japanese politics. At the same time, his focus on Japan as the unit of analysis neglects the dramatic international dimensions impinging on the long process of state building in Northeast Asia, without which it cannot be understood.

War, Revolution, Land Reform

The reader may have noticed that we have said a great deal about the Korean (and Japanese state), whether in its developmental or its premodern condition, and we are nowhere near the presumed tipping point of 1960 (as in: "Korea had a GNP per capita of $100 in 1959 but after the onset of export-led policies its GNP took off. . . ."). The years from 1945 to 1960 are mostly blank in the literature on Korean development, except to criticize the irrational policies of the first Korean president, Syngman Rhee. Yet, the decade after World War II was more critical than any other for Korea, being the source of national division (1945), the emergence of two Koreas (1948), and the eruption of one of the century's most devastating wars in 1950. Any attempt at an incremental account of state building or continuity in economic development gets lost amid these wrenching changes; instead these years highlight the importance of unexpected and unpredictable crises, that is, ruptures that render elusive any coherent narrative.

Two things happened in this first postwar decade, however, that deeply affected state building and development. First, Americans occupied southern Korea in September 1945 and proceeded to rule through the massive central state that the Japanese left behind, promoting Koreans with civil service experience under the Japanese (whether in Korea or Manchuria) and after a few months, leaving them mostly to their own devices. A separate southern state thus emerged very quickly in 1945 and 1946 (even though the U.S. military government lasted until August 1948), but because of the extraordinary centralization of everything in Seoul and the truncation of the peninsula into two, the reach of this state was effectively doubled. From 1945 to 1953 the primary function of this state was coercive, seeking to suppress a strong left wing in the south, aggressive labor unions, and subsequently a guerrilla movement (Cumings 1981). But the state was among those Korean institutions least changed by the post-1945 turmoil, and after the Korean War ended, this highly centralized and bureaucratized entity would be the handmaiden of any Korean president interested in development.

The other critical event of the 1940s was the end of a landlord system stretching back centuries. The North Koreans carried out a quick and relatively bloodless land revolution in early 1946, allowing many landlords to run off to the south, where they predictably joined with their southern counterparts to block the land reform that the Americans and Korean liberals hoped to accomplish. In 1948, the U.S. military Government succeeded in selling off about 20 percent of the arable land that had been held by Japanese companies and individuals, to tenant farmers who ended up with small parcels of land basically sufficient to support their families. The Korean National Assembly passed a land reform law in 1949, but it was not implemented before the Korean War began. In the summer of 1950, the North Koreans occupied the South for nearly three months, and carried out a revolutionary redistribution in about two-thirds of southern Korea. When U.S. and South Korean forces recovered the South, Americans would not allow landlords to simply reoccupy their land, and so finally the 1949 reform was consummated. It left millions of small-holding owners in the place of equal numbers of former tenants, and broke the back of the landed aristocracy. In so doing, this reform decisively reconfigured the relationship between the state and the localities. If the colonial state had penetrated the villages like no previous government, now the localities had little wherewithal to resist the central state. Korea thus had one of the most strongly centralized states in the world, with little or no local autonomy.

After the Korean War, the first president, Syngman Rhee, followed what specialists call "import substitution industrialization" or ISI, with nearly full American support and indulgence. Korea had become a front-line state in the Cold War by 1950, a key "Free World" ally, and Rhee milked that relationship for all it was worth: "said to be an economic failure, the ROK was still an unaccountably expensive one, making unprecedented inroads on the U.S. Treasury in the form of billions of dollars in aid" (Woo 1991, p. 44). Was this ISI program "irrational"? Rhee knew perfectly well that the unvoiced American strategy for South Korea was to restitch its economic relations with Japan; by substituting Korean industries for Japanese, duplicating them if need be, the seams for the stitching would no longer be there. Eisenhower, for example, told General Van Fleet in 1954 that he was going to tell Rhee that "we have got to get Japan backing up Korea as a 'big brother,'" but soon Rhee shot this back to Ike,

> What [aid coordination with Japan] means is that [Korean] recovery is slowed as we are expected to buy more from Japan, and accordingly

to use less to build up our own productive facilities. This has an immediate effect of once more placing our economy at the mercy of the Japanese. (Woo 1991, p. 57)

Korea again to be the handmaiden of Japan's growth? Better to be "another Japan" than a dependency. This was the logic behind Rhee's policies.

Latin America was then the continent of import substitution. Inaugurated in the depression as a way to survive in a collapsed world economy and having a certain intimacy with the Iberian corporate politics of the region, and given that World War II passed this continent by, import substitution lasted far longer than anywhere else. Behind walls of protection the people and firms involved with production for domestic markets built up extensive networks of personal and political ties, as scholar Guillermo O'Donnell has shown. Therefore, when all the world told these nations in the 1960s that they had to begin exporting and dropping their barriers to trade, the question was how to break the thick nexus of interests that had grown up around the previous strategy. Here military coups and strong states have advantages: after Park Chung Hee made his coup in 1961, the junta arrested the import-substituting businessmen who had fattened at Syngman Rhee's trough and marched them through the streets Cultural Revolution-style, with dunce caps and sandwich placards saying "I am a corrupt swine," "I ate the people," and other such slogans. Park's accession to power also marked an end to 15 years of turmoil in South Korea, and a return to the developmental model of the 1930s (Park had been an officer in the Japanese Army in Manchukuo), with much Japanese and American help and aid.

The essence of this model was state-mediated finance going to firms in targeted industries, with the firms soon growing to enormous size and dominating the economy, and political leaders getting rewarded with huge political funds to maintain themselves in power. The state also developed new guidance mechanisms for the economy, in particular the Economic Planning Board that became the Korean equivalent of Japan's Ministry of Trade and Industry. This model took hold in Korea in the early 1960s, and propelled industrial development until it was broken up in the 1990s. The highly conscious agents of the "miracle on the Han" were state bureaucrats willing to hand out something for something: no-cost money if you put it to good use, building up another industrial prodigy. They were called, policy loans for export performance, and they seemed to show that sometimes there is a free lunch in capitalist economics. The state deployed money in the magical way that Joseph

Schumpeter imagined, as a mysterious poof of energy for the incessant innovation that he saw as the motive force of growth. A man goes to a bank with an idea for a better mousetrap, the banker signs a piece of paper, greenbacks pour out like cheese in Wisconsin, and all the mice run for cover. In the American system it is typically the private bank and the entrepreneur whose symbiosis creates this energy, but Schumpeter said that other institutions could perform this function—which they did in Korea, even if *chaebol*s coupling with the finance ministry isn't quite as romantic as the entrepreneur looking for the main chance.

Here was the state's role in the bargain: it will arrange for, say, a bank in Japan to give a person $10 million at below-market interest rates to make 12-inch black-and-white TVs, and guarantee the loan to the bank. It will set aside property for him in a free-export zone, build the roads to the plant, provide heat and electricity at preferential rates, and set aside American surplus cement for the buildings. State planners will find a foreign firm with established markets, know-how, and channels of distribution, who will sell the TVs everywhere in the United States, even in grocery stores. The state guarantees a steady supply of educated and disciplined labor at a set price (also well below market), prevent unions, and send in the army whenever dangerous combination occurs at the workplace. The state will decide how many competitors this firm will have, provide annual targets for production (with bonuses for going beyond them), and make sure there's room enough for these firms to grow.

This is a simple sketch, but if it worked intermittently in the 1960s, it worked like clockwork in the 1970s and became the essence of the "Korean model." With huge amounts of petrodollars sloshing through world markets after the OPEC quadrupling of oil prices, and with bankers begging people to take loans, the Korean state mediated that flood of money, pointing it toward the immensely expensive "Six Industries" of Park's heavy-industrial "big push." For the next 15 years, Korea borrowed abroad at Latin American rates: foreign debt rose 42 percent shortly after the oil shock, but investment also shot up, to an historic high of 32 percent of GNP in 1974. By the end of the decade, Korea was among the big four debtors in the world, led by Brazil; its foreign borrowing from 1976–1979 placed it third, behind Mexico and Brazil, but in the decade 1967–1978, Korean debt grew 15-fold, twice the rate of all less-developed countries and well ahead of Mexican and Brazilian borrowing. Korea also, however, grew by an average of 11 percent from 1973 to 1978, with heavy industry accounting for 70 percent of total manufacturing investment. To get the big loans of that period, however, you had to be big already: a *chaebol*. To keep getting them, you "had to be gigantic."

The central element in the Korean model, then, was state-mediated finance: and "the main goal of Korea's finance was to hemorrhage as much capital as possible into the heavy industrialization program":

> The financial policy of *Yushin* was this: the government set financial prices at an artificial low to subsidize import-substituting, heavy, chemical, and export industries. . . . The political economy of this bifurcated financial system was illiberal, undemocratic, and statist. . . . Every bank in the nation was owned and controlled by the state; bankers were bureaucrats and not entrepreneurs, they thought in terms of GNP and not profit, and they loaned to those favored by the state. (Woo 1991, pp. 149–153).

The average cost of such loans through much of the 1970s was −6.7 percent, whereas even the black market rate was positive—well above the inflation rate in fact. The result was that each favored *chaebol* "for all practical purposes, was a private agency of public purpose" (Woo 1991, p. 169). The public purpose, of course, was to herd them into specific, selected industries that would build the "rich country, strong army" of Park's dreams.

If this sounds like a capitalist heaven, it was: South Korea was a cornucopia of state supports to business. But so were many other poor countries, and they are still poor. The question for Korea is how a state bureaucracy could allocate credit resources efficiently, that is, rationally; and how could they be wizards of finance, gnomes of Seoul, when every political calculation would push in the direction of rewarding friends and benefactors at the expense of the commonwealth? The answer to this question comes in four Korean parts.

First, political leaders do not pay attention to efficiency and rationality, but to political and, in this case, national efficacy. All kinds of risks disappear when a company knows that a long-term investment has the backing and the resources of a highly nationalistic political leadership behind it (like, let's say, the American aerospace industry in the 1960s), and politicians who will sink or swim with the investment. Second, the Korean ideal and tradition of the civil servant does produce many well-educated people devoted to what is best for their country and government, and by the 1960s many were also foreign-trained technocrats who knew how to plan and allocate resources. Third, there *were* many rewards for friends, as one "slush fund" scandal after another has shown. The firms that got policy loans were quasi-state organizations who shared common interests with government, who sank or swam by following government dictate, and who were personally connected (often by marriage) to the ruling elites. This third element led to a kind of rational or efficacious corruption, in which relatives in the government lent money to relatives in business, piling money upon growth expectations and growth upon money expectations, somewhat like a chain letter or crap game that worked year in and year out as long as the pie kept expanding. The carrot-and-stick that the government always held was the complete dependency of the big firms on it for capital. If performance was poor or the firm did not do what the state wanted, it could be bankrupted the next day. This gave the state tremendous influence on investment patterns, mobility into new industries, and simple day-to-day corporate performance (Woo 1991, pp. 10–13).

The last Korean difference is that the proof of success was export performance in the hothouse of international competition—something that in the 1960s was simultaneously a discipline on firm performance *and* easier than the same thing today, because the world economy was much less crowded in the 1960s. South Korea was well placed in the 1960s to receive declining light industries from the United States or Japan (textiles, footwear, transistor radios, black-and-white TVs, wigs, small appliances), and export them to the low end of the American market. Because it had such a small market of its own, however, Korean firms were precariously poised in the flows of global commerce, very vulnerable to recessions and slowdowns—another reason for the Korean government to be a good partner, benefactor in good times and insurance agent in bad times. South Korean interests frolicked for years in the yawning maw of the American market (usually in cooperation with American firms that had moved to Korea for coproduction), long before China, Indonesia, or Thailand got into the act.

The Anomalous States of Northeast Asia

The state is not purely a domestic product, of course, but South Korea and Japan have existed and developed within an American security network that is now six decades old. If the Cold War ended on a world scale, that did not mean that national security structures built during that 40-year struggle disappeared. Indeed, the watershed changes of 1989–1991 had relatively little effect on Northeast Asia: no Communist state collapsed and the United States did not retreat; Soviet power in the region just evaporated, leaving the structure of unilateral American power continuing in place. The rationale for containment collapsed, of course, but that was merely one part of U.S. strategy: the American bases that still dot Japan and South Korea (containing nearly 100,000 troops) were agents both to contain the communist enemy and to constrain the capitalist ally. After World War II, Japan and South Korea were the subjects of this dual containment policy, while their economies were posted as engines of growth for the broader world economy. Americans revived Japan's formidable industrial base, reconnected former colonial hinterland territories that were still accessible to it (South Korea and Taiwan above all), and enmeshed them in security structures that made them into semi-sovereign states.

Since that distant but determining point of origin American generals have had operational control of the huge South Korean army and Japan, which is long the second largest economy in the world, and has depended on the United States for its defenses and the flow of its vital resources. Meanwhile both countries were showered with all manner of support in the early postwar period, as part of a Cold War project to remake both of them as paragons of noncommunist development. Japan became the paradigmatic example of non-Western growth for the "modernization school" that dominated American policy and scholarship in the 1950s and 1960s, just as South Korea subsequently became the first Asian "tiger." The central experience of Northeast Asia in the postwar period, in short, has not been a realm of independence where autonomy and equality reigned, but an alternative form of political economy enmeshed in a hegemonic web. Japan, South Korea, and Taiwan industrialized within this web, and thus had states "strong" for the struggle to industrialize, but "weak" because of the web of enmeshment: they are semi-sovereign states. North Korea and China defined themselves as outside the web, thereby endowing the web with overriding significance—and so they structured their states to resist enmeshment. They have had states "strong" for industrialization, and "total" for hegemonic resistance.

If the transnational security structure of Northeast Asia has not changed, the end of the Cold War left the United States less certain of its backing for the Korea–Japan type of developmental state. This was in part the result of increasing trade competition from Japan, and more importantly a reflection of the increasing American support for a global model of free markets and the rule of law—neoliberalism. The global financial crisis that began in the summer of 1997 and spread from Thailand and Singapore to Indonesia and South Korea was the occasion for a dramatic invocation of new rules of the game in the Northeast Asian political economy. A systematic failure of capitalism struck precisely those economies long held up as models of industrial efficiency—the Asian "tigers"—and standing behind the travail of the smaller afflicted countries was perhaps a more stunning phenomenon: the shaky financial condition and political immobilism of the world's second largest economy, Japan, with perhaps $1 trillion in bad loans and (for a country long praised for its efficient "administrative guidance"), a genuine crisis of governance in the 1990s.

In the early stages of the crisis, a dominant view emerged among mainstream analysts that Asian economies were at fault for their "crony capitalism" with its many market irregularities and "moral hazards." From the mid-1960s onward, South Korea and Taiwan were the fastest-growing economies in the world, with China outstripping them in the past decade. In the 1990s, the East Asian countries accounted for nearly two-thirds of all capital investment (excluding Japan with its long-term recession) and for half of the growth in world output, even though they constitute only 20 percent of the world's GDP. So how could the "miracle" economies of East Asia turn overnight into cesspools of "crony capitalism?"

The unexpected liquidity crunch in 1997 had a certain serendipity for an America with an ever-deepening global position and a resurgent growth in productivity and technological prowess in Silicon Valley and elsewhere; it gave American leaders the chance to try and dismantle the remaining alternative model of capitalist political economy, before it organized not just Japan and South Korea, but China as well. Paradoxically, the economic debacle also gave the people of these countries a new and sudden chance at democratic opening: they became Washington's best ally in implementing lasting reform, because just as politics could not be separated from economics during the era of the "Asian miracle," in the past decade demands for democratization have gone hand in hand with faltering economies in the Asian region. The deep meaning of the 1997–1998 Asian crisis thus lay in the American attempt to ring down the curtain on "late" development of the Japan/Korea type, and the likelihood that they would succeed—because the strong, nationalistic developmentalism of Japan and South Korea was propagated in the soft soil of semi-sovereignty, and because the Americans had willing accomplices in Northeast Asian peoples who have sought to reform or nullify this same model themselves, in the interest of economic equity and democratic politics. The best place to witness this conjuncture is South Korea, but the Korean case will also hold important lessons for China and Japan.

After the IMF bailout, influential analysts inveighed against a model of development that had been the apple of Washington's eye during the decades of authoritarianism in Korea. Deputy IMF Director Stanley Fischer said true restructuring would not be possible "within the Korean model or the Japan Inc. model." "Korean leaders are wedded to economic ideals born in a 1960s dictatorship," an editorial in *The Wall Street Journal* said, leading to "hands-on government regulation, ceaseless corporate expansion, distrust of foreign capital and competition"; the 30 largest *chaebols*, accounting for a third of the country's wealth, were "big monsters" who "gobbled up available credit" and relied on "outdated notions of vertical integration for strength." Perhaps the chief economist at Deutsche Morgan Grenfell, Ed Yardeni, trumped all the pundits in heaping scorn on Seoul: "the truth of the matter is that Korea, Inc. is already bankrupt. . . . All that's left is to file the papers. This is a zombie economy."[3] If it wasn't a zombie, the crisis certainly cut the economy down to size. In November 1997, South Korea ostensibly had a GNP of almost $500 billion and a per capita GNP of about $11,000; it accounted for about 6 percent of total world GDP (compared to 2.5 percent in 1980), and ranked eleventh among industrial countries. By January per capita GNP had fallen to $6,600 and GNP to $312 billion, or seventeenth place (behind Mexico, India, and Russia).[4] (By the end of 1998, the economy had lost a further 6 percent of GNP.)

The IMF's ministrations came in the middle of the most important presidential campaign in South Korean history. For the first time, it appeared that a former dissident, a person of unquestioned democratic credentials with a base in the abused and underdeveloped Southwest, might finally come to power. And so, Washington and Wall Street insiders openly suggested that Kim was the wrong leader at the wrong time in the wrong place: a U.S. diplomat told a reporter,[5]

> We could be in a position in which Kim Dae Jung takes office in the midst of a financial emergency that is going to require a lot of pain and downsizing of South Korean businesses. . . . Almost no one thinks he will command the authority to pull it off.

In fact no other conceivable political leader was better positioned than Kim truly to change the Korean system; indeed he had called for reforms analogous to those of the IMF throughout his long career, and directed particular attention toward breaking up the powerful nexus between the state, the banks, and the big business conglomerates (Kim 1985). Even before his inauguration Kim legalized labor's participation in politics and brought union leaders together with government and business leaders in "peak bargaining" negotiations, something that had never occurred before in South Korean history. This master stroke gave to Korea's labor movement a key goal that it had long sought and a stake in the system, and encouraged seasoned labor leaders to shape and discipline President Kim's reform program, not to destroy it. The democratization movements of all stripes during and after the period of military dictatorship were the basis of these changes, a clear example of a state building process that "embodies conflict, antagonism, winners and losers," in Rueschemeyer's terms. Thereafter, a strong and mature civil society subjected every move by President Kim and his party to thorough (and often withering) democratic debate, but nothing remotely comparable to the disorders that afflicted the successive dictatorial regimes occurred. South Korea returned to double-digit growth in 2000, and even though its growth slowed modestly after the American economy stagnated in 2001, in recent years it is has been far better off than other Asian countries afflicted by the 1997 crisis.

Another reformist president Roh Moo Hyun, was elected in 2003 and he continued to hack away at the state-bank-*chaebol* nexus. The most successful conglomerate, Samsung, is now a vibrant multinational corporation; Hyundai, formerly the largest firm, is broken up into several subsidiary corporations; the third largest, Daewoo, completely collapsed amid massive bad loans and bankruptcy. With nearly half the banks in Korea now foreign-owned, the old Korean model barely exists anymore; the state continues to have a strong hand in the economy, but there is much more distance and transparency between it and the *chaebol* groups. The South Korean reform process itself has been heavily state-directed, predictably, while Western "rule-of-law" dictums often seem like just another strategy to open Korean markets and firms to predatory competition and buyouts by bigger and stronger Western banks and corporations.

The Korean reforms, the aftermath of the Asian financial crisis, and the continuing inertia of the Japanese economy do raise new questions about the viability of the developmental state model in the new century, however. In the aftermath of this crisis, it appeared that the era of "late" industrial development pioneered by the Japanese was over, and certainly the wave of democratization in South Korea has drastically decompressed the bureaucratic-authoritarian nature of this state. If this model worked effectively to build the sinews of the second industrial revolution (in steel, railroads, autos, etc.), it seems bereft in the face of the third industrial (or information-age) revolution. Leaders of the Japanese economy have tried the same stratagems over and over in search of renewed growth, like Aladdin rubbing the same lamp again and again; reducing interest rates to zero for years on end did not suffice to get Japanese consumers to spend more, just as Keynesian government pump-priming may have extended highways and bullet-train lines to the remote far reaches of the country, but barely kept the economy from falling into prolonged recession year after year. It seems unlikely that any lasting verdict on the fate of the developmental state will be possible until we see the shape of the Japanese political economy after it returns to sustained economic growth.

Democracy Makes a Difference

We have barely discussed a key element of state building in Korea, namely its enormous coercive force. The colonially formed National Police combined with a draconian National Security Law in postwar South Korea to make for a highly authoritarian police state, and the rise of enormous military institutions during the Korean War provided the basis for two major military coups, in 1961 and 1980. The Korean Central Intelligence Agency emerged in the 1970s as a ubiquitous repressive force, with agents throughout Korean society. Despite all this coercive capacity, however, Korean political development was never smooth and the population was continuously restive. Every Korean republic until the one created in 1992, under Kim Young Sam, began or ended in massive uprisings or military coups. The longest one, the Third Republic under Park Chung Hee (1961–1979), began with a coup and ended with Park's murder at the hands of his own intelligence chief. The next longest under Chun Doo Hwan (1980–1987) began and ended with popular rebellions that shook the foundations of the system.

With the accession to power of Kim Young Sam in February 1993, however, the military was finally retired to the barracks. In November 1995, amid daily revelations of the enormous political "slush funds" that militarists Chun Doo Hwan and Roh Tae Woo had accumulated in the 1980s, President Kim suddenly arranged to indict both of them for treason, for the coup in December 1979 and the bloodletting at Kwangju five months later. Unlike most former military dictatorships, the new democratic regime in Korea did not allow bygones to be bygones: Kim Young Sam jailed the two former presidents and launched official investigations into their crimes; eventually Chun was sentenced to death and Roh to life in prison (however both received pardons from Kim Dae Jung in 1998).

If the road to state building is long, and if over centuries Korea built a state that successfully intervened in and directed economic growth, its protracted and stormy process of democratization speaks volumes to the sharp conflicts and crises that this same state helped to create. Finally, in the new century the previous autonomy of this strong state is hamstrung in many salutary ways, by a strong civil society, periodic free elections, and the disciplines of world market competition.

Conclusion

The history of state building and development in Korea suggests that a focus on policy changes in the direction of economic activity ca. 1960, a year often taken as point zero in Korea's industrial "take-off," elides a much deeper and longer background, and makes the lessons of Korean development less transferable to other situations. Clearly the long tradition of civil service and modified meritocracy, stretching back more than a millennium, is of central importance to the continuing prominence of elite bureaucrats in directing Korea's economy. To refer back to the introduction, "the development of institutions and norms" had a centuries-long provenance through the long history of the Korean civil service. The emergence of a modern state occurred mostly under Japanese colonial auspices, but many Koreans were involved in it, yielding "a complex alignment of interests and the coordination of many different actors and units." Finally, Korean development and the emergence of a strong state, particularly after 1945, embodied to a high degree "conflict, antagonism, winners and losers, and long-term stalemates"—with the stalemates often broken violently (as with the military coups in 1961 and 1980).

The very high average level of education, which has been so important to Korea's comparative advantages in development, also has roots that are centuries old. Yet Korean and Japanese state building were also rooted in mid-nineteenth-century German conceptualizations of the state: state science (as opposed to political science), and national economy (as opposed to market economy), both conceived in the context of "late" industrialization in a predatory world economy. The Japanese period, remembered by Koreans as one of almost pure exploitation, was in fact a rare colonial experience of bureaucratic and administrative intervention throughout the economy and society that added on to Korea's native state traditions a highly articulated, centralized authority that penetrated to the lowest villages—another way of highlighting "the coordination of many different actors and units."

During the American occupation the mostly unreformed central state in Seoul was the unquestioned winner. It is the singular element of continuity through the eight years of turmoil after the Japanese empire collapsed. Likewise, land reform was the critical outcome of that same period of revolution and war, ending a millennium of local power and relative autonomy that had constrained state power historically. But this strong, highly articulated state was also a semi-sovereign state, socked into Northeast Asian security arrangements that the Uinted States fashioned in the period 1947–1951, and that remain dominant today. In the 1960s, South Korea rejoined the high-growth political economy of the region that got its start in the 1930s, if in modified form (only Japanese economic and technological influence returned to Korea; politically and culturally there was little influence). The Korean state has changed markedly in the past decade, as it was whipped by waves of democratization, crisis, and reform. The key achievements put the military out of politics and back in the barracks, sharply limited the domestic purview of intelligence agencies, and attenuated the directing function of the state in the economy; above all, the nexus of state-bank-*chaebol* that defined the Korean model of development, is a shadow of its former self and subject to sharp supervision by a host of new state agencies, civil society groups, and through free speech and free elections, the Korean people themselves.

Notes

1. Itò, quoted in Jon Halliday. 1975. *A Political History of Japanese Capitalism*. New York: Pantheon Books. In 1872 the Japanese government directed its chargé d'affaires in Berlin, Aoki Shùzò, to draft a constitution for Meiji Japan. He sought the aid of Rudolf von Gneist, then a professor at the University of Berlin and a famous constitutional scholar. Aoki submitted his draft in 1873, entitled "Governmental Principles of Great Japan" (*Dainihon seiki*). Other provisional drafts followed in 1876, 1878, and 1880, guided by the constitutions of Prussia, Austria, and Denmark. When he was in Germany, Itò Hirobumi met principally with von Gneist and Lorenz von Stein. Itò later asked his close aide, Inoue Kowashi, to draft a constitutition, and the latter was guided in turn by Herman Roesler, a German political scientist in Tokyo. See Helen Hardacre. 1989. *Shintō and the State, 1968–1988*. Princeton: Princeton University Press, pp. 115–118.
2. The English title is a bit clipped; von Stein's German title was *Der Begriff der Gesellschaft und die soziale Geschichte der Französischen Revolution bis zum Jahre 1830*. See Wallerstein (1992), pp. 65–67.
3. Editorial by Joseph Kahn and Michael Schuman, *The Wall Street Journal*, November 24, 1997; Fischer quoted in *The Wall Street Journal*, December 8, 1997; Yardeni's "zombie" remark was broadcast widely on CNN TV News; see the full quotation in *The Washington Post*, December 11, 1997.
4. *World Development Indicator*. 1997; Asian Development Bank. 1996. *Key Indicators of Developing Asian and Pacific Countries* (GNP figures assume purchase power parity or PPP; 1995 and 1996 figures are multiplied by 1996 and 1997 growth rates); 1998 figures from LG Economic Research Institute, reported in *The Korea Herald*, February 21, 1998.
5. Quoted by David Sanger, *The New York Times*, November 20, 1997.

References

Amsden, Alice. 1989. *Asia's Next Giant: South Korea and Late Industrialization*. New York: Oxford.
Cumings, Bruce. 1997. *Korea's Place in the Sun: A Modern History*. New York: Pantheon Books.
———. 1981. *The Origins of the Korean War, vol. 1*. Princeton: Princeton University Press.
———. 1999. "Webs With No Spiders, Spiders With No Webs: Reflections on the Developmental State." In *The Developmental State*. Edited by M. Woo-Cumings. Ithaca: Cornell University Press, 61–92.
Eckert, Carter J. 1991. *Offspring of Empire: The Koch'ang Kims and the Origins of Korean Capitalism*. Seattle: University of Washington Press.
Gale, James Scarth. 1972. *History of the Korean People*. Seoul: Royal Asiatic Society.
Johnson, Chalmers. 1982. *MITI and the Japanese Miracle: The Growth of Industrial Policy, 1925–1975*. Stanford: Stanford University Press.
Kim Dae Jung. 1985. *Mass Participatory Economy*. Cambridge: Harvard East Asian Center.
Lautensach, Hermann. 1945. *Korea: A Geography Based on the Author's Travels and Literature*. Trans. Katherine and Eckart Dege. Berlin: Springer-Verlag.
Lowell, Percival. 1888. *Chosön: The Land of the Morning Calm*. Boston: Ticknor and Company.
Palais, James. 1975. *Politics and Policy in Traditional Korea*. Cambridge: Harvard University Press.
Polanyi, Karl. 1957. *The Great Transformation*. New York: Beacon Press.
Tsurumi, E. Patricia. 1967. "Taiwan under Kodama Gentarö and Gotö Shimpei." *Papers on Japan, v. IV*. Cambridge, MA: Harvard University, East Asian Research Center.
Wallerstein, Immanuel. 1992. *Unthinking Social Science*. New York: Basic Books.
Woo, Jung-en. 1991. *Race to the Swift: State, Finance and Industrialization in Korea*. New York: Columbia University Press.

PART IV
Conclusion

CHAPTER ELEVEN

States and Development: What Insights Did We Gain?

MATTHEW LANGE AND
DIETRICH RUESCHEMEYER

An Emerging Consensus

There are those to whom the idea that states have a major role to play in advancing social and economic development is anathema. To them, state intervention of any kind equals distortion of economic allocation and the proliferation of unproductive rents for a few. They have their counterpart in others who morally reject the market as nothing more than institutionalized greed and selfishness. Yet both of these positions have lost support and become marginal.

In international institutions like the World Bank, in academic discussion, and in national policy making, there are disagreements about important policy directions, for instance about the relative priority to be given to economic growth, to environmental sustainability, or to the consequences of different development paths for the distribution of wealth and equity. However, these disagreements typically do not negate shared views that acknowledge the critical role states play in promoting economic and social development nor do they question the importance of mobilizing private resources and intelligence through the market. What are the major elements of this consensus?

There is first the recognition that the state is indispensable for many prerequisites of economic and social development. This goes well beyond the Smithian acknowledgment that the market needs protection from violent disorder and a legal framework that secures contract and property rights. Most agree, for instance, that needed investments—in schooling, public health, or the infrastructure of transportation and communication—require public resources because they do not pay off fast enough to attract private capital. Fundamental agreement on needed state action also extends to reasonable macroeconomic management, to an effective system of the rule of law that creates not only secure expectations for economic transactions but also lays the foundation for autonomous cooperation in civil society, and even to the many regulations that make efficient markets possible (a point that must not be obscured by blanket arguments for and against "market deregulation"). In addition, it is recognized that states have to respond to the dynamics of the political sphere as such and to the challenges presented by the international system and that these responses inevitably shape economic and social policies as well.

At the same time, market exchange is appreciated as a formidable mechanism of coordination that in complex economies cannot be replaced by central political decision making. At the heart of the emerging consensus, then, is the notion of a synergy between state action and market functioning. Both are necessary, and while one can be at odds with the other, they do not necessarily stand in stark opposition to each other. The supreme task—and this is a political task—is to aim for a balance of mutual compatibility. This may mean to choose policy tools in the pursuit of political goals that least interfere with functioning markets. It may require policies to ameliorate market failures. And it may call for policies to mitigate market outcomes that otherwise would create severe political pressures against a successful synergy of market and politics.

Despite the indispensable role of states in developmental processes, there is also agreement that they do not always further that end. States can also stand in the way of forward action due to sluggish inertia; they can act in self-serving ways and create wasteful advantages for select clients; and they can choose mistaken policies and with that possibly create collective disasters. This negative potential of state action is not a figment of the neoliberal imagination. To contain it and to realize the positive contributions of the state to social and economic development, state action must be disciplined.

How can states be disciplined? In his contribution to the introductory part of this volume, Peter Evans emphasizes the combined impact of bureaucratic organization, the market, and democratic guidance and control. Bureaucratic organization and oversight have long been recognized as a critical tool for controlling the machinery of states; but we now have quantitative empirical evidence to demonstrate its contribution to economic growth (Evans and Rauch 1999). The role of the market—offering a metric for economic costs and benefits, providing indications for the efficient allocation of public resources, and keeping public expenditures from chronically exceeding revenues—is part of the synergy conception of the state-economy relationship. The importance of an active and demanding civil society for making state action both effective and responsive has recently been recognized more and more. Much of its effect depends, of course, on the balance of power within society. While even a political influence that is confined to the strongest economic interests may have positive effects on aggregate economic growth, the political demands made on the state will change as the balance of power in society changes.

Matthew Lange's chapter on the rule of law expands the discussion of how states are disciplined. Rule of law rather than personal discretion is at the heart of bureaucratic organization. Extended beyond the state apparatus, it means that the state binds itself to rule observance. At the same time, the rule of law not only enables markets to function; it also creates the institutional conditions for cooperation in associations and other specifically modern social relations, relations that are not based on family, kinship, and clan, that are not held together by an asymmetric dependence of the participants on dominant patrons, and that can deal with a wide variety of objectives. In short, the rule of law is a critical ingredient of synergy not only in state-economy but also in state-society relations.

The emergent consensus on the important role of states in development does not extend to specific policies of economic development beyond the broad agreements sketched above. As we concluded in our introductory overview, much of the knowledge to develop such policies and to evaluate them remains contested. The ambiguities and gaps in policy-relevant knowledge leave the future of development in many countries uncertain. There is a wide variety of potentially relevant conditions, and their impact changes over time. Inevitably, it is politics and state action that have to respond to such uncertainty and change. Over any prolonged period of time, then, we have to expect a complex interaction of state action and economic and social developments.

Some examples may illustrate these uncertainties. A policy configuration such as the Korean developmental state, which was a winning formula for more than a generation, is being readjusted if not radically abandoned, and this readjustment may yet involve more disturbing political and social developments than we have observed in Korea so far. The

Soviet system of central planning was not always the evident failure it now seems in retrospect; but it proved to be increasingly dysfunctional, and the difficulties of radically transforming economy and society toward a completely different order are still apparent in Russia. China has achieved impressive aggregate growth rates, but its rapidly increasing disparities in wealth and well-being are contained by an authoritarian political system that may well not be able to cope with these problems in the future. Many of the Middle Eastern oil states have not been able to convert their vast natural resources into sustained development, and the outlook is worse in much of sub-Saharan Africa where the starting conditions were far less favorable. The purpose of these examples is not to advocate a pessimistic outlook. After all, not only difficulties and blockages but many positive developments as well came as surprises during the last 50 years. The point is simply to underscore that uncertainty is pervasive and that images of a linear progression toward ever greater and more inclusive development across all conditions are misleadingly simplistic.

Long-Lasting Effects of States on Development

The second part of the volume deals with the question whether states have long-term effects on developmental processes. It thereby provides empirical analyses that bring to life some of the conclusions of the earlier part. What is at stake here are not different development policy designs, but the unintended consequences of state structures. Theda Skocpol has labeled these effects "Tocquevillean," because they played a central role in Alexis de Tocqueville's works on *The Old Regime and the French Revolution* and *Democracy in America*:

> When the effects of states are explored from the Tocquevillean point of view, those effects are *not* traced by dissecting state strategies or policies and their possibilities for implementation. Instead, the investigator looks more macroscopically at the ways in which the structures and activities of states unintentionally influence the formation of groups and the political capacities, ideas, and demands of various sectors of society. (Skocpol 1985, p. 21)

All three chapters in this part suggest that state structures have in fact had lasting consequences for later development. However, each stresses different aspects of the state and therefore suggests different mechanisms through which states affect developmental outcomes over extended periods of time.

Using data for approximately 100 countries, Areendam Chanda and Louis Putterman investigate the correlates of economic growth between 1960 and 1995, the level of GDP per capita in 1995, and state institutional quality between 1982 and 1995. Their primary explanatory variable measures the historic presence of states between either 1 and 1950 CE or 1 and 1500 CE. They find that these age measures are positively and significantly related to economic growth between 1960 and 1995. This relationship holds even if controls are introduced for the level of GDP per capita in 1960, for the extent of secondary schooling in 1960, and for the rate of investment. And it remains significant with and without the inclusion of the most developed countries and even if controls for different areas of the world are introduced.

Yet, this astoundingly stable relationship between the age of states and economic growth in the second half of the twentieth century presents a number of intriguing puzzles. There is first the finding that *both* state age measures—the measure that covers the whole 2,000-year period of the common era as well as the one that breaks off in 1500 CE—are related to economic growth in the last half of the twentieth century. This is quite unexpected and suggests that the effect of state age has its roots in conditions that are ancient indeed. Just as surprising, the state history variables, while closely associated with economic *growth* after 1960, are only weakly related to current *levels* of GDP per capita. Finally, state age is not stably related to different measures of the institutional quality of states, which itself is positively related to economic growth. These latter findings in combination suggest that: (1) the age of states did not affect recent economic growth through its impact on state institutional quality and (2) that the age of states is strongly related to economic development over the past half century but not before.

What, then, can account for these findings? If long state histories are not related to the institutional quality of states, their influence on economic growth may run through the other side of the state-society relation. States may create certain preconditions for economic growth through their effect on economic structures and on the culture of subject populations. Alternatively—or concurrently—measures of state age may be proxies for broader early changes in economy and social structure. The authors speculate that an evolutionary process underlies the relationship in which human capital—and, we would add, social capital—increases as societies grow and become more diverse. Such an argument suggests that states and intensive agricultural production interact to promote a readiness for economically productive activities by increasing societal division of labor, unifying populations linguistically and culturally, enhancing individual propensities to participate in labor-intensive economic production, and expanding individual demand for education. From these, we can distinguish two interrelated sets of mechanisms that may well link states—in interaction with settled agriculture—to preconditions for later economic growth: (1) structural effects on the division of labor and the development of urban life and (2) long-term cultural effects.

Both states and intensive agriculture promote increases in the division of labor, as the former establish a political elite that demands certain goods and services and the latter allows many individuals to live without directly participating in the production of food. As a result, communities come to include political elites, religious authorities, artisans, as well as agricultural producers. While communities with such a division of labor have greater inequities, they also induce market exchange. Greater specialization and the extension of a sense of community beyond kinship groups facilitate the organization of more complex social relations.[1] In addition, formal education becomes increasingly important with a division of labor. Most basically, political elites require record keeping for the management of state assets and revenue, something that encourages writing and mathematics, and early states almost always use education as a status signal and thereby increase societal demand for it.

Considering the long-term cultural effects, settled agriculture requires a tremendous discipline of labor as well as consumption. It involves toilsome and monotonous work that has to be performed at set times. Since food is often scarce and some seed must be saved for spring planting (a possible reason for the religious fasting periods that precede the Spring Equinox), agriculture also imposes sharp limits on consumption. Historically, a triad of disciplining agents responded to this need: the extended family with its hierarchies of age and gender, religion organized above the village and tribal level, and the patrimonial state. All three supported a system of norms and an ingrained ethos that had at its center labor commitment and deference to authority. Such a normative culture clearly represents an asset for advances in economic development, though it is equally clearly not a sufficient condition for accelerated economic growth.

If the historic presence of states promotes economic development through such mechanisms, the question arises why this effect has come about only so recently.[2] Out of the many possible explanations, one seems most likely. Nearly all ancient states depended on various forms of patrimonial authority. As Weber (1968) recognized, patrimonialism—a kin-based system of personal rule and traditional legitimacy—is deeply averse to social and economic change. Furthermore, the systems of stratification typically associated with patrimonial rule constitute incentive structures that encourage exploitation and inhibit innovation. Consequently, the historic presence of states may actually constrain economic development and industrialization. Indeed, only in particular critical periods did patrimonial forms of rule morph into less traditional systems of rule—western Europe during the eighteenth and nineteenth centuries, the Meiji Restoration, the Russian and Chinese Revolutions, the Korean War, and so on—and these transitions also preceded large-scale economic change and industrialization.

The twentieth century was a period of dramatic changes of this kind throughout the world. Communist Revolutions and two world wars occurred; colonialism, which had spread to all corners of the world, came to a rapid halt; and transnational economic and political relations expanded and gained new powers. All of these events, in turn, weakened patrimonial forms of authority and promoted industrialization efforts. Thus, the historic staple of intensive agriculture began to decline, and the human and social capital of historic civilizations was increasingly employed for modern forms of production.

In the chapter following that of Chanda and Putterman, James Mahoney and Matthias vom Hau analyze the developmental legacies of Spanish colonialism. Their analytic focus is on the state, and they find that the intensity of Spanish colonialism is inversely related to postcolonial developmental trajectories. Specifically, through the comparative-historical analysis of 18 former colonies, they discover that the colonial centers were encumbered by three negative legacies that did not exist or were much weaker in the Spanish colonial backwaters: (1) the centers had powerful patrimonial states while the backwaters were nearly stateless; (2) the states in the centers were controlled by conservative elites uninterested in increased economic production whereas the states in the backwaters became dominated by more liberal elites participating in international trade; and (3) the colonial centers were much more dependent on Spain for their economic well-being than the backwater areas. These "advantages of backwardness" were not due to endowments that enhanced economic growth through developmental state policy. Rather, the areas that lacked intensive colonialism were able to avoid the same state institutional impediments that characterized the colonial centers. Thus, the legacies of Spanish colonialism were never advantageous for economic development, some were simply worse than others. The chapter, therefore, helps to explain the development levels among Spanish colonies today as well as their mediocre positioning within the world.

The final chapter of the part is by Matthew Lange. Like Mahoney and vom Hau, he investigates colonial state legacies yet focuses on the British Empire. The chapter finds that the British left different colonial state legacies that, in turn, differentially affected postcolonial development. Specifically, indirect colonialism, which used indigenous elites to rule peripheral areas, created a very negative legacy compared to the directly ruled colonies, which had centralized and bureaucratic legal-administrative institutions throughout the territory. Using a set of 33 former British colonies for multivariate statistical analysis, the extent of indirect rule is negatively and significantly related to (1) several indicators of state governance in the late 1990s; (2) per capita GDP and life expectancy in 1960; and (3) average annual change in per capita GDP between 1960 and 2000 and absolute change in life expectancy between 1960 and 1990. The chapter, therefore, provides quantitative support to past qualitative works finding that indirect rule institutionalized decentralized and despotic forms of rule that negatively affected governance and development, while direct rule endowed countries with rule-based legal-administrative institutions that promoted diverse developmental processes.

As the synopses just rendered demonstrate, all three chapters provide evidence that states affect developmental processes over extended periods of time. Patrimonialism emerges in all three as a major explanatory factor. Mahoney and vom Hau as well as Lange find that patrimonial states have negative effects on long-term development. Mahoney and vom Hau see a main channel of influence running through state autonomy, which allowed rent-seeking patrimonial elites to impede development. Lange, on the other hand, contends that patrimonialism inhibited development through its effects on state structures. In indirectly ruled British colonies, the combination of patrimonialism in rural areas and bureaucracy in the center resulted in fragmented states lacking the capacity to act corporately. The mechanisms highlighted by Mahoney and vom Hau in Latin America and by Lange in former British colonies likely have an elective affinity to one another. Mahoney and vom Hau recognize, for instance, that Spanish colonialism institutionalized ineffective states, which prevented the Spanish authorities from controlling local elites and therefore made possible an instrumental state serving rent-seeking interests. Alternatively, although stressing state structure and its effects on the capacity of the state to act corporately, Lange contends that indirect rule made the central state dependent on local powerholders and therefore allowed non-state actors to unduly control state policy. The combination of these two factors—a fissiparous and incapacitated state as well as an instrumental state controlled by a conservative elite—therefore appear to reinforce one another and to account for the vitality of patrimonialism over time, a point that brings us back to the chapter by Chanda and Putterman.

In their chapter, Chanda and Putterman show that the historic presence of states is negatively related to present state institutional quality once the currently most developed countries are excluded or controls for geographic location are introduced, although the relationship is not always statistically significant. Since nearly all states up until the past few centuries have been patrimonial, this finding suggests that patrimonialism undercut the positive effects of old states. In addition, their findings that per capita GDP in 1995 is negatively related to the historic presence of states when other factors are controlled for, provide evidence that old patrimonial states have not promoted significant economic growth. Instead, only the states that overcame patrimonial impediments—such as western Europe, Japan, and South Korea—have become truly developmental.

When combined, these findings suggest that patrimonialism is an important obstacle that must be overcome for broad-based development and that the inability to do so has caused countries that were once among the world's most developed to stagnate and fall further and further behind. As such, the findings provide a new interpretation to the influential work of Acemoglu, Johnson, and Robinson (2001, 2002), which all three chapters in this part cite and draw upon. Acemoglu, Johnson, and Robinson contend that colonialism caused a reversal of fortunes throughout the world by affecting the nature and quality of institutions. Their primary explanation focuses on settlement and extraction, with the former promoting growth and the latter inhibiting it. In the world's least developed societies, the colonial powers established settlement colonies, which created liberal institutions that protected property rights. In the world's most developed societies, on the other hand, colonial powers established extractive institutions to exploit the wealth of the colonized. This volume suggests an alternative yet partially complementary account: colonialism generally strengthened patrimonialism in the more developed societies yet provided the basis for more bureaucratic states when no previous patrimonial structure was present. Cumings's chapter on the rapid construction of the South Korean state also lends credence to this argument: Japanese colonialism and civil war helped undermine patrimonial elements in the Korean system of rule, thereby sparking rather remarkable state building and industrialization.[3]

Despite these similarities, Chanda and Putterman, Mahoney and vom Hau, and Lange stress different avenues through which states affect development. The main thrust of the chapter of Chanda and Putterman suggests that the historic presence of (mostly patrimonial) states shaped human and social capital and thereby created conditions that were ultimately favorable to economic growth. The focus is therefore not on the direct effects states can have on developmental processes but on indirect effects: states shape structural developments as well as social norms and cognitive frameworks in ways that eventually enhance economic development. The argument is, therefore, a prime example of an historic cause that is constructed over a long period of time, lays dormant, and only affects the outcome once other conditions are right.

Alternatively, Mahoney and vom Hau focus on state effects that are more direct than those described by Chanda and Putterman. Their primary emphasis is on how the economic regime supported by both states and national elites affects the mode and type of economic production. In particular, Latin American states that supported liberal economic policy prescriptions ended up having superior economic growth to those that implemented mercantilist policy. While the former promoted export-led growth, the latter led to rent-seeking by conservative elites. Mahoney and vom Hau also provide an account of different types of historic effects. Instead of being a cause that built up over long periods of time, they describe a cause that emerged rather quickly, yet depended on historical conditions (i.e., the presence or absence of pre-Columbian populations) and had long-term repercussions due to lock-in effects and the continuation of economic regimes over extended periods of time.

Finally, Lange analyzes state effects that are even more direct than those described by Mahoney and vom Hau. Instead of simply being midwives that shape developmental processes through policy that influences the action of others, states can also be demiurges that independently affect developmental outcomes (Evans 1995). For this to occur, however, states must have the institutional capacity to act corporately and engage societal actors. This, in turn, requires that states are organized in ways that promote corporate coherence. Lange's findings suggest that states that are centralized and bureaucratically organized have superior capacities for this than those that are fissiparous and patrimonial. Considering historical causes, Lange describes one that emerged over several decades yet that has shaped long-term outcomes through institutional reproduction and constant institutional effects.[4]

The Difficult Process of Building Effective States

A state that proves to be an effective tool in the hands of rulers—capable of exerting coercive or hard power as well as infrastructural or soft power—is a necessary if not sufficient condition for successful development. Yet, an effective state of this kind is not available just because it is needed. Building it is an arduous task. In Part III of this volume we looked into past history to learn more about the timescales and social processes involved in state building. Is it inherently a long-term process? What are the conditions for the emergence of effective states?

For this analysis, a rough metric is needed to arrive at judgments of slow and fast in the development of states and state-society relations. We propose one based on two considerations, the time horizons of political actors and generational turnover. The planning perspective of political actors varies of course a great deal, depending for instance on their expected tenure in office or on a culture of *raison d'etat* that encourages a longer-term outlook. Still, intentional planning tends to be constrained by whatever the time horizon of the decisive actors happens to be. Generational turnover is significant in the development and consolidation of normative orientations, the establishment of a new ethos, and the functioning of institutional innovations. Taking the two considerations together, developments that approach 25 to 30 years in duration can reasonably be called long-term. Some developments will take much longer. This is especially the case where the rationalization of rule is a matter of contention among major social interests inside and outside the state apparatus. Even more drawn-out periods of "stasis"—diagnosed from different problem perspectives as stagnation or remarkable stability—are characteristic of centuries of patrimonial rule where a persistent impulse toward a rationalization of rule is hardly discernible.

In this part's first chapter, Dietrich Rueschemeyer lays out theoretical arguments why building a bureaucratic state is likely to be a protracted affair. Referring to the long history of state building in Europe that began after the collapse of the Carolingian Empire and the rise of a proto-bureaucratic church in the eleventh century and that came to a conclusion with the full bureaucratization of northwestern European states only in the second half of the nineteenth century, he combines ideas of the theory of norms and institutions with insights from the study of conflicts in search of a better understanding of the construction of effective states. Norm theory and conflict theory elucidate what it takes to build effective state organizations as well as what obstacles state builders are likely to encounter. The same basic ideas also help in understanding how state-society relations conducive to effective state action come about. It is critical to realize that normative developments and conflicts over state building interact with each other. Thus, opposition to more effective states, whether located within the state or in the wider society, is likely to interfere with the establishment and consolidation of a new ethos of state officials, while a more effective state apparatus can be a powerful tool in overcoming opposition to the rationalization of rule. Many of the propositions advanced by Rueschemeyer point to incremental and time-consuming processes. However, more rapid developments seem possible under certain conditions.

While normative and institutional change often requires generational turnover to consolidate and opposition against state reform frequently prolongs the time needed for moving toward more effective forms of governance, it is also possible to specify some of the conditions for accelerated developments. Most prominent are crisis situations such as severe economic difficulties, wars, and postwar as well as postrevolutionary situations, which may both create a sense of urgency and shift the balance of power in favor of those seeking a more effective government. However, crises may have the opposite effect as well, if the challenges they pose overwhelm the resources of state elites. Crises are likely to engender advances toward a more bureaucratic state organization only where strong foundations already exist on which state elites are then able to build. This qualification can be generalized. Pushed to the extreme it states: wherever significant organizations of a bureaucratic or proto-bureaucratic character are already in existence and where well-functioning social relations independent of personal, family, and kin ties are common in society, states can be reformed with considerable speed.

Thomas Ertman juxtaposes to these theoretical arguments a crisp overview of European state development. Following leads of Max Weber, he offers powerful conclusions. He emphasizes that the period from the eleventh to the sixteenth century cannot be taken as part of a single gestation period of the bureaucratic state that ended only 150 years ago. It was a period of premodern patrimonial rule. Yet, this patrimonialism had four characteristics that set it apart comparatively and that turned out to be necessary conditions for the unique and unexpected later rise of capitalism and the modern state: (1) a separation of religious and secular authority; (2) self-governing cities and conceptions of community that transcended kinship and clan; (3) autonomous markets; and (4) strong traditions of procedural rather than substantive justice. These particular features of European premodern states may have been necessary but they were not sufficient for modern state building. This occurred only after the sixteenth century. Ertman focuses on two further conditions: the rapidly expanding supply of laymen with higher education and the maturing of markets. The former improved the bargaining position of rulers vis-à-vis their staffs, while creating a distinct status group of civil servants, the latter opened ways of state finance that avoided dependency on officeholders and a few financiers.

When modern state building came about, it took different forms in different parts of Europe. In England, it was pressure from Parliament that initiated the process. The government could use public credit markets to finance long-term needs. In line with the strong role of public opinion and broader-based politics, the dominant ethos of the English civil servants emphasized service to the public. State building in the German territories and in Scandinavia came about in the aftermath of the Reformation and the related wars. Diffusion of innovations was aided by commonalities of culture and situation. As state building was less induced by developments in society and economy, the ethos of the civil service was, in these countries, much more oriented to the state itself. Developments in other European countries fell between these more clear-cut trajectories.

Ertman emphasizes that state building efforts did not necessarily take extremely long periods of time, although it was still long-term according to our metric of 25 to 30 years and depended on preexisting state and societal characteristics that took considerable time to emerge. He points to several junctures at which intentional action engineered breakthroughs in the process of bureaucratization. In France and in the countries occupied by French forces in the early 1800s, revolution and military imposition made for radical breaks with the old state structures. However, while similar successes can be located at specific points in time in other countries, they typically were partial advances to be complemented later by others, and they often took a longer time to become fully embedded. Still, Ertman stresses that the qualitative shifts in European state development took place in a matter of decades—less than forty years in England and similar periods in the German and Scandinavian states—and that the process then became irreversible: none of the European proto-bureaucracies reverted to patrimonialism.

The next two chapters were conceived as critical tests of the proposition that state building is inherently a long-term process. After all, the best-known revolutions were followed in their wake by fast state construction. Similarly, the developmental state of South Korea seemed to emerge with great speed from the crisis of the Korean War.

Jaime Becker and Jack Goldstone emphasize in their overview of postrevolutionary developments the resulting balance of power between opposing forces as a major factor. Under pressure to gain and maintain territorial control, revolutionary elites were aided by often dramatic shifts in the power balance. Interests associated with the *ancien régime* were weakened significantly. And large segments of the elites and of the population at large were mobilized for political and social change. In combination, these factors made for outcomes that qualify our overall finding that state building is inherently a slow process.

The time required for attaining territorial control varied a great deal (as did the specific alignment of opposing forces), but overall revolutionary elites established their power in quite short time periods. Yet, establishing territorial control is not tantamount to building a modern bureaucratic state. Becker and Goldstone show that in some cases the strong element of charismatic rule characteristic of revolutionary elites is replaced by patrimonial features. In others, preexisting bureaucratic foundations could be used in state reconstruction, while in still others, postrevolutionary state building made substantial advances toward an effective modern state even without strong elements of a rational state organization existing already in the *ancien régime*. The most famous example of the latter possibility is the Napoleonic reforms in the aftermath of the French Revolution and their diffusion in western Europe.

Becker and Goldstone review the major resources for state building after revolutions, the variation of which is critical for understanding different outcomes—the quality of the existing state organization and its military, aggregate human capital as well as cultural capital, leadership of the charismatic-visionary and the pragmatic variety, and external support or interference. They see the major obstacles to successful state reconstruction in the persistence of strong patrimonial interests and in ethnic fragmentation. Becker and Goldstone therefore suggest that rapid postrevolutionary state building requires not only the removal of entrenched elites from power but also fortuitous preexisting conditions.

State building inevitably involves state-society relations; and here, Becker and Goldstone develop a major argument. Taking off from Michael Mann's distinction of "despotic" and "infrastructural" state strength as, respectively, "power over civil society" and "power through civil society" (Mann 1986, p. 477), they make a case that revolutions often result in states that retain a "despotic" power over society for long periods of time, unchecked by either effective self-organization of society or the impersonal rule of law. They relate this outcome to a historical bifurcation of modern "state design"—constitutional democracy and one-party states. One interpretation of these findings is that forces that allow postrevolutionary regimes to build states rapidly—the removal of opposition and political control of a mobilized population—stifle civil society and therefore limit the long-term effectiveness and durability of states.

The last chapter of this part deals with the history of the Korean state. Bruce Cumings describes an astounding historical trajectory of long-term stability followed by a sequence of contingent ruptures. This history is instructive indeed for the questions at hand. Centralized government in Korea goes back to the fifth century CE. A few centuries later, it equipped itself with a body of trained and examined civil servants, though hereditary restrictions limited access to the examinations. An educational system infused with Confucian norms and values had a thoroughgoing impact on Korean society for more than a thousand years. Within the state, it created a consistent ethos of the select corps of officials.

However, this bureaucratic state rested in its power over society, if not in its internal workings, on compromises with powerful rural landowners. "The administrative setup was strong from the center down to the county level . . . Below the counties . . . local influentials (meaning clans and elders) controlled everything (p. 215)." This system—so different from, and yet also very similar to more common patrimonial forms of rule—had a remarkable stability until the twentieth century. It was changed in rapid succession by a series of contingent developments—Japanese colonialism from 1910 upto the end of World War II, American occupation, division into North and South, the war of the Korean peninsula, and the seizure of power by the military in 1960. The Japanese carried the bureaucratization of the central government radically further, while landed interests lost their power in the wake of World War II and the Korean War. Yet, the beginning of the authoritarian developmental state in 1960, which was dramatically successful economically, was not in itself a radical new beginning in state development. It could build on ancient foundations that were remarkably undisturbed by the abrupt changes in 1910, in the mid-1940s, and during the Korean War. Remarkable continuities were evident in fundamental policy as well: in an international situation that was dominated by American hegemony, the Korean state nevertheless retained policy orientations that had deeper roots that were shaped by ancient traditions as well as by continental European influences implanted by the Japanese.

Of the two inquiries designed to further explore the conditions of rapid state building, one, Cumings's analysis of the history of the Korea state, broadly confirms the expectation that state building tends to be a long-term process, even though important specific developments came about in relatively short periods of time. Relatively rapid and successful state building was promoted by colonial conquest and war, both of which weakened patrimonial classes that stood in the way of bureaucratization. Thus, external as well as internal conflict emerges as an important factor shaping state building, and social upheavals provide an opening for rather punctuated trajectories of state reforms. Yet, the most far-reaching transformations occurred over a 50-year period, demonstrating that state building was a moderately long-term process in this seemingly rapid instance. Moreover, even these transformations depended on historical foundations, such as the long history of a trained and coherent civil service, an advanced educational system, and a unified national culture.

The review of postrevolutionary state building by Becker and Goldstone, on the other hand, suggested three qualifying conclusions. First, building or reconstructing a state able to secure effective territorial control is often achieved in a relatively brief time. Second, there are some instances where revolutions created, fairly rapidly, a modern bureaucratic state, though this was often contingent on fortuitous preexisting conditions. Third, postrevolutionary states often display state-society relations that lack the reciprocity through which states are guided and disciplined and therefore have problems with long-term stability and effectiveness.

Conclusions and Implications

What, then, did we learn about states and development? Looking at the history of states in a number of very different ways, we gained insights into their construction as well as their long-lasting effects on developmental processes. First, once again, state building is difficult and time consuming. The construction of huge legal-administrative apparatuses—with effective lines of communication and authority and a suitable *esprit de corps* among its officials—and the development of productive state-society relations take decades even under the most fortuitous conditions. And, once built, state institutions of very different kinds tend to persist over long periods of time and to affect a variety of social processes. Persistent state structures can inhibit social and economic development, and states can adopt dysfunctional policies; yet states can also reinforce developmental trajectories through continuous effects over extended periods of time and devise solutions to new developmental dilemmas as they emerge. The evidence suggests that much of the variation in global developmental inequalities can be explained by different histories of state building and different effects these states have had on developmental processes.

Yet, a reader may well wonder whether these are not rather "academic" insights. Are they at all relevant in the face of the pressing policy problems in today's world? Indeed, if state building takes a long time, if legacies of state building have long-lasting effects, both positive and negative, and if the outcomes of state policies often are hard to predict, what good is it to know that some states promote developmental outcomes while others do not? We do not share this skepticism. Acknowledging uncertainty and ignorance, as we have done repeatedly, is an eminently important element of responsible policy making. Even more so is recognition of the inconvenient facts that state building is difficult and typically drawn out in time and that stubborn blockages to development may be built into state-society relations. Diagnoses, even partial diagnostic insights, are indispensable for adequate policy formation, even if these diagnoses mean that certain avenues seem blocked or at least difficult to pursue. Without such recognition, it is impossible to arrive at reasonable estimates of the chances of alternative policies.

In addition, by showing that effective states are necessary for various types of policy implementation, the findings suggest faults in one-size-fits-all policy prescriptions. Whatever policies may be desirable in principle, they must be within the realistic capabilities of a state as it exists in a particular country. Too often economic modelers as well as social idealists stipulate tasks that many states cannot possibly meet. If a state's capacity is limited, less may well be more. Overextending state responsibilities can have dangerous consequences. Tragically, it is possible that the limitations on a state's capacity are so severe as to foreclose successful development in a country for the near or medium-term future. However, this must not be assumed as inevitable in even the poorest countries.[5]

Do the difficulties of state building that we have identified, then, suggest an unconditionally poor development outlook for those countries that are not blessed with favorable historical conditions? That would be a crude overinterpretation of our results. We suggest that recognition of the role of states in combination with an historical view may help specify—at least in hypothetical form—some pathways to more effective state action that promise success in a tolerably short period. The chapters on state building contain a number of important qualifications on the otherwise strong empirical generalization that state building tends to be a long-term process. The first point to note is that our historical generalization is similar to a significant but not perfect correlation in quantitative research. It cannot be used to rule out various kinds of "exceptions" that contradict the modal picture.

But theoretically informed comparative historical investigation can do more than correlational analysis. It can point to specific conditions that make for variation and exceptionalism. Rueschemeyer divides the ensemble of his hypotheses into four sets, those focusing on normative and institutional change and those focusing on opposition and overcoming of opposition both within state organizations and in the wider society. While it is clear that these sets of factors interact with one another, it is imperative not to see them as a closely fused bundle. In general, we must recognize that in every country where state building is a concern, very particular constellations of obstacles are present. Here is one sense in which the epigram of the late House Speaker Tip O'Neill—"All politics is local"—is surely correct. This particularism opens up a wide field for investigation, but it is critically important when it comes to drawing policy relevant conclusions. Locating the problems in a given country may highlight promising avenues for advancement.

For instance, it may at some point become possible to break the resistance of vested interests to more effective state functioning, and that may then make the creation of well-functioning bureaucratic organizations a much more manageable task. Both the theoretical arguments of Rueschemeyer and the work on postrevolutionary state developments of Becker and Goldstone see crises as possibly decisive accelerators of state development, as they affect both the sense of urgency on the part of different decisive actors and at the same time may have weakened contrary interests decisively. Crises that have this result may well turn into critical junctures that open up steady, self-reinforcing, and not easily reversed change toward effective state action and productive state-society relations.

Rueschemeyer cautions not to consider diffusion and learning from other countries a panacea. This does not mean, however, that they are irrelevant. Ertman found that diffusion and learning was very important in continental Europe, especially where linguistic, cultural, and political conditions were similar. For many countries in today's world, this can be a significant factor in accelerating state building, provided that the indigenous obstacles are not too steep. If a close consideration of local conditions reveals possibilities of proceeding, cross-national learning may become important indeed. It may make it possible to tackle the problem of building effective state organizations even if, in the end, they still may meet the two to three decades threshold of long-term change. One important effect of cross-national learning is that it can extend the time horizon of policy makers, allowing them to realize that any serious attempt to construct effective states must be approached from a long-term perspective that demands vigilance, ingenuity, and persistence.

Besides highlighting the configuration of domestic power relations and the diffusion of bureaucratic models across international boundaries, the chapters point to other specific conditions that help advance the cause of constructing effective states. Ertman emphasized the supply of trained staff as a critical variable. He also argued that secure financing, which did not create particular dependencies, was decisive in England. Secure financing of the tasks undertaken is similarly a critical priority in today's state building efforts, a priority that leads us back to the synergies between states and markets. Overlapping with this is a third consideration stressed by Ertman, which has a close correspondence to Peter Evans's triad of mechanisms disciplining states. The influence of interests without access to rent-seeking—of popular pressure represented by Parliament, of a relatively free press, and of financial markets—was decisive in promoting proto-bureaucratic reforms in England. Their absence and the despotic character of many of the postrevolutionary states documented by Becker and Goldstone is equally relevant.

The Korean story, as reviewed by Cumings, adds a number of important insights. If one does not succumb to the temptation to see actual historical trajectories as developments that *had* to happen, it is not easy to imagine less promising interventions than the impositions of foreigners, first the Japanese and later the Americans. And yet the thoroughgoing completion of bureaucratization and the eventual weakening of large landowners' hold on power was the result of precisely these impositions in combination with the devastation of the Korean War.

While such disruptions opened pathways to relatively rapid state building in Korea, the latter also depended on the maintenance of other precolonial characteristics. Thus, radical transformations can build on ancient foundations, even if at first sight the developments in question seem far from promising. In fact, building on existing foundations is probably the most important way of constructing effective states. That was, after all, the way state building proceeded in Europe. In his ingenious comparative study of developmental state action Peter Evans has pointed to the chance of extending pockets of bureaucratic rationality in the states of Brazil and India (Evans 1995). Partial moves toward the bureaucratic pole of state organization can be fast, but often they were not. Still, important things can be accomplished by these effective parts of the state and building on these advances is the most promising route for many countries. At the same time, the Korean case clearly shows that certain aspects of preexisting arrangements must be discarded or changed in order to implement capacity enhancing reforms, patrimonial state relations being a notable example.

This project began with a simple and hardly controversial idea: searching for avenues of developing state capacity with greater dispatch than is typical of the past record is an eminently worthwhile undertaking. The overall picture of the slow historical processes typically involved in building states and transforming state-society relations and of their often long-lasting consequences at first seems to undercut any such hopes. On close inspection, however, our findings say something different. They warn against futile policy ambitions and they give indications of realistic possibilities to shorten the gestation period of desperately needed developments.

Notes

1. For a recent discussion of the association of agrarian economies with specialization, overall inequality, and political authority located three or four levels above the local community see Nielsen (2004), who reviews and reanalyses with new data the earlier work of Lenski (1966).
2. In an as yet unpublished paper "Early States, Reversals, and Catching up," Chanda and Putterman have found a positive relationship between early states or early agriculture and levels of income in 1500 as best they can be guessed. However, the international differences in living standards in 1500 were small compared to those of today.
3. Incidentally, in Korea, what appears to have been a vital determinant of economic expansion was not the protection of property rights but their disregard: forced land reforms weakened the patrimonial elite and paved the way for industrialization.
4. Our thinking about the time dimensions of cause and effect relations has benefited greatly from the work of Paul Pierson, now available in one volume (Pierson 2004).
5. Jeffrey Sachs, for instance, makes this clear in his recent review of promising interventions in sub-Saharan African development (Sachs 2004).

References

Acemoglu, Daron, Simon Johnson, and James Robinson. 2001."The Colonial Origins of Comparative Development: An Empirical Investigation." *American Economic Review*, 91, 5: 1369–1401.

Acemoglu, Daron, Simon Johnson, and James A. Robinson. 2002. "Reversal of Fortune: Geography and Institutions in the Making of the Modern World Income Distribution." *Quarterly Journal of Economics*, 117: 1231–1294.

Evans, Peter. 1995. *Embedded Autonomy: States and Industrial Transformation*. Princeton, NJ: Princeton University Press.

Evans, Peter, and James Rauch. 1999. "Bureaucracy and Growth: A Cross-National Analysis of the Effects of 'Weberian' State Structures on Economic Growth." *American Economic Review*, 64: 748–765.

Lenski, Gerhard. 1966. *Power and Privilege*. Chapel Hill, NC: University of North Carolina Press.

Mann, Michael. 1986. *The Sources of Social Power*. Vol. I. Cambridge and New York: Cambridge University Press.

Nielsen, Francois. 2004. "The Ecological-Evolutionary Typology of Human Societies and the Evolution of Social Inequality." *Sociological Theory*, 22, 2: 292–314.

Pierson, Paul. 2004. *Politics in Time: History, Institutions, and Social Analysis*. New York: Cambridge University Press.

Sachs, Jeffrey. 2004. "Doing the Sums on Africa." *The Economist*, May 22: 19–21.

Skocpol, Theda. 1985. "Bringing the State Back: Strategies of Analysis in Current Research." In *Bringing the State Back In*, edited by P. Evans, D. Rueschemeyer, and T. Skocpol. New York and Cambridge: Cambridge University Press, 3–37.

Weber, Max. 1968. *Economy and Society*. Trans. Ephraim Fishoff. New York. Bedminster Press.

INDEX

Abers, Rebecca, 45n8
Acemoglu, Daron, 77, 90n5, 92, 118, 121, 128, 247
Adelman, Irma, 82
Afghanistan, 191, 201, 206
Africa: age of state, 70, 77; colonial legacy, 12, 117, 118; democracy, 131, 137n8; development, 23n3, 29, 96, 127, 133, 242, 258n5; diseases, 121, 136n6; French Africa, 135; state building, 181
agriculture, settled, 70–1, 213, 243
Albania, 184
Aminzade, Ronald, 199
Amsden, Alice, 4, 18, 57, 61, 118, 212
Andrien, Kenneth, 96–102 *passim*, 106
Aoki Shùzò, 234n1
Aquino, Corazon, 196, 199
Aragon, 166
Argentina: colonialism, 93, 100, 105–12 *passim*; the state, 70, 90n11, 95, 111
Aristide, Jean-Bertrand, 191, 200
Armenia, 197
ascenso, 101, 103
Asia: the cold war, 17; democratization, 131; economy, 12, 16, 17, 18, 27, 70, 228–31; state building, 181, 213
associations, 50–2, 58–9, 61–2
audiencias, 100, 101, 102
Australia, 77, 90n9, 124
Austria, 169, 234n1

authority: charismatic, 192, 252; rational-legal, 52–4, 55–6, 192; traditional, 52–3, 192; *see also* Weber, Max
Aylmer, G.E., 172
Azores, 117

Ba'athist party, 192
Baiocchi, Gianpaolo, 45n8
Balazs, Etienne, 214
Baltic states, 159, 184, 191, 203, 207
Banerjee, Abhijtit, 136n5
Bangladesh, 125, 136n4
Bantus, 71
Barbados, 128
Barrett, Richard, 17
Barro, Robert, 79
Barzelay, Michael, 36
Bates, Robert, 12, 18, 23n3, 62
Bavaria, 169, 172
Bayart, Jean-François, 122, 135
Becker, Jaime, 251–2, 254, 256–7
Beckford, George, 128
Belarus, 159
Belgium, 176, 179
Bergeron, Louis, 176
Berlin, Germany, 234n1
Berman, Harold, 162n2
Berman, Sheri, 52
Bertucci, Guido, 41
Birnbaum, Pierre, 52

Bishop, Maurice, 199, 201
Bjerre Jensen, Birgit, 171
Blom, J.C.H., 176
Bloom, David, 90n13
Bockstette, Valerie, 74, 82, 90n6
Bogotá, Colombia, 108, 110
Bolivar, Simon, 196
Bolivia, 90n11, 100, 103, 106, 111, 196
Bollen, Kenneth, 122
Bolsheviks, 191, 198–206 *passim*
Boone, Catherine, 12, 118, 120, 122, 135
Boserup, Ester, 90n1
Bosnia, 203
Bourbon Reforms, 93, 98, 100, 103–5, 108–9, 111
Bourdieu, Pierre, 198
Brading, David, 97, 99, 102
Brandenburg, 169
Brazil: debt, 225, 257; development, 45n1; public transportation, 39–40; the state, 34–6, 70, 90n11
Bresser Pereira, Luis Carlos, 45n1
Brewer, John, 174
British colonialism: administration, 217; determinants of, 120–2; and direct rule, 118–25, 246; and indirect rule, 12, 119–25, 136n7, 246; legacies of, 117–36, 246; list of colonies, 123*t*
Brittany, 202
Brown, David, 118, 122
Brunei, 131
Bryce, James, 117
Buddhism, 213
Buenos Aires, Argentina, 100, 106–10 *passim*
bureaucracy, 7–8, 50–2, 145; and development, 32–6, 55–6, 61–2; and norms, 147; origins of, 144, 206; qualitative indicator of, 90n7; *see also* state building; states; Weber, Max
Burkett, John, 72, 73, 79, 81, 88, 90n6
Burkholder, Mark, 100–10 *passim*
Burt, Ronald, 51

California, 37–8, 45n2
Callaghy, Thomas, 63n7
Calvinism, 160
Cambodia, 200, 206
Camdessuss, Michel, 17
Cameroon, 124
Canada, 90n9, 124, 130
Canary Islands, 117
Capdequí, José Marí, 101
capitalism, 3, 13, 15–16, 23n3, 152, 160
Caracas, Venezuela, 100, 108, 109, 110
Carnoy, Martin, 114
Carolingian Empire, 177, 249
Carranza, Venustiano, 200
Carruthers, Bruce, 27
Castile, 166
Castro, Fidel, 192, 199, 200
Castro, Raúl, 200
caudillismo, 53
Ceara, Brazil, 34–6
Centeno, Miguel Angel, 113–14n4, 161
Central America, 28
Ceuta, 117
chaebols, 225–6, 230, 231, 234
Chanda, Areendam, 74, 243–8, 258n2
Chandler, D.S., 102, 104
Chanock, Martin, 120
charisma; *see* authority: charismatic
Charles I, 204
Charles II (England), 172–3
Charles II (Spain), 102
Charles X, 195
Chechnya, 197, 203
Chester, Sir Norman, 175
Chiapas, 198
chiefs, 119–20, 122, 125
Childe, V. Gordon, 10
Chile, 70, 90n11, 107, 109, 110
Chin, Soomi, 17
China: development, 71, 77, 82, 85, 90n14, 227, 229, 242; under Mao, 197, 198; revolution, 184, 190, 195–207 *passim*, 245; the state, 70, 162n7, 166, 177, 193, 204, 215, 221

Index

Chosôn Dynasty, 215
Chun Doo Hwan, 232
Church, Clive, 176
civil service, 194–6, 212–16 *passim*, 233, 250–3 *passim*
civil society, 43, 231, 241, 252
Clapham, Christopher, 120
clientelism, 50–2, 73
Coard, Bernard, 201
Coatsworth, John, 105, 106, 110
cold war, 17, 163n9, 223, 227–8
Coleman, James, 60, 160
Colombia, 100, 107
colonialism, 77, 93–9, 97–9, 122, 199, 217; *see also* British colonialism; Japan: colonialism; Spanish colonialism
Confucianism, 213–14
Congo, Democratic Republic of, 53, 70
consulados, 102, 107
coordination structures, 49–52
corruption, 17, 86, 90n7, 126, 194, 207
Coser, Lewi, 63n2
Costa Rica, 93, 95, 106, 107, 111
Cote D'Ivoire, 135
Creoles, 101–4, 107
Croatia, 203
Cromwell, Oliver, 172, 198
Cruise O'Brien, Donal, 122, 135
Cuba, 184, 191, 192, 197–200 *passim*, 207
cultural capital, 198, 252
Cumings, Bruce, 17, 213–17 *passim*, 222, 247, 253–4, 257
Curitaba, Brazil, 39, 45n6
Czechoslovakia, 197, 201, 203
Czech Republic, 159, 200, 203; *see also* Czechoslovakia

Dabee, Rajen, 19
Daewoo, 231
da Silva, Lula, 42
Declaration of the Rights of Man and Citizen, 205
democracy, 40–3, 126, 130–1, 135, 152, 204–5, 213, 229–34 *passim*,

Deng Xiaoping, 200
Denmark, 166, 171, 172, 234n1
despotic power, 162n1, 193–4, 207–8, 252
Depression, the, 160
development policy, 13–19
Deyo, Frederic, 16
Diamond, Jared, 70–1, 127
Díaz, Porfirio, 199
Dipper, Christof, 170, 171, 175
division of labor, 244
Doha, A.H.M.S., 136n4
Downing, Sir George, 172–3
Doyle, William, 167, 175
Dror, Yeheskel, 163n10
Durkheim, Emile, 147, 162n8
Duvalier, Francois, 191, 200
Duvalier, Jean-Claude, 191, 200

Easterly, William, 37, 72, 86, 128
Eckert, Carter, 218
Ecklund, Robert, 14
Ecuador, 100, 103, 105, 106, 111
education: and civil servants, 169–70, 179, 212–14 *passim*, 233, 250–3 *passim*; historical development of, 244; state provisioning of, 56
Edwardes, Michael, 136n5
Egypt, 70, 166, 196
Eisenhower, Dwight D., 223
Eisenstadt, S.N., 11, 150
El Salvador, 105
encomienda, 101, 107
Encyclopedia Britannica, 74, 75
Engels, Friedrich, 11
Engerman, Stanley, 92, 118
England: Bank of, 173; Civil War, 172; economy, 14, 23; Glorious Revolution, 173, 184, 191, 198; Hanoverian Succession, 174; Parliament, 172–4, 179, 203, 204–5, 251, 257; state building, 166–81 *passim*, 204, 251, 257; Treasury, 173; *see also* Great Britain; British colonialism

Englebert, Pierre, 127
Enlightenment, the, 3
Enron, 38
Ertman, Thomas, 162n, 167–73 *passim* 181, 203–4, 250–1, 256–7
Esman, Milton, 8, 49, 59, 61
Ethiopia, 82, 206
ethnicity, 73, 128, 181, 202–3, 252
Europe, 4, 12, 14, 53, 58, 82, 128, 159; *see also* state building: Europe
Evans, Peter: developmental state, 4, 57, 63n3, 163n10, 248; embedded autonomy, 10, 59, 60, 95, 113n2, 257; international environment, 97; predatory state, 32, 52; state building, 8; state discipline, 31, 240–1; synergy, 34, 43, 45n6, 52, 61, 63n6; Weberianness, 90n15–16
Export-Oriented Industrialization (EOI), 17, 18, 19

Fanon, Frantz, 118
Ferguson, Niall, 117
Fiji, 122
Firmin-Sellers, Kathryn, 135
Fisher, John, 109
Fisher, Michael, 119, 135
Foran, John, 198
France: colonialism, 217; development, 211; mercantilism, 14; and Napoleon, 197; National Assembly, 175, 179, 203–4; revolution, 169, 175–6, 179–80, 195–208 *passim*, 220, 252; the state, 166–70 *passim*, 175–6, 179–80, 205, 214; Third Republic, 179
Franklin, Benjamin, 200
Freedheim, Sara, 34–6, 63n6, 63n8
Freedom House, 126, 130
Fronde, the, 162n6
functionalism, 151, 163n9
Fung, Archon, 45n8

Gaetani, Francisco, 45n1
Gale, James Scarth, 213
Gaunt, David, 171

Germany: Hohenzollern, 203; ISI, 16; late development, 4, 12, 57, 211, 220–1; Nazis, 51–2, 197; revolution, 197; the state, 169–80 *passim*, 213, 214, 220–1, 233, 234n1, 251
Gerschenkron, Alexander, 4, 163n12
Ghana, 135
globalization, 17
Godolphin, Sidney, 173–4
Goldsmith, Arthur, 63n3
Goldstone, Jack, 251–2, 254, 256–7
Gootenberg, Paul, 97
Gopal, Ram, 136n5
Gorski, Philip, 8, 52, 63n3, 163n15
Göto Shimpei, 216
Grampp, William, 15
Granovetter, Mark, 57
Great Britain, 18, 27, 28, 211; *see also* British colonialism; England
Greenaway, David, 19
Grenada, 201
Grier, Robin, 118, 122
Griffiths, Percival, 125, 136n4
Gross Domestic Product (GDP), 72, 79–85, 126, 131–2
Guardino, Peter, 102
Guatemala, 79, 100, 103, 105, 111
Guatemala City, Guatemala, 100
Guerra, Francisco-Xavier, 99
Gustav, Vasa, 171

Haber, Stephen, 106
Hadenius, Axel, 63n8
Hailey, William, 117
Haiti, 82, 191, 200
Halliday, Fred, 202
Halliday, John, 234n1
Halperín Donghi, Tulio, 97, 108, 109
Hamilton, Alexander, 200
Hanover, 169
Hansen, Roger, 106
Hardacre, Helen, 234n1
Hardin, R., 5
Harling, Philip, 175
Havel, Vaclav, 200

INDEX

Hays, William, 136n2
Hazeldine, Tim, 45n4
health, 34–6, 56, 126, 133–4
Heckscher, Eli, 14, 23n4, 113n1
Hegel, G.W.F., 220
Heller, Patrick, 41, 45n8, 49, 57, 60, 63n5–6, 63n8
Herbst, Jeffrey, 127
Herlitz, Lars, 14
Hibbs, Douglas, 71, 72, 73, 90n9
Hirschman, Albert, 4, 22n1
Hoff, Karla, 37
Holland, 8, 163n15, 172; *see also* Netherlands
Holy Roman Empire, 169, 170
Hong Kong, 130, 136n1
Houtzager, Peter, 17, 39, 90n16
Huff, W.G., 118
human capital, 197–8, 243, 252; *see also* education
Human Development Index, United Nations, 39
Humblet, Catherine, 72
Hundred Years War, 167
Hungary, 159, 166, 191, 197, 201
Huns, 71
Hunt, Lynn, 198
Huntington, Samuel, 40
Hussein, Saddam, 192
hybridity, 27–32
Hyundai, 231

Import-Substitution Industrialization (ISI), 16, 18, 223–4, 226
India: colonialism, 121, 125, 136n4–5; early state, 70, 177; economic development, 77, 82, 90n14, 230, 257
Indonesia, 70, 77, 227, 228
Indus Valley, 70
infrastructural power, 151–2, 162n1, 192–3, 207–8, 252
Inoue Kowashi, 234n1
International Country Risk Guide (ICRG), 37, 39–40, 45n5, 81, 86–7, 90n7, 90–1n16

International Monetary Fund (IMF), 17–18, 31, 34, 41, 42, 229–30
Iran, 184, 190–1, 195, 200–1, 205, 207
Iraq, 191, 192, 201
Ireland, 14
Isaac, Thomas, 45n8
Islamoglu, Uri, 162n7, 163n11
Italy, 9, 167–81 *passim*, 211
Itō Hirobumi, 220, 234n1
Iyer, Lakshmi, 136n5

Jackman, Robert, 137
Jackson, Robert, 63n3
Jamaica, 122, 128
James II, 204
Japan: colonialism, 212, 216–19, 247, 257; economic development, 4, 16, 17, 57, 82, 85, 157, 211, 227, 229, 231–2; relations with Korea, 224, 228, 230; the state, 70, 213, 214, 219–22, 234n1, 247; *see also* Colonialism: Japanese; Meiji Restoration; Ministry of International Trade and Industry (MITI)
Jefferson, Thomas, 200
Jeserich, Kurt, 169
Johnson, Chalmers, 4, 57, 219–21
Johnson, Lyman, 100, 105, 107, 108, 110
Johnson, Paul, 82
Johnson, Simon, 77, 90n5, 92, 118, 121, 128, 247
Jones, Richard, 127, 128
Joseph II, 176

Kahn, Joseph, 234n2
Kalberg, Stephen, 52, 63n
Kanbur, Ravi, 45n1
Kaufmann, Daniel, 86–7, 126
Keefer, Philip, 90n7
Kelley, Jonathan, 197
Kemal, Mustapha, 196
Kenya, 12, 62, 82
Kerala, India, 41, 49
Khmer Rouge, 200–1
Khomeini, Ayatollah, 195, 199, 200
Kicza, John, 96, 104

Kim Dae Jung, 230–2
Kim Sông-su, 218
Kim Young Sam, 232
King, Lawrence, 38
Kiser, Edgar, 162n6
Kish Nobosuke, 219
Klaus, Vaclav, 200
Klein, Herbert, 105, 106, 197
Knack, Stephen, 90n7
Knight, Alan, 109
Knudsen, Tim, 171
Kohli, Atul, 95, 118
Korea: agrarian bureaucracy, 213–16; colonialism, 212, 216–19, 233, 253; Korean National Assembly, 223; land reform, 223, 258n3; state-led development, 211–34, 253; war, 222–3, 257; *see also* North Korea; South Korea
Korean Industrial Bank, 218
Kosovo, 203
Kraay, Aart, 86, 126
Kronman, Anthony, 63n1
Krugman, Paul, 45n2
Kuczynski, Robert, 127, 128
Kuethe, Alan, 108
Kumar, Anand, 136n5
Kuomingtang regime, 196
Kwangju, South Korea, 232
Kwantung Army, 219
Kyôngbang Textile Company, 218
Kyongju, South Korea, 213

Lamberts, E., 176
land reform, 223
Lange, Matthew: acknowledgement, 113n, 162n; colonialism, 118, 120, 125, 136n7, 246–8; law and development, 59, 241; Mauritius, 62
Laos, 201
LaPorta, Rafael, 122, 128
Latin America: colonialism, 92–113, 205; debt, 225; economic development, 16–17, 19, 29, 224; the state, 78, 90n11, 181, 204

Lautensach, Hermann, 219
law: customary law, 120, 125; and economic development, 23n3, 58, 240; kadi justice, 177; neo-utilitarian view, 94; Roman law, 144, 177, 203–4, 206; *see also* authority: rational-legal; rule of law
leadership, 199–201, 252
Leavy, Jennifer, 90n16
Lee, John Michael, 124
Lee Kwan Yew, 219
legal rule; *see* authority: rational-legal; rule of law
Lenin, V.I., 199, 200, 205, 206
Lenski, Gerhard, 10, 258n1
Lenski, Jean, 10
Levine, Ross, 72, 79, 86, 128
Levy, Marion, 162n8
Lima, Peru, 100, 107
Linton, April, 162n6
Li Peng, 200
Lipset, Seymour Martin, 60
List, Friedrich, 221
Litchfield, R. Burr, 176
Lockart, James, 100, 101
López Alves, Fernando, 110
Louis Philippe, 195
Lowell, Percival, 214
Lugard, Frederick, 119
Lynch, John, 99, 103, 108

Macedonia, 203
Macropedia, 75
Madero, Francisco, 199
Magnusson, Lars, 23n4
Mahoney, James: acknowledgement, 63n, 113n, 162n; Central America, 27, 28; Spanish colonialism, 92, 105, 111, 118, 245–8; time and comparative history, 20
Maine, Sumner, 162n8
Malaysia, 122, 128, 131
Malettke, Klaus, 170
Mali, 70

INDEX

Malta, 124
Mamdani, Mahmood, 12, 51, 57, 63n7, 118–22 *passim*, 135
Manchuria, 212, 216, 218, 219, 224
Mandela, Nelson, 199
Mann, Kristin, 120
Mann, Michael, 120, 151, 162n1, 192–3, 252
Mao Tse-tung, 198, 200, 201
markets, 4, 36–40, 50–62 *passim*, 177–8, 240–2
Marx, Karl, 11
Mauritius, 19, 62, 128
Maximilian, Emperor, 169
Maya, 79
Mayntz, Renate, 43
McEvedy, Colin, 127, 128
McFarlane, Anthony, 108
McKinley, P. Michael, 109
Meiji Restoration, 157, 160, 245
Mendez, Juan, 59
mercantilism: economic policy, 13–15, 19, 23n4, 113n1; the state, 92, 93–9, 100–6, 111
Merry, Sally Engle, 120
Mesopotamia, 166
Mexico: age of state, 70, 90n11; colonialism, 100, 103, 104, 106, 109, 111; economy, 225, 230; revolution, 197–201 *passim*, 205, 207; *see also* New Spain; Chiapas
Mexico City, Mexico, 107
Middle East, 24, 166, 181, 204, 242
Migdal, Joel, 63n7, 95, 97, 113n4, 118, 120
military, 12, 196–7
Minh, Ho Chi, 199
Ministry of International Trade and Industry (MITI), 219, 221, 224
modernization theory, 163n9
Mongols, 71
Montgelas, Count, 171–2
Moore, Mick, 39, 45n5, 90n16
Mörner, Magnus, 107

Morocco, 130
Morris, Cynthia, 82
Myanmar, 125, 136n3–4

Namibia, 130
Napoleon, 176, 179, 200
Napoleonic Wars, 181
Nasser, Gamel Abdul, 196
National Science Foundation, 113n
Navarre, 166
Neo-Europes, 77, 90n9
neoliberalism, 15, 18–19, 31, 213; *see also* neo-utilitarianism
neo-utilitarianism, 94
Netherlands, 14, 176, 179, 184; *see also* Holland
New Guinea, 70
New institutionalism, 38
New Jewel Movement, 199, 201
Newson, Linda, 107
New Spain, 92, 97, 101, 103, 110
New Zealand, 45n4, 77, 90n9, 124
Nicaragua, 191, 197, 198, 201
Nielsen, Francois, 258n1
Nigeria, 70, 122, 125
Nine Years War, 173
North America, 77
North, Douglas, 3, 37–8, 45n3, 58, 153, 194
North Korea, 201, 223; *see also* Korea
North, Lord, 174
Norway, 166, 171, 178, 251

Obregon, Alvaro, 200
O'Donnell, Guillermo, 57, 59, 224
Oestreich, Gerhard, 169
Olivier-Martin, Francois, 168
Olson, Mancur, 5
Olsson, Ola, 71, 72, 73, 90n9
O'Neill, Tip, 256
Onis, Ziya, 61, 63n6
Organization of Economic Cooperation and Development (OECD), 18, 90n10

Organization of Petroleum Exporting Countries (OPEC), 225
Oriental Development Company, 217
Ostrom, Elinore, 49, 62, 63n8
Ottoman Empire, 162n7

Pakistan, 125, 136n4
Palais, James, 215–16
Panama, 100
Paraguay, 100, 109
Paris, France, 201, 202
Park Chung Hee, 224, 225, 226, 232
Parsons, Talcott, 48, 51, 55, 153, 162n1, 162n3, 162n8
Party of Institutionalized Revolution (PRI), 197
Paterson, William, 173
patrimonialism, 53, 102, 119–20, 135, 175–80, 244–8, 250–1; *see also* authority: traditional; Weber, Max: patrimonial and rational-bureaucratic states
Pelletier, Jacques, 34
Perdue, Peter, 162n7, 163n11
Perotta, Cosimo, 15
Perrow, Charles, 51
personal rule, 53, 55, 57, 59
Peru: colonialism, 92, 100–5 *passim*, 109, 110; the state, 70, 90n11, 97, 103, 111
Peter, Leopold, 176
Peterson, Claes, 171
Peter the Great, 171
Philippines, 82, 122, 191, 196, 199, 207–8
Piedmont, 176
Pierson, Paul, 20, 258n4
Pinheiro, Paul, 59
plantations, 128
Poland, 159, 166, 197
Polanyi, Karl, 4, 56, 221
Political Risks Services (PRS), 39, 45n5
population density, 73, 127
Porter, Bernard, 121
Portes, Alejandro, 49
Porto Alegre, Brazil, 39

Portugal, 166–9 *passim*, 181
Potosí, Bolivia, 106
Prussia, 8, 163n15, 170, 204, 234n1
Przeworski, Adam, 41
Putnam, Robert, 9, 57, 60, 63n
Putterman, Louis: acknowledgement, 136n; human capital, 127; social evolution, 88; states and development, 72, 74, 81, 243–8, 258n2

Rabe, Horst, 170
Rauch, James, 32, 63n3, 90n15, 241
Reformation, the, 170, 178, 251
Relative Income Conversion Efficiency (RICE), 39–40, 90n16
Renelt, David, 79
Reno, William, 118, 120
revolutions, 183–210, 212. 251–2
Rheinstein, Max, 63n1
Rhodes, Cecil, 216
Roberts, Michael, 171
Roberts, Richard, 120
Robespierre, Maximilien, 200
Robinson, James, 77, 90n5, 92, 118, 121, 128, 247
Robinson, Ronald, 122, 135
Rock, David, 107, 109, 110
Rodik, Dani, 56
Roh Moo Hyun, 231, 232
Romanelli, Raffaele, 176
Roman Empire, 71, 166, 177, 193
Rosberg, Carl, 63n3
Rosenberg, Hans, 148
Roseveare, Henry, 173
Rothstein, Bo, 144
Rueschemeyer, Dietrich: acknowledgement, 63n, 113n, 136n; *Power and the Division of Labour*, 162n4; state building, 165, 203–4, 208–9, 212, 231, 249–50, 255–6; state organization, 8, 95, 97, 163n10; time and comparative history, 20
rule of law, 11–12, 13, 86, 90n7, 126, 231, 240–1; *see also* authority: rational-legal;

law; Weber, Max: patrimonial and rational-bureaucratic states
Russia: development, 4, 12, 230, 242; revolution, 16, 184, 191, 195–207 *passim*, 245; Romanovs, 199, 203; the state, 159, 171, 178; *see also* Soviet Union
Rwanda, 161

Sachs, Jeffrey, 72, 258n5
Said, Edward, 118
Samsung, 231
Sandinistas, 197, 198, 201
Sanger, David, 234n5
Santiago, Chile, 108
Saxenian, Annalee, 49
Saxony, 169
Schulze, Winfried, 169
Schumpeter, Joseph, 224–5
Schwarz, Brigide, 168
Schwartz, Stuart, 100, 101
Scotland, 166
Scott, Graham, 45n4
Scott, James, 6, 8, 51, 120
Selbin, Eric, 199
Sen, Amartya, 43, 49
Seoul, South Korea, 216, 217, 226
Seven Years War, 174
Shi'a Islam, 195, 198
Shin, Gi-Wook, 12
Shue, Vivienne, 95
Shuman, Michael, 234n3
Sicily, 166
Sieyes, Emmanuel Joseph, 200
Silicone Valley, 229
Silla Dynasty, 213
Simmel, Georg, 58
Singapore, 122, 131, 219, 228
Skocpol, Theda, 62, 95, 199, 207, 242
Slovakia, 203; *see also* Czechoslovakia
Slovenia, 203
Smith, Adam, 3, 14–15, 38, 56, 221, 93
Socolow, Susan, 100, 108, 109
Sokoloff, Kenneth, 92, 118

Solomon Islands, 128
Somalia, 53, 69, 124
South Africa, 57, 124, 199
South Korea: Central Intelligence Agency, 232; Economic Planning Board, 224; industrialization, 17, 82, 85, 211–12, 257; late development, 4, 12, 57, 223; the state, 70, 77, 158, 161, 212, 241, 247; *see also* Korea
Soviet Union, 38, 195–202 *passim*, 242; *see also* Russia
Spain: economic development, 14, 15; empire, 103–5, 107, 108, 109; state building, 167, 168, 169, 181, 204; *see also* Spanish colonialism
Spanish colonialism: administration, 99–106; "great reversal," 111; independence, 104, 110; legacy of, 92–113, 122, 245; state, 100–11
Sperling, John, 174
Squire, Lyn, 45n7
Stalin, Joseph, 205
state building, 19–20, 143–62, 248–54; "advantages of backwardness," 157–8, 245; and the church, 144, 167–8, 177, 203; and conflict theory, 147–50, 154*t*, 156, 249–50; diffusion of states, 251–2; in Europe, 144–6, 165–81, 249–51; and norm theory, 146–7, 154*t*, 150–3, 156, 249–50, 255; and revolutions, 183–210, 250, 251, 252, 254; and state-society relations, 149–53, 154*t*, 156–7, 254; temporal aspects of, 153, 155–7, 158–61, 249; *see also* states
states: and administration, 53; age of, 69–72, 73–4, 82, 88, 243; autonomy of, 7, 54, 95–7, 101–2, 112, 246; and coercion, 5, 10; and collective action problems, 5–6; corporate coherence of, 7, 8, 9, 35, 154; developmental, 57, 95–6, 113n3, 219–22, 228, 232; discipline of, 26–44; and infrastructure, 56; instrumental, 96, 111, 240; legitimacy of, 9; minimal, 93–9,

states—*continued*
106–11; predatory, 32, 95–6, 113n3, 135; quantitative indicators of, 37, 39–40, 45n5, 78, 86–7, 90n7, 90–1n16, 125–6, 129; and reforms, 28–9, 34; and revenue, 101–2, 103, 108, 178; state-society relations, 8–9, 43, 59–62, 95–6; statism, 15–18; and welfare, 4, 56, 158–9; *see also* authority; mercantilism: state; rule of law; state building; Weber, Max
St. Augustus, 10
Steiner, Jüerg, 181
Stephen, Francis, 176
Stiglitz, Joseph, 17, 19, 37, 41, 56, 61
Stinchcombe, Arthur, 53
St. Kitts and Nevis, 124
Stolleis, Michael, 170
Strayer, Joseph, 4
sultanism, 53
Sun-Yat Sen, 199
Sweden, 144, 158, 166, 170–2, 178–80 *passim*, 251
synergy, 59–62, 240, 241, 257
Syngman Rhee, 222–4 *passim*

Taiwan: colonialism, 12, 212, 216, 219, 228; economic development, 17, 77, 85, 229
T'ang Dynasty, 213
Taylor, M., 5
Temple, Jonathan, 82
Tendler, Judith, 34–6, 63n5–6, 63n8
Thailand, 70, 77, 227, 228
Thirty Years War, 171
Tilly, Charles, 10, 12, 20, 53, 122, 161, 191
Tocqueville, Alexis de, 202, 242
Tokyo, Japan, 234n1
Tollison, Robert, 14
trade, 15, 16, 102, 109–11
traditionalism; *see* authority: traditional
Trimberger, Ellen Kay, 202
Trotsky, Leon, 199, 200, 205
Trow, Martin, 60

Trubek, David, 23n3, 63n4
Tsurumi, Patti, 216–17
Tucumán, Argentina, 107
Turkey, 196, 202
Turks, 71
Tuscany, 176

Ugaki Kazushige, 218
Uganda, 70, 122
Uggla, Frederick, 63n8
Ukraine, 159
United Kingdom; *see* England; Great Britain
United States, 90, 100, 106, 124, 158, 205, 206; economy of, 14, 38, 42, 211, 225, 227, 231; and foreign intervention, 17, 198, 201, 222–3, 227–8, 233, 253, 257; revolution, 196, 199, 200, 205, 207–8
University of Bologna, 144
Uphoff, Norman, 9, 49, 59, 61, 63n6
Uruguay, 93, 95, 105–12 *passim*
Uvin, Peter, 162n

Van Fleet, James, 223
Veblen, Thorstein, 10, 163n12
Venezuela, 100, 105, 107, 108, 109, 112
Viceroyalty of New Granada, 100, 108
Viceroyalty of New Spain, 100; *see also* New Spain
Viceroyalty of Peru, 100; *see also* Peru
Viceroyalty Río de La Plata, 100, 106, 108
Vietnam, 17, 191, 199, 201, 207, 217
Villa, Pancho, 200
Visigoths, 71
vom Hau, Matthias, 63n, 245–8
von Gneist, Rudolf, 234n1
von Pyhy, Conrad, 171
von Stein, Lorenz, 220, 221, 234n1–2

Wade, Robert, 4, 12, 16, 17, 57, 61, 118
Walker, Charles, 102
Walker, Geoffrey, 98, 99
Wallerstein, Immanuel, 220, 234n2

Wang, Xu, 63n6
Warner, Andrew, 72
War of the Spanish Succession, 173, 174, 184
Washington, George, 196, 199, 200
Weber, Max, 48–63; and bureaucracy, 7–8, 30, 144–6, 162n8, 212, 221; and habits and norms, 162n5; and law and economy, 3, 7, 23n; and modernization, 163n14; and patrimonial and rational-bureaucratic states, 93–5, 112, 165–7, 192, 244; and the Protestant ethic, 160; and state and development, 4, 32–3, 55–6, 95; and state building in Europe, 171–4 *passim*, 177–81, 250–1; *see also* authority
Weingast, Barry, 23n2
Whigham, Thomas, 109
Whigs, 174
White, Howard, 90n16
William III, 173, 205

Williamson, Jeffrey, 90n13
Woloch, Isser, 195
Woo, Jung-en, 219, 223–4, 226, 227
Woodward, Ralph Lee, 105
Woolcock, Michael, 63n5
Woolf, Stuart, 176
World Bank, 18, 31, 34, 41, 73, 158, 239
WorldCom, 38
Wright, Erik, 45n8
Wuerttemburg, 169
Wunder, Bernd, 170, 171

Yardeni, Ed, 230, 234n3
Yôngdûngp'o, South Korea, 218
Young, Crawford, 117
Yugoslavia, 203
Yusuf, Shahid, 41

Zapata, Emiliano, 200
Zapatistas, 198
Zoido-Lobaton, Pablo, 86, 126